Ring-tailed cat   *Mallette Dean*

SIERRA NORTH

100 Back-Country Trips in the High Sierra

by Thomas Winnett and Jason Winnett

 WILDERNESS PRESS • BERKELEY

First printing May 1967
Second printing July 1967
Third printing July 1969

SECOND EDITION May 1971
Second printing April 1972
Third printing September 1974

THIRD EDITION January 1976
Second printing February 1978

FOURTH EDITION May 1982

Photos by the authors except as noted
Drawings by Lucille Winnett
Design by Thomas Winnett

Library of Congress card number 81-70344
ISBN: 0-89997-017-6
Manufactured in the United States

Published by Wilderness Press
2440 Bancroft Way, Berkeley, CA 94704

Write for free catalog

ACKNOWLEDGEMENTS

A guidebook like this requires a lot of input, and I have been fortunate enough to meet many gracious and generous Sierra lovers who have helped me bring the old trail descriptions up to date and to present the descriptions of the new trips: Jeff Schaffer, Ron Felzer, Margaret and the late Bob Pierce, Ben Schifrin, Ken Fawcett, Joe Grodin, J. C. Jenkins, Raleigh Ellisen, Don Parachini, Earl Schnick, John Jencks, Grant Barnes, Harold Furst, Cecelia Hurwich, Norman Jensen, Edwin Rockwell, Jason Winnett and Caroline Winnett.

The chapter on "The Care and Enjoyment of the Mountains" was adapted from an article by Michael Loughman.

Table of Contents

Looking south from Donohue Pa

Introduction

This Book's Purpose

The Sierra Nevada is the longest and most extensively trailed mountain range in the United States. With its complex valley-ridge makeup, its lofty eastern escarpment, and its mild weather, it is a backpacker's paradise unequalled in intrinsic beauty and scenic grandeur. Much of the finest scenery and best fishing lie in the back country, accessible only by trail. There has been, therefore, a growing trend toward wilderness trips, and with the trend has come a demand for reliable backcountry trip suggestions. This book is a selective effort to meet that demand.

Galen Clark, Yosemite's beloved "Old Man of the Valley," was once asked how he "got about" the park. Clark scratched his beard, and then replied, "Slowly!" And that is the philosophy the authors have adopted in this book. Hiking descriptions, with the exception of a few "Moderate" ratings and an occasional "Strenuous" trip, are based on a leisurely pace, in order that the hiker can absorb more of the sights, smells and "feel" of the country he has come to see. Pace may not be everything, but Old Man Clark lived to a ripe old age of 96 and it behooves us to follow in his footsteps.

This Book's Terms

Sierra North encompasses the region from the volcanic battlements of Carson Pass to the aspen-lined banks of Mono Creek, where the companion volume, *Sierra South*, takes over. The individual trips were selected on the basis of (1) scenic attraction, (2) wilderness character (remoteness, primitive condition) and (3) recreational potential (fishing, swimming, etc.) After walking the trip, the author decided how long it should take if done at a leisurely pace, how long at a moderate pace, and how long at a strenuous pace. In deciding, he considered not only distance but also elevation change, heat exposure, terrain, availability of water, appropriate campsites and finally, his subjective feeling about the trip. For each trip, then, we suggest how many days you should take to do it at the pace (*Leisurely, Moderate* or *Strenuous*) you prefer. Some trips simply don't lend themselves to a leisurely pace—maybe not even a moderate pace—and some are never strenuous unless you do the whole thing in one day. Such trips have a blank in the number-of-days spot for the corresponding pace at the beginning of the trip.

The last decision about pace was the decision of which pace to use in describing the trip, day by day. Since this book is written for the average backpacker, we chose to describe most trips on either a leisurely or a moderate basis, depending on where the best overnight camping places were along the route.

Subjective considerations also carry over to the evaluation of campsites. Campsites are labeled *poor, fair, good* or *excellent.* The criteria for assigning these labels were amount of use, immediate surroundings, general scenery, presence of vandalization, availability of water, kind of ground cover and recreational potential—angling, side trips, swimming, etc.

Angling, for many, is a prime consideration when planning a trip. The recommendations in this book are the result of (1) research into the California DF&G's fresh-water fish-stocking program, (2) study of DF&G-sponsored surveys ("Anglers' Guides"), (3) on-the-trail sampling and feed evaluations and (4) interviews with commercial packers. When a conflict arose between paper research and trail sampling, the latter was given precedence. Like the campsites, fishing was labeled *poor, fair, good* or *excellent.* It should be noted that these labels refer to the quantity of fish in the stream or lake, not the fishes' inclination to take the hook. Experienced anglers know that the size of their catch relates not only to quantity, type and general size of the fishery, which are given, but also to water temperature, feed, angling skill, and that indefinable something known as "fisherman's luck." Generally speaking, the old "early and late" adage holds: fishing is better early and late in the day, and early and late in the season.

Deciding when in the year is the best time for a particular trip is a difficult task because of altitude and latitude variations. Low early-season temperatures and mountain shadows often keep some of the higher passes closed until well into August. Early snows have been known to whiten alpine country in late July and August. Some of the trips described here are low-country ones, offered specifically for the itchy hiker who, stiff from a winter's inactivity, is searching for a "warm-up" excursion. These trips are labeled *early season,* a period that extends roughly from late May to early July. *Mid season* is here considered to be from early July to the end of August, and *late season* from then to early October.

Most of the trails described here are well maintained (the exceptions are noted), and are properly signed. If the trail becomes indistinct, look for *blazes* (peeled bark at eye level on trees) or *ducks* (two or more rocks piled one atop the other). Two other significant trail conditions have also been described in the text: (1) degree of openness (type and degree of forest cover, if any, or else "meadow," "brush" or whatever); and (2) underfooting (talus, scree, pumice, sand, "duff"—deep humus ground cover of rotting vegetation—or other material).

Three other terms used in the descriptive text warrant definition. *Packer campsite* is used to indicate a semipermanent camp (usually constructed by packers for the "comfort of their clients") characterized by a nailed-plank table and/or a large, stand-up rock fireplace. *Improved campsite* is a U.S. Forest Service designation for a place where a simple toilet has been installed. A *use trail* is an unmaintained, unofficial trail that is more or less easy to follow because it is well worn by use.

The text contains occasional references to points, peaks and other landmarks. These places will be found on the appropriate topographic maps cited at the beginning of the trip. ("Point 9426" in the text would refer to a point designated simply "9426" on the map itself.)

The Care and Enjoyment of the Mountains

The mountains are in danger, particularly the High Sierra. About a million people camp in the Sierra wilderness each year. Backpacking is something everybody knows about and almost everybody is going to want to try. With California's population edging toward 25 million, the wilderness is threatened with destruction, particularly the High Sierra.

Litter is not the problem! Increasingly, wilderness campsites, even when free of litter, have that "beat out" look of overcrowded roadside campgrounds. The fragile high country sod is being ground down under the pressure of too many feet. Lovely trees and snags are being stripped, scarred, and removed altogether for firewood. Dust, charcoal, blackened stones and dirty fireplaces are accumulating. These conditions are spreading rapidly, and in a few years *every* High Sierra lakeshore and streamside may be severely damaged.

The national park service and the forest service are faced with the necessity for reservation systems, designated campgrounds, restrictions on fire building, increased ranger patrols, and perhaps even rationing of wilderness recreation. Not only the terrain but the wilderness experience is being eroded. Soon conditions may be little different from those we wanted to leave behind at the roadhead.

The solution to the problem depends on each of us. We must change our habits so as to have as little effect on the terrain as possible. We must try to leave no traces of our passing. This was the rule in the wilderness when Indians and trappers traveled through other people's territory. It is still a good rule today. It does take a little trouble. In an earlier day that extra trouble was the price of saving one's scalp or load of beaver pelts. Today it is the price of saving the wilderness. A few basic principles of wilderness preservation—particularly aimed at High Sierra conditions but applicable elsewhere too—are offered below.

Learn to go light. This is largely a matter of acquiring wilderness skills, of learning to be at home in the wilderness rather than in an elaborate camp. The *free spirits* of the mountains are those experts who appear to go anywhere under any conditions with neither encumbrances nor effort but always with complete enjoyment. John Muir, traveling along the crest of the Sierra in the 1870s with little more than his overcoat and pockets full of biscuits, was the archetype.

Modern lightweight equipment and food are a convenience and a joy. The ever-practical Muir would have taken them had they been available in his day. But a lot of the stuff that goes into the mountains is burdensome, harmful to the wilderness, or just plain annoying to other people seeking peace and solitude. Anything that is obtrusive or that can be used to modify the terrain should be left at the roadhead: gigantic tents, gas lanterns, radios, saws, hatchets, firearms (except in the hunting season), etc.

Pick "hard" campsites, sandy places that can stand the use. The fragile sod of meadows, lakeshores and streamsides is rapidly disappearing from the High Sierra. It simply cannot take the wear and tear of campers. Its development depends on very special conditions. Once destroyed, it does not ordinarily grow back.

Be easy with the trees! In the timberline country wood is being burned up faster than it is being produced. The big campfires of the past must give way to small fires or to no fires at all. Wood is a precious resource; use it sparingly. Where it is scarce use a gas stove, not a saw or hatchet. Trees, both live and dead, are part of the scenery. They should never be *cut*. The exquisite golden trunks left standing after lightning strikes should be left completely alone. Sadly, in some popular areas they have already been destroyed for firewood, and you would never know they *were* there.

In established, regularly used campsites a single, small, substantial fireplace should serve for both cooking and warming. If kept scrupulously clean it should last for many years. Unfortunately, fireplaces (and campsites) tend to become increasingly dirty and to multiply. There are now, by actual survey, a hundred times as many fireplaces as are needed in the High Sierra. The countless dirty fireplaces should be eradicated. Many campsites situated at the edge of the water should be entirely restored to nature and not used again. It is a noble service to use and clean up established campsites where they are present, and to restore them to nature where called for.

Elsewhere build a small fireplace, if one is legal, and always eradicate it and restore your campsite to a natural condition before you leave. This is facilitated if you build with restoration in mind: two to four medium-sized stones along the sides of a shallow trench in a sandy place. When camp is broken the stones are returned to their places. The coals are thoroughly burned down and pulverized under a heavy foot until nothing is left but powder. The trench is filled with clean sand. *Fires should never be built against cliffs or large boulders.*

Protect the water from soap and other sources of pollution. Abundant pure water is one of the joys of the mountains. Imagine having to purify every cupful before you drank it.

Scatter organic garbage in dry, out-of-the-way places. It disappears most quickly when dry and exposed to the air. Talus slopes and dry brush are the best hiding places. Garbage should never be burned in the fireplace. Orange peels are an exception. They seem to be destructible only in a hot fire.

Thoroughly cold and pulverized charcoal may be broadcast away from camp in a fireproof site. Charcoal is part of the natural scene.

Pack cans and foil back to the roadhead. Smelly or oily cans and foil can be cleaned easily in a hot fire but please do remove them. The accumulation of garbage, cans, and charcoal around fireplaces is the principal reason campsites are abandoned and new, redundant fireplaces and campsites are created.

Latrines should be located at least 50 yards from any camping area, stream, or dry stream course. Again a little extra trouble will alleviate one of the most annoying wilderness problems. Please be willing to walk a little farther and cover up a little more carefully.

Maps and Profiles

Today's Sierra traveler is confronted by a bewildering array of maps, and it doesn't take much experience to learn that no single map fulfills all needs. There are base maps (U.S. Forest Service), shaded relief maps (National Park Service), artistically drawn representational maps (California Department of Fish and Game), aerial-photograph maps, geologic maps, three-dimensional relief maps, soil-vegetation maps, etc. Each map has different information to impart, and the outdoorsman contemplating a backcountry trip is wise to utilize several of these maps in his planning.

For trip-planning purposes, the reader will find a plan map in the back of this book. Trails and trailheads used in the trip descriptions are shown on this map in red, the access roads in black, water in blue, and the topographic map grid in orange.

The profile of each trip in this book gives a quick picture of the ups and downs. All profiles are drawn with the same *ratio* of horizontal miles to feet of elevation except 44 and 87. The vertical scale in all is exaggerated.

On the trail most backpackers prefer to use a topographic (*topo*) map, because it affords a good deal of accurate information about terrain and forest cover. Topo maps come in a variety of sizes and scales, but the best, because it covers the whole Sierra in one useful scale, is the U.S. Geological Survey's 15′ Topographic Quadrangle series. The 15′ series scale is approximately $1'' = 1$ mile; the contour interval (elevation difference between contour lines) is 80 feet in the Sierra; and the area covered by each map is about 14×17 miles. They show most of the maintained trails (exceptions are noted in the text of this book), the elevations, the relief, the watercourses, the forest cover and the works of man. Learning to read these maps takes a little practice, but the savings in shoe leather and frayed tempers make it a worthy undertaking. For the reader's convenience, the appropriate 15′ topo maps for each trip are cited in the text.

By far the best topo maps—for the quadrangles for which they are available—are the 15′ quadrangle maps published by Wilderness Press. These maps are based on the USGS versions, but were completely updated in the late 1970s and early

1980s after thorough fieldwork. Trails are much easier to see on these maps because they are shown as solid black lines. And each map has an index grid and an index for locating all the features on it. In the area of *Sierra North,* Wilderness Press 15′ maps are available for these quadrangles: Hetch Hetchy, Tuolumne Meadows, Yosemite, Merced Peak and Devils Postpile. In addition, Wilderness Press will publish an updated topographic of Yosemite National Park and Vicinity in 1982. This map alone will show more than half of the trails described in *Sierra North.* In the tabular matter at the start of each trip in this book, the topo maps needed for the trip are listed. If the map's name is in ***boldface,*** that quadrangle is available in the Wilderness Press series, and it is the best one available.

Another useful map series is the ½″ = 1 mile series published by the U.S. Forest Service. Being base maps, they lack contour lines, but they are revised with some frequency, and they show newer roads and trails. They also show water, man-made structures and some elevations.

HOW TO ACQUIRE YOUR MAPS

USFS base maps:

U.S. Forest Service,
630 Sansome St.,
San Francisco, CA 94111
An index map is free.
Individual forest maps are $1.00 each.

Wilderness Press
15′ *Topo* maps:

Wilderness Press
2440 Bancroft Way
Berkeley, CA 94704
Write for free catalog

USGS 15′ *Topo* maps:

U.S. Geological Survey,
Federal Center, Denver, CO 80225
$2.00 each
State index map is free

Topo maps plus free state index maps can be obtained *in person* from USGS offices located at:

7638 Federal Building
300 North Los Angeles Street
Los Angeles, CA

345 Middlefield Road
Menlo Park, CA

504 Custom House
555 Battery Street
San Francisco, CA

Wilderness Permits and Quotas

The wilderness traveler will need a permit from the Forest Service (for federally designated wilderness areas) or from the National Park Service (for national-park backcountry and wilderness). You may obtain a permit from the Park Service or Forest Service ranger station or office that administers the area. In Yosemite permits are available on a first-come-first-served basis not more than 24 hours before your departure into the backcountry. In Tuolumne Meadows you can get your permit from a booth in the parking lot near the west end of the Tuolumne Lodge spur road. The Park Service realizes that many Yosemite hikers are weekend visitors, so from late June through Labor Day weekend they keep the booth open on Friday nights and open it early (sometimes 6 a.m.) on Saturday mornings. In Yosemite, you can also get a permit in person at the Big Oak Flat entrance station on Highway 120, in Yosemite Valley and at Wawona.

Rules for obtaining a permit for a national-forest area have been in flux, so we suggest that you write the supervisor of the national forest you plan to visit, to find out the procedure in force at the time of your trip, using the addresses below. In addition, permits for Yosemite may be obtained by mail *between Feb. 1 and May 31* by writing: Wilderness Permits, Box 577, Yosemite National Park, CA 95389. After May 31 you must appear in person. Groups of 15 or more are requested to make mail reservations for any trip between Memorial Day and October 1.

Emigrant Wilderness
Stanislaus National Forest
19777 Greenley Rd.
Sonora, CA 95370

Hoover Wilderness
(for eastside entry)
Toiyabe National Forest
Bridgeport, CA 93517

Hoover Wilderness
(for southside entry)
Inyo National Forest
P.O. Box 10
Lee Vining, CA 93541

Minarets Wilderness
(for westside entry)
Sierra National Forest
North Fork, CA 93643

Minarets Wilderness
(for eastside entry)
Inyo National Forest
P.O. Box 148
Mammoth Lakes, CA 93546

John Muir Wilderness
(for westside entry)
Sierra National Forest
1130 "O" Street
Fresno, CA 93721

John Muir Wilderness   *Mokelumne Wilderness*
(for eastside entry)   El Dorado National Forest
Inyo National Forest   100 Forni Road
873 N. Main   Placerville, CA 95667
Bishop, CA 93514

If your trip extends through more than one national-forest wilderness, or through more than one national forest, or through both a national forest and a national park, obtain your permit from the forest or park where your trip starts.

A wilderness permit is issued for a single trip during a specified period of time. A separate permit is necessary for each trip.

The wilderness permit also serves as a campfire permit while you visit the wilderness area. A campfire permit is required for campfires outside of wilderness areas.

Capacities have been established for high-use areas in the region covered by this book, including all the backcountry of Yosemite. If the capacity of the area where you want to go has been filled, you must select another overnight destination. A number of other rules exist for backcountry use, many of which are simply codifications of the principles in the chapter "The Care and Enjoyment of the Mountains." One rule that is all too often broken is that you must camp at least 100 feet from lakes and stream—where terrain permits. In a few places, such as Barney Lake and Peeler Lake, that distance is increased to 200 feet. Copies of all these special regulations are available from the government agencies that issue wilderness permits.

Land of Fire and Ice

Called the "land of fire and ice" by one awestruck pioneer emigrant, this large slice of the northern Sierra encompasses the area stretching south from U.S. 50 to the North Boundary of Yosemite National Park. The pioneers who first trod this wilderness recognized the black basaltic crests of this region for their fiery origins, and in stories of arduous crossings over snow- and ice-capped summits, they expressed a profound appreciation for the evolutionary contrasts. Today's geologists tell us that lava once covered that area from around Sonora Pass west to Knights Ferry to a depth of 1500 feet. Millions of years passed before the juggernaut forces of time, glacial ice and water cut through this thick layer, and today more than half of this region consists of re-exposed white-and-gray granite, the hallmark rock of the Sierra. The traveler passing through the backcountry cannot help but notice the sharp delineation between the older batholithic granites and the volcanic overlays.

Historically, this region offers much to intrigue the visitor—particularly if this visitor is on foot (either on two or four). Many of the trips described here trace old emigrant trails, and it is easy for backpackers, afoot like the emigrants, to identify with these pioneers. Preceding the emigrants were the footloose pathfinders. Explorers like John Fremont, Joseph Walker and Jedediah Smith first looked upon these mountains, and Fremont and Walker made crossings that cut across some of the routes described here. Before the white man, however, the Indian established hunting trails that made a network over the foothills on both sides of the Sierra crest. The Maidu and the Miwok occupied and hunted the west side of the crest, and the Washoe and Piute coexisted on the east. It is of interest to the mountaineer to know that most of these Indian trails are located on top of the ridges, and not, as is the white man's custom, along the muddy, snowy canyon bottoms.

After the Indians and the explorers came the emigrants. The Bartleson-Bidwell party of 1841 was the first overland emigrant group to cross the Sierra, and its route, tentatively identified, showed the way—later changed in places—for those who followed. This route still bears blazes cut in trees by westward-bound emigrants. There is, for example, a blazed tree near Emigrant Lake in Emigrant Basin which still shows the epitaph of a traveler who died there in October 1853. Still another emigrant route followed Fremont's old route up the West Carson River to Caples (formerly Twin) Lake, and thence descended the west slope past yet another Emigrant Lake.

These routes were the predecessors of roads—first toll roads, and finally public highways. Today, with the devastating intrusion of roads into these wild spots, Californians have come to a reluctant recognition of the necessity of preserving wilderness integrity. To this end they have established, through federal auspices, wilderness areas that are supposed to preserve a wild area in its intrinsic primitive state. The Mokelumne Wilderness was established in 1964, and in 1974 the Emigrant Basin Primitive Area was enlarged and renamed the Emigrant Wilderness. There is also a plan for a Carson-Iceberg Wilderness that would encompass the area between the Ebbets Pass highway and the Sonora Pass highway. Unfortunately, in the Emigrant Wilderness it was decided to exclude the mining claims and their access road, which cuts across the Sierra crest at Emigrant Pass. And in the planning stages of the Carson-Iceberg Wilderness it is proposed that the present Clark Fork road be left to intrude like a dagger into the heart of the wilderness area. Administrative decisions of this caliber offer slim hope that future decisions will be made to extend the protective mantle of a wilderness area designation to other deserving areas such as that scenic east-side region in the West Walker River drainage. Here the present policy remains one of wilderness attrition by "recreation roads" (a gross contradiction) and unless prompt action is taken, it too will become another dusty traffic jam suitable only for trail bikes and tent cities.

The backcountry hiker who knows the beauty of unspoiled wilderness comes to know the threat implicit in the unrestrained use of machines. With an objectivity born of an appreciation of fundamentals, and an individual wholeness that results from relying on his own resources, he recognizes the automobile as a cultural blight that is responsible for the destruction of thousands of acres of Sierra wilderness. Only recently have Forest Service officials begun to realize the burgeoning threat of trail bikes and snowmobiles, and this dawning awareness has prompted an administrative procla-mation that has closed many of the trails on the Eldorado and

Stanislaus National Forests to jeeps and trail bikes. One hopes similar restrictions will be placed upon the equally disastrous presence of snowmobiles in the backcountry.

The Emigrant Basin area has long been a fisherman's mecca, and for good reason. Hundreds of lakes and miles of streams offer excellent angling for brook, rainbow, brown and golden trout. Some of the better fishing in the area may be found at Wire Lakes, Cow Meadow Lake, the North Fork of Cherry Creek, and the upper reaches of Falls Creek (Jack Main Canyon). California fishing licenses are required.

The Trailheads

Horse Canyon Trailhead. Go 0.6 mile on State Highway 88 from the Silver Lake Ranger Station, north of Silver Lake, to Oyster Creek Roadside Rest, where there is plenty of parking, and walk 100 yards farther up the highway to the signed trailhead. There is room for a very few cars right by the trailhead.

Plasse's Resort. Go east on State Highway 88 to the last downhill stretch before arriving at the shore of Silver Lake and turn right on a road signed *Stockton Municipal Camp.* At the bottom of the hill, turn right toward the resort and go about 300 yards beyond to some unofficial parking areas near a seasonal stream just before a sign saying there is a wilderness area 6 miles ahead.

Echo Summit. Go ½ mile south from Echo Summit (on U.S. 50) to the end of an oiled summer-home-tract road.

Carson Pass. Go 1 mile west of Carson Pass on State Highway 88 to a small parking area.

Upper Wolf Creek Meadows. About 2½ miles south on State Highway 4 from State Highway 89, turn left and go southeast up Wolf Creek Road 3⅓ miles to a fork left, where you could descend northeast to the north end of Wolf Creek Meadows. Continue straight ahead—south—1½ miles beyond the fork to road's end, from which a short, rocky road veers northeast to signed *Wolf Creek Meadows Undeveloped Camping Area.* The Wolf Creek Trail heads south up a creekside jeep road.

Wolf Creek Meadows. Follow Wolf Creek Road 3⅓ miles to a fork left and descend northeast on it to the north end of Wolf Creek Meadows. In ⅔ mile from the fork, the road reaches a spur road heading southeast. This spur climbs ¼ mile to two adjacent trailheads, but it is best to park on a small flat, on your right, about midway along this spur road, before the road curves left. The two trailheads serve the High Trail and the

East Carson River Trail.

Ebbetts Pass. This is the highest point on State Highway 4. The Pacific Crest Trail crosses State Highway 4 only 0.1 mile northeast of the pass, and in another 0.3 mile a short spur road veers right up to a PCT parking lot. A short spur trail up to the PCT leaves from the lot's south end.

Heiser Lake Trailhead. From the east end of Lake Alpine go 6 miles northeast up State Highway 4 to the west end of Mosquito Lake, beside which is the signed trailhead.

Bull Run Lake Trailhead. From the east end of Lake Alpine go 4 miles northeast up State Highway 4 to a spur road branching right signed *Stanislaus Mdw, Bull Run Trail.* Follow this road ½ mile to its end.

Lake Alpine. At the east end of Lake Alpine on State Highway 4 turn right ⅓ mile to the Silver Valley Overnight Campground. Just within the campground, at a *Speed Limit 10* sign, is the trailhead for the Highland Creek Trail.

Rodriguez Flat. From the State Highway 4/89 junction with U.S. 395, go 5½ miles south on U.S. 395 to Coleville, then another 2¼ miles to a road west, signed both *Lost Cannon Creek Road* and *Mill Canyon Road.* Alternatively, from the State Highway 108/U.S. 395 junction, drive 13 miles north to Walker, then another 2½ miles to Lost Cannon Creek Road. This dirt road west quickly becomes the Golden Gate Road. Go up it 6¼ miles; following *Little Antelope Pack Station* signs. From the mountain crest junction at broad, open Rodriguez Flat, drive ½ mile south to road's end at signed Trail 1020.

Kennedy Meadow. Go 1 mile up an oiled road from State Highway 108, 29 miles east of the Pinecrest **Y**. You can let passengers out at the resort, and park there for a fee or drive ½ mile back to a public parking area.

Crabtree Camp. From the traffic light in downtown Sonora, go 25½ miles northeast on State Route 108 to tiny Cold Springs, and 1.2 miles beyond turn right on signed Crabtree Road. Follow this paved road 6.8 miles to a junction just before a pack station. Go straight ahead onto dirt road and drive 2.65 miles to a junction. Go right here for 0.7 mile to the trailhead parking lot beside Bell Creek.

Gianelli Cabin. Proceed as above to the last-named junction. Turn left and go 4 miles to road's end.

Sonora Pass West. About 0.85 mile west of Sonora Pass on State Highway 108, turn north to park on a closed-off dirt road.

Sonora Pass. This is the highest point of State Highway 108, 67 miles northeast of Sonora and 15 miles west of the U.S. 395 junction.

Silver Lake to Scout Carson Lake **1**

TRIP   From Silver Lake to Scout Carson Lake (round trip). Topo map *Silver Lake*. Best mid season; 11 miles (17.8 km).

Grade	Trail/layover days	Total recommended days
Leisurely	2/1	3
Moderate	2/0	2
Strenuous	....	....

HILITES   The mountains around Silver Lake are a startling amalgam of light-gray granite and dark-brown lava, the granite being gently rounded, but the lava arrayed in tiers of jagged cliffs. This trip follows a boundary between the two types of terrain, ascending gently southward under the soaring lava cliffs of Thunder Peak and Thimble Peak to a lovely, small lake near timberline.

DESCRIPTION

1st Hiking Day (**Silver Lake** to **Scout Carson Lake,** 5.5 miles—8.9 km): From the aspen grove at the trailhead just north of Oyster Creek Roadside Rest, the duff-colored trail ascends gently, sometimes moderately, through a red-fir forest in which some wind-toppled firs across the trail require small detours. In early season, open patches in the forest are carpeted with lupine, and showy red columbines grow here and there. Eroded blocks of lava beside the trail have taken on grotesque and fascinating shapes which your imagination can identify as what it will. Even more compelling are the dark lava cliffs on the northern skyline, the crenelated battlements of a 3-mile-long igneous castle. About 2 miles up from the trailhead an unsigned trail comes in on the right beside a large boulder; this is one route up from the Boy Scout Camp below. A more-used path from the camp, the trail shown on the topo map, meets our route ½ mile farther up, on an open hillside, and 70 yards beyond this junction is the first water you will

cross in midsummer, flowing very slightly but fit to drink.
From this cooling pause, we break out onto an open slope
dotted with red fir and great numbers of yellow-flowered mule
ears, mixed with bits of blue lupine. Then the blazed trail
re-enters red-fir forest, and just how brittle the wood of this
conifer species is, is shown by the tremendous amount of
broken wood littering the forest floor—seemingly enough for a
thousand campfires.

Leaving the forest, our rocky trail climbs across an open
hillside dotted with many large granite boulders, a large
assortment of wildflowers and a few lodgepole pines, red firs
and Sierra junipers. As we come into earshot of a plunging
stream, we turn steeply uphill and in 100 yards reach and
jump-ford this creek. The walk up the far bank is enhanced by
the gurgling sounds and by the brilliant chutes and cascades of
this unnamed stream, which drains the bowl between
Thunder Peak (not named on the topo map) and Thimble Peak.
About 300 yards later the trail veers away from the stream to
make an unrelenting steep ascent, then levels off just before it
tops out on a granite ridge. Here again the hillside is very
open, and we now have excellent views of Silver Lake and
mountains surrounding it. Then a short, strolling descent
brings the hiker to an all-year stream with flanking flower
gardens, a good place to stop for lunch. The many mountain
birds around here will eat any crumbs you leave.

Beyond the stream our trail contours along an open hillside
where the flower display in season is among the best for miles
around. Using one of the guides listed in the Recommended
Reading chapter, the budding botanist will recognize woolly
sunflower, Indian paintbrush, sulfur flower, scarlet gilia,
pennyroyal, mule ears, corn lily and sagebrush, among others.
Soon our route passes the signed-but-hard-to-find trail to
Kirkwood Meadow and Caples Lake, and ½ mile farther, at a
ford of an unnamed stream, meets the signed lateral trail to
Scout Carson Lake. From this junction an unmaintained trail
leads south for a good ¼ mile to this small, grass-and-heather-
fringed lake with good campsites.

2nd Hiking Day: Retrace your steps, 5.5 miles (8.9 km).

Silver Lake to Summit City Canyon

2

TRIP   From Silver Lake to Summit City Canyon (round trip). Topo map *Silver Lake*. Best mid season; 20 miles (32.2 km).

Grade	Trail/layover days	Total recommended days
Leisurely	4/1	5
Moderate	3/0	3
Strenuous	2/0	2

HILITES   The first leg of this trip is a long traverse of very flowery open hillsides with fine views of the Silver Lake basin and its surrounding battlements. Then the trail enters a new stream valley and winds down through solitude-filled Horse Canyon to a variety of streamside campsites along beautiful Summit City Creek.

DESCRIPTION (Leisurely trip)

1st Hiking Day: Follow Trip 1 to **Scout Carson Lake**, 5.5 miles (8.9 km).

2nd Hiking Day (**Scout Carson Lake** to **Summit City Canyon**, 4.5 miles—7.2 km): First we retrace the long ¼ mile of use trail to the Horse Canyon Trail and turn right (east) on it. Our sometimes muddy trail ascends moderately through a thinning tree cover almost to timberline, passing through upland meadows rife with flower color in early season. Approaching Squaw Ridge, we cross a set of little-used jeep tracks and in 100 yards arrive at an unnamed pass which is the border of the Mokelumne Wilderness, a region of 50,450 acres where only foot travel is permitted and trails are generally kept up to a standard sufficient for walkers but not horses or mules.

The descent into steep Horse Canyon proceeds on a great number of switchbacks that zigzag down among tall, elegant silver pine trees past plentiful patches of daisies, groundsel, phlox, brodiaea, paintbrush and whorled penstemon, among other blossoms. At a natural overlook spot less than a mile down, the far-gazing hiker can see deep into Summit City Canyon and the Mokelumne River Canyon. Farther south, standing above the south canyon rim, are some peaks beyond Kennedy Meadow, including Cooper Peak, Granite Dome and Three Chimneys. Shortly after, our descending trail passes a trail that leads back to Squaw Ridge. After a few more switchbacks, the trail grade abates to moderate, and then almost to level, as it winds through a delightful meadowy area with lots of grass growing underneath a moderate cover of lodgepole pines, and flower swaths flanking bubbling little streams. This would be a fine camping area for lovers of seculsion. It was not always so secluded. Horse Canyon was part of the route of one emigrant trail, and eye bolts can still be found in some trees, where they were used to rope the wagons up or down.

After a mile of this meadowy forest, our trail crosses the Horse Canyon stream to its east side and leaves the main draw of the canyon, passing east over a ridge. Then the trail plunges down a rocky way where it is disguised as a rock-filled watercourse, and one had best watch one's footing. A brief stop will allow the careful descender to lift his eyes to enjoy the surrounding greenery and flowers, and to look down to the bottom of Summit City Canyon, far below. Soon the steepness decreases, and the rocky chute gives way to gentle switchbacks that lead ½ mile down to the Tahoe-Yosemite Trail beside Summit City Creek. Fair-to-good campsites lie near the junction. Fishing is fair-to-good for rainbow (to 10″) in Summit City Creek.

3rd and 4th Hiking Days: Retrace your steps, 10 miles (16.1 km).

Silver Lake to the Mokelumne River   **3**

TRIP   From Silver Lake to the Mokelumne River (round trip; part cross country). Topo map *Silver Lake*. Best mid season; 29 miles (46.6 km).

Grade	Trail/layover days	Total recommended days
Leisurely	6/2	8
Moderate	5/1	6
Strenuous	4/0	4

HILITES   The largest wilderness river in the northern Sierra is the goal of this trip. Virgin forests here shade the cool, green river, brown trout often rise to the fly, and except at trail crossings solitude is plentiful.

DESCRIPTION (Leisurely trip)

1st and 2nd Hiking Days: Follow Trip 2 to **Summit City Canyon**, 10 miles (16.1 km).

3rd Hiking Day (**Summit City Canyon** to the **Mokelumne River**, 4.5 miles—7.2 km): Some readers have complained that previous editions didn't mention the rattlesnakes in Summit City Canyon and along the Mokelumne River. Now they are mentioned. But we have yet to see one there.

Several hundred yards below the Horse Canyon Trail junction, our route, following the Tahoe-Yosemite Trail, easily crosses the Horse Canyon stream and then winds down Summit City Creek to cross Telephone Gulch. The main canyon narrows, but not so much as to force our path right next to the creek, and we follow a sandy duff tread across flats dotted with many lodgepole pines and aspens. The commonest

flower here, as it has been since before we reached the floor of
Summit City Canyon is the pink-cupped sidalcea. The second
commonest has been squaw root, also called yampa, with
hundreds of little white flowers making up flattish
flowerheads. An overgrown sign points to *Grouse Creek,* and
finally the regular trail ends just beyond a charming if now
illegal campsite.

From here to the Mokelumne River, the essentially
cross-country route is variously marked, and sometimes more
clear, sometimes less, but at worst you will be delayed in your
passage; you can't get lost. You should cross Summit City
Creek about 200 yards downstream from the illegal campsite,
at a point where deep, narrow channels in the bedrock can
contain all the stream flow except in early season, and
immediately scramble up the east slope before veering south
to parallel the stream. You will go behind a knoll about 30 feet
high with a small Jeffrey pine on it, and then proceed parallel
to the creek but separated from it by a series of rocky
prominences. From time to time ducks give some guidance, as
do a few remaining orange plastic ribbons tied by trail
surveyors when the Forest Service intended to construct a
trail here.

About ½ mile from the main stream crossing, we dip down
beside a very small stream and parallel it for ½ mile, then
cross it and contour high on a red-fir-shaded hillside, looking
down on a green, aspen-dotted flat where Summit City Creek
meanders south. After a little bushwhacking through willow
thickets, we descend on open granite to an almost flat area
near the stream, then on a fallen log cross a tributary that
runs till late summer. After penetrating more brush, we again
descend on open granite, this time to a large, sandy-bottomed
pool below a spectacular cataract on Summit City Creek. This
pool makes a fine lunch spot.

From the pool we pick up the ducked route again and make
two half-loops away from the creek and back to it. In some
places there are competing ducks, but they all lead in the
correct general direction. About ¼ mile from the pool we get a
good look down into the river canyon, and see that it is not too
far below us now. After the second half-loop returns to the
creek momentarily, our route veers east, tops a small ridge,
and descends steeply south for ¼ mile to a crossing of Summit
City Creek. A fallen tree here still with its bark, which does
not quite reach the north bank, would help one across the
creek during high water. About 100 yards beyond the crossing,
a faint trail forks left and we follow it 300 yards to an unsigned

junction in a sandy flat. Turning right here, we reach, in 300 more yards, a sign indicating *Cedar Camp Trail*. A few yards farther is the beautiful, clear Mokelumne River.

If you miss these faint trails, you can of course just follow Summit City Creek down to its confluence with the river. There are good campsites near the confluence. Fishing in the river for brown and rainbow trout (to 14″), is good—better if you go upstream, because that's tough walking.

4th, 5th and 6th Hiking Days: Retrace your steps, 14.5 miles (23.3 km).

Mokelumne River near Summit City Creek

4   Silver Lake to Long Lake

TRIP   From Silver Lake to Long Lake (round trip). Topo
            map *Silver Lake*. Best mid season, 13 miles—21
            km (maximum).

Grade	Trail/layover days	Total recommended days
Leisurely	2/0	2
Moderate	....	....
Strenuous	....	....

HILITES   This easy weekend trip is even shorter for those
            with mountainworthy cars, and the very swimmable lake which is the destination makes a fine
            base from which to explore the gentle plateau
            north of the Mokelumne River Canyon.

DESCRIPTION

If your car has good clearance you can probably drive past
Allen's ranch to a parking area just beyond a runoff stream not
long before Squaw Ridge (see the description below). You find
the start of your dirt road at the top of the hill on State
Highway 88 southwest of Silver Lake, and just east of Tragedy
Spring, beginning among some summer homes. The parking
area is 5 miles in from the highway. About 1¾ miles up this
dirt road a signed fork to the right leads past Mud Lake and
then back to the main dirt road before you reach Allen's ranch,
and cars with only medium clearance can probably reach the
parking area by taking this detour. Using either road will save
you 2½ miles of walking each way.

1st Hiking Day (**Silver Lake** to **Long Lake**, 6.5 miles—10.5 km):
This hike begins on a dirt road that goes south from Plasse's
resort, south of Silver Lake. Just beyond the resort
campground the road fords a small, unnamed stream and
heads past Stockton Municipal Camp on the right. Our wide,
dusty trail leaves the road as we continue southbound in a
moderate forest of small lodgepole pines east of the creek. Soon
the trail begins to rise gradually and then more steeply, under

a welcome forest canopy of red fir and lodgepole pine. It passes several long, grassy meadows flanking the unnamed stream, fine spots for a breather stop or an early lunch. In 1½ miles our route passes a junction with a trail to Hidden Lake and then reaches the steep south wall of the basin we have been ascending. Here the path proceeds by way of long switchbacks up a mountain-hemlock-shaded volcanic slope. Views from the ridgetop include Silver Lake and Hidden Lake in the northern foreground, the Crystal Range and the Jacks Peak-Dicks Peak range farther north in Desolation Wilderness, and in the south, the meadow that we will walk through south of Allen's ranch, and the top of buff-brown Mokelumne Peak.

About 75 yards downhill from this saddle we meet the dirt road referred to above. (The northbound hiker could identify the place to leave the dirt road by noting that beyond Allen's ranch a two-track rough road veers right from the main dirt road at a pile of several hundred tan volcanic rocks.) Our route on the dusty dirt road descends gently past the entrance to Allen's ranch and crosses the signed headwaters of the Bear River—at this point not even a trickle in late summer. Then we soon ford running water in the lee of hundreds of brilliant yellow mimulus flowers and reach the parking area referred to above. Just beyond, we veer right on a trail as the jeep road ascends leftward, and traverse gently up in the shade of pine and hemlock to Squaw Ridge.

The junction on the ridge is in the middle of a forest of signs, identifying the Squaw Ridge Trail going northeast and southwest, the site of Plasse's Trading Post of Gold Rush days, the road-trail to Pardoe Lake, and our Cedar Camp Trail, numbered 17E27. About 200 yards down from this sign "forest" is Horsethief Springs, where amid more yellow mimulus a pipe delivers the best drinking water on this entire trip, a fine place for lunch. Continuing on the 2-track road, our route arrives at the signed border of the Mokelumne Wilderness, created by Congress in 1964, where 50,450 acres are forever held in trust for those who prefer their outdoors unmechanized.

In the wilderness our route for the next mile is almost level, slightly down, past several large meadows awash in corn lilies, groundsel and lupine in midseason. After a short descent on open hillside, the trail leads down through cool forest with a very green understory. Then it levels again in a moderate forest cover of pine and fir and passes the trail to Black Rock Lake. The next descent, over open granite slabs that look south to the plateau around our destination and to

Mokelumne Peak, passes a signed trail to Cole Creek Lakes. The sign is nailed to a lodgepole pine near its base, and easily missed. These lakes are a fine alternative campsite for this trip. The largest lake is ½ mile south on the lateral trail, and swimming and fishing for rainbow and brook trout are excellent.

Continuing on the Cedar Camp Trail, we wind among boulders shaded by silver and lodgepole pine and descend rockily to cross the dwindling outlet of a small lakelet which is the southernmost of the Cole Creek Lakes. A use trail up its east side leads to the main lake, mentioned above.

Now in red-fir forest, our path switchbacks down for a mile of decreasing gradient, recrossing the dwindling outlet, to the signed turnoff to Long Lake. Here we turn east and wind levelly beside snowmelt ponds for a short ½ mile to the west end of warm, reedy, tree-bound Long Lake. There is no stream, but the lake water is drinkable. In late season Halazone would be an extra precaution. Fishing for brook trout (to 14″) is fair, with a midsummer slowdown, and swimming from the granite slabs at the east end is first-rate. At night, you may be entertained by the excited calls of convening coyotes. On my first visit here, before I knew any were around, I let out a yip-yip, and was astounded that two real ones answered.
2nd Hiking Day: Retrace your steps, 6.5 miles (10.5 km).

Brook trout from Long Lake

Silver Lake to Camp Irene

5

TRIP   From Silver Lake to Camp Irene (round trip). Topo map *Silver Lake*. Best mid season; 25 miles (40.4 km).

Grade	Trail/layover days	Total recommended days
Leisurely	5/1	6
Moderate	4/0	4
Strenuous	3/0	3

HILITES   The hiker taking this trip will stop overnight at two highly contrasting places. Long Lake is at 8000 feet elevation, in the cool belt, and the green water is still, with no visible inflow or outflow after early season. In contrast, the Mokelumne River is a good-sized, clear-flowing river at an elevation of only 5000 feet, where middays can be very hot.

DESCRIPTION (Moderate trip)

1st Hiking Day: Follow Trip 4 to **Long Lake**, 6.5 miles (10.5 km).

2nd Hiking day (**Long Lake** to **Camp Irene**, 6 miles—9.7 km): After retracing the short lateral trail to Long Lake, this day's route turns left (south) on the Cedar Camp Trail and rises gradually through a dense forest of fir and pine. Many rivulets lace this slope into midseason, and their courses are fertile growing grounds for lavender shooting stars and other meadow flowers. As the grade levels off, the trail swings eastward and soon arrives at green, sloping Munson Meadow, where in late season you will find the first flowing water since Horsethief Springs. For northbound hikers, it is the first water since the beginning of the long, unshaded climb up the manzanita-lined sandy trail from the "oasis" in the Mokelumne River canyon.

From Munson Meadow the trail wanders southeast over a forested plateau for a mile before it starts to descend in earnest into the river canyon. At first, the trail is rocky and dusty, shaded by a sparse forest cover of red firs. Then it steepens and becomes completely exposed to the sun as it leads down a series of long switchback legs on very sandy underfooting. Views across the canyon are quite expansive, and time passes quickly—for the descending traveler. Coming back is a very different story.

Nearly 2 miles from the start of the switchbacks, the trail, still steep, enters much more hospitable territory where all-year water allows alders, willows, aspens and a great panoply of wildflowers to flourish. About 100 yards below the first of these wet "oasis" areas is a flat spot where one could camp if he were up-bound and exhausted. The trail continues to descend, moderately to steeply, but it is well shaded much of the time, and it often crosses unmapped streams that flow all year. At these streams the thirsty hiker can pleasure his mouth with the sweet pure water, and pleasure his eyes with the multicolors of orange tiger lily, pink columbine, yellow groundsel and white milfoil flowers, and the rich green of bracken ferns. After about four stream crossings—depending on the season—it is a steep 200-yard descent on a rocky-dusty trail to the junction of the unmapped trail up the river canyon and the trail down to Camp Irene.

Turning right here, our route descends to a stream not shown on the map and follows it down to the river, passing a 1974 burn shortly before reaching Camp Irene. This camping area has a sandy beach, fine granite slabs, lovely pools—and a lot of campers, since it is a popular overnight stop along the Tahoe-Yosemite Trail. Those who need solitude will find it up or down the river. Fishing in the Mokelumne is good for brown and rainbow trout (to 14").

3rd and 4th Hiking Days: Retrace your steps, 12.5 miles (20.9 km).

Silver Lake to the Mokelumne River   6

TRIP   From Silver Lake to the Mokelumne River via
Summit City Canyon, return via Munson Meadow
and Long Lake (shuttle trip). Topo map *Silver
Lake*. Best mid season; 28.2 miles (45.4 km).

Grade	Trail/layover days	Total Recommended days
Leisurely	6/2	8
Moderate	5/1	6
Strenuous	4/0	4

HILITES   This tour visits examples of all the landscapes of
the Carson Pass region—volcanic peaks, rounded
granite domes, deep-cut river canyons and lake-
dotted plateaus. Anyone in good condition who has
the basic skills for hiking cross country will enjoy
this long shuttle trip.

DESCRIPTION (Moderate trip)

1st, 2nd and 3rd Hiking Days: Follow Trip 3 to the **Mokelumne
River**, 14.5 miles (23.3 km).

4th Hiking Day (**Mokelumne River** to **Long Lake**, 7.2 miles—11.6
km): (This trail description as far as the junction with the
trail to Camp Irene is quite detailed because the multiplicity
of trails and paths in the region west of Summit City Creek
makes route finding a problem.) From the *Cedar Camp Trail*
sign, retrace your steps 300 yards to the unsigned junction in a
sandy flat and turn left. A bare hundred yards south of this
junction, very noticeable ducks lead up a granite slab, more or
less straight ahead. Don't follow them. Instead, veer right, and
when you top the crest of granite a few feet above you, you will

(if it's still there) see a duck which will lead you onto the little-used trail on which you came here from the Tahoe-Yosemite Trail. If you do accidentally follow the proscribed ducked route, you will soon find yourself going down beside the river. Eventually you will have to leave the riverside and climb some cliffs above a gorge, perhaps using rope to haul your pack once or twice. Finally you will arrive at Camp Irene, and from there you can take the Tahoe-Yosemite Trail north 1 mile to its junction with the Munson Meadow Trail, a junction described in later paragraphs.

Back at the Tahoe-Yosemite Trail where we left it yesterday, we turn left, top a small ridge, cross a tributary stream, and descend into a dense forest of second-growth ponderosa pine and incense-cedar with a few delicate ferns on the level forest floor. Then, emerging from this forest, we see that we are close under granite cliffs on the right (north). From here a gentle downgrade takes us past a 5-foot-thick ponderosa, burned through at the base, into a fine forest of first-growth sugar pines, their great cones strewn about the forest floor. After crossing a stream that flows in early season, our route soon leaves the forest and climbs more than 100 feet on rocky-dusty underfooting, leveling off under a sparse-to-moderate cover of Jeffrey pines, incense-cedars and black oaks. In ⅛ mile after the climb, the eastbound hiker would notice a fork veering right, but he should keep left. From this junction our path makes a steep, sandy ascent for several hundred yards, then drops slightly across exposed granite outcroppings. Just after it swings right, there is another unofficial junction that might beguile an eastbound hiker: he should keep right at this junction. Then one arrives at the signed junction of the trails to Camp Irene (left) and Munson Meadow (right). From here, retrace the steps of most of the 2nd hiking day, Trip 5, to Long Lake. The ascent you will make out of the Mokelumne River canyon is very stiff indeed, and the earlier you start this hiking day, the better.

5th Hiking Day: Reverse the 1st hiking day of Trip 4, 6.5 miles (10.5 km).

Carson Pass to Showers Lake

7

TRIP From Carson Pass to Showers Lake (round trip). Topo map *Silver Lake*. Best mid season, 8.6 miles (13.8 km).

Grade	Trail/layover days	Total recommended days
Leisurely	2/1	3
Moderate	2/0	2
Strenuous	....	....

HILITES Showers Lake is one of the best camping places between U.S. 50 and State Highway 88, with numerous campsites and good angling for brook trout. En route, the trail through the upper Truckee Valley offers panoramic views of immense volcanic formations and promises potential close-up glimpses of many birds and mammals.

DESCRIPTION

1st Hiking Day (**Carson Pass** to **Showers Lake**, 4.3 miles—6.9 km): From a small parking area (8350') 1 mile west of Carson Pass our dusty route climbs steadily northward on an old jeep road now closed to motor vehicles. The slope is moderately forested with red fir, lodgepole pine and clumps of aspen. Leaving the tree cover behind, we climb steeply up a slope covered by sagebrush and mule ears. In the warm sun of this open slope the sage odor adds spice to the thin, clear air. After ascending 400 feet in ½ mile, the trail reaches a saddle on the divide between Truckee River drainage and American River drainage. From this saddle views southward of Round Top Peak and its snow-draped satellites are excellent. In the north, we see Mt. Tallac, Dicks Peak and Jacks Peak, all west of Tahoe. Here we begin a descent down the long, green, tree-dotted valley of the upper Truckee. Nearby on the east, Red Lake Peak is topped by slablike volcanic outcroppings resembling a stegosaur's back plates. Little runoff streams that spring from porous volcanic rocks trickle their water onto flower gardens of iris, yarrow milfoil, Mariposa lily, sulfur flower, lupine and paintbrush. Descending moderately to

steadily from the summit, we cross three runoff streams (dry
in late season), then a westward-flowing tributary, and finally
the infant Truckee River—all via easy fords.

Just past another easy ford are the buildings of a cow camp,
and near them the Round Lake Trail (not shown on the topo
map) branches right. The meadows here are full of little gray
Belding squirrels, commonly called picket-pins, and often a
Swainson hawk soars overhead, hoping to surprise one of
them. Continuing the level walk from the Round Lake
junction, we pass an unsigned trail to Meiss Lake, visible as a
meadow-fringed blue sheet in the northeast. Then one last
time we ford the river, on boulders, and a few feet beyond the
ford an old jeep road forks right toward Meiss Lake, as our
route bears left. (From this point on our route is not shown on
the topo map.) We pass a trail to Schneider Camp (not shown
on the topo map and unsigned but marked by a blazed **S** on the
lodgepole), and ascend out of Dixon Canyon on a gentle grade.
From the crest of this little ascent, the trail dips past a
shallow, weedy pond and continues on the old two-track jeep
road. After crossing two runoff streams (dry in late season), we
begin a steady-to-steep ascent of ¼ mile, first up a wash filled
with smoothed, round rocks, and then on a rocky-dusty trail,
under moderate-to-dense forest cover of red fir, hemlock,
silver pine and lodgepole pine. Sixty yards after the jeep tracks
emerge from this forest onto a meadowy slope lush with lupine
and mule ears, a trail veers slightly left and uphill from the
tracks, and we take the trail. (The old jeep road also goes to
Showers Lake.) This trail section traverses a bountifully
flowered, meadowy slope to a forested saddle overlooking
Showers Lake, from where it descends to the fair-to-good
campsites on the west and east sides of the lake (8650').
Fishing is good for eastern brook (to 12"). From a base camp
here, one may easily walk cross country to Four Lakes, where
fishing and swimming are often good in mid-to-late season.
2nd Hiking Day: Retrace your steps, 4.3 miles (6.9 km).

Carson Pass to Echo Summit 8

TRIP From Carson Pass to Echo Summit (shuttle trip). Topo maps *Silver Lake, Fallen Leaf Lake.* Best mid season; 10.8 miles (17.4 km).

Grade	Trail/layover days	Total recom- mended days
Leisurely	2/1	3
Moderate	2/0	2
Strenuous	....	....

HILITES This trip offers one of the easiest ways in the whole northern Sierra to get away from the crowd, and it is an excellent choice for a two-party shuttle. With a minimum of effort, the hiker can traverse some high, scenic, little-used country, where the wildlife is as plentiful as the people are scarce.

DESCRIPTION

1st Hiking Day: Follow Trip 7 to **Showers Lake,** 4.3 miles (6.9 km).

2nd Hiking Day **(Showers Lake** to **Echo Summit,** 6.5 miles —10.5 km): Heading northwest from the southwest shore of Showers Lake, we soon find the trail, and then ascend gently for several hundred yards through mixed conifers. Coming out onto open slopes, we ford a year-round stream fed by the snow cornice that drapes the ridge of Little Round Top above. Where we cross this stream, its banks are lined with thousands of blossoms of the showy yellow flower *Arnica chamissionis*. In fact, this whole open bowl is laced with runoff streams and lavishly planted with colorful bushes and flowers: blue elderberry, green gentian, swamp whiteheads, mountain bluebell, aster, wallflower, penstemon, spiraea, cinquefoil, corn lily and columbine. As we walk around this bowl on the boundary between volcanic rocks above and granite below, we have good views of Stevens Peak and Red Lake Peak, both built up of layers of richly colored volcanic flows.

Finally, the trail ascends out of the bowl and enters a sparse cover of lodgepole and silver pine. At the crest of this ascent, the pine gives way to hemlock as we pass a cattle drift fence (close the gate) and level off through open high country. Reaching a willowy meadow, one may lose the trail momentarily, but it is easy to find if one continues straight across the meadow. A short distance beyond is a junction with a signed trial to Schneider Cow Camp, which leads west. One third of a mile beyond this junction our route crosses, at right angles, an unsigned but well-grooved trail which is used by local stockmen, and then continues its almost level, winding course northward under a sparse-to-moderate mixed forest cover.

We then pass a collapsed stock fence and make a short, steep descent down a hemlock-covered hillside to a meadowy slope where marsh marigolds, their white and yellow petals set off by their rich green leaves, bloom in the wetness of melting snows until late in the season. Our sandy footpath soon passes a trail that winds down Sayles Canyon, and then we continue north to a summit from where views of the Crystal Range, including Pyramid Peak, are good. From here it is a gentle descent under hemlock, silver and lodgepole pine to Bryan Meadow. Here one may camp except in late season, when the stream is dry. A collapsed log cabin in the meadow sprawls near the confluence of routes leading to Showers Lake, U.S. 50 and Benwood Meadow.

Heading for Benwood Meadow, we ascend a gently rising sandy trail through meadowy, open stands of lodgepole pine, with some sagebrush. The alert hiker here may spot a red-shafted flicker on one of its characteristic undulating flights between trees. At the top of this sandy climb the trail levels off and becomes indistinct, but the route is well marked by blazes. A short, steep descent then brings us to a willow-filled bowl where an unnamed stream rises. We cross the young stream and on the far slope veer right, on a trail that soon switchbacks steeply down a red-fir-covered slope. At the foot of the slope is another willowy meadow, and shortly beyond that another steep downslope, also shaded by red fir, where following the route may require attention to the occasional ducks. The trail then levels out in a large meadow that was once a lake, skirting the west side of it.

The trail from this meadow to Benwood Meadow is sometimes indistinct, but there are sufficient blazes and ducks. At Benwood Meadow the flora is quite noteworthy: along the wet meadow margin the flower-spotter is kept busy by the plenitude of aster, corn lily, snow plant, alpine lily, monkey flower, penstemon, false Solomon's seal, squawroot, pennyroyal, groundsel, columbine, larkspur and mountain bluebell, to say nothing of the ferns, grasses and sedges.

Past Benwood Meadow, our nearly level trail meets a junction with a new segment of trail that goes left to Echo Summit. Then it dips to cross the outlet of a lily-filled pond, and ascends gently up a rather exposed slope, where a few mixed conifers partially shade a ground cover of huckleberry oak, pinemat manzanita and Sierra chinquapin. Finally, the rocky-dusty trail ends at an oiled road (7520′) that serves a small tract of summer homes ½ mile south of Echo Summit.

Showers Lake

9   Mosquito Lake to Bull Run Lake

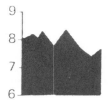

TRIP
From Mosquito Lake to Heiser Lake, Bull Run Lake, return to Stanislaus Meadow (shuttle trip). Topo maps *Markleeville, Dardanelles Cone* (this new trail is not shown on either map). Best mid season; 8 miles (12.8 km).

Grade	Trail/layover days	Total recom-mended days
Leisurely	3/0	3
Moderate	2/0	2
Strenuous	....	....

HILITES
Two of the better, scenic, trout-stocked lakes of the Lake Alpine area are visited on this easy hike. Dayhikers and fishermen may wish to hike only to Heiser Lake via the Heiser Lake Trail or only to larger Bull Run Lake via the Bull Run Trail, thereby avoiding the short 2½-mile shuttle.

DESCRIPTION (Leisurely trip)

1st Hiking Day (**Mosquito Lake** to **Heiser Lake**, 2 miles—3.2 km): At the west end of Mosquito Lake in a picnic ground, look for a faint trail that follows old blazes southeast, directly up a forested slope. In about 30 yards, the trail becomes obvious, leading up granitic bedrock that has a veneer of volcanic rocks. The steep trail quickly levels off, then makes a short, moderate descent and winds south close to a pond that is erroneously labeled "Heiser Lake" on the *Markleeville* topo map. The true Heiser Lake is seen on the *Dardanelles Cone* topo as the lake one mile north-northeast of Bull Run Lake.

Leaving the pond's environs, we climb steeply through a thinning forest of silver and lodgepole pine and mountain hemlock, and surmount a granitic ridge at its low point. On fresh-looking, glacially scoured rock we descend from the ridge and follow a winding route that takes the path of least resistance down slabs. After leveling off in deep forest, we climb ⅓ mile to a junction on a little flat. Tomorrow we'll head southwest from here down a creekside trail, but since our immediate goal is Heiser Lake, we turn east, hike a short ¼ mile uphill, then switchback and climb south over a low granitic ridge that hides the shallow lake. Dotted with several small islands of granitic rock, this conifer-fringed lake presents the fisherman with a picturesque distraction while he contemplates a meal of fresh brook trout. Campsites lie on the north and south shores under a pleasant canopy of red fir, lodgepole pine, silver pine and mountain hemlock.

2nd Hiking Day (**Heiser Lake** to **Bull Run Lake**, 2.5 miles—4 km): First, retrace your steps ½ mile to yesterday's trail junction. From here our route, usually well blazed and ducked, takes us southwest to the brink of a rocky slope, and then down the slope via very steep switchbacks. We then stay fairly close to Heiser Lake's outlet creek, paralleling it west across a flat basin shaded by mountain hemlocks. Approaching the basin's west edge, we cross four closely spaced branches of a tributary that joins the outlet creek just south of the trail. After a brief climb west, our trail turns south and leads to a signed junction with the Bull Run Trail.

From the junction, this route almost immediately fords Heiser Lake's outlet creek, a ford that could require a little doing in early season when it is a small torrent of white water. After following an almost level granitic bench for ⅓ mile, this route angles south and crosses the first of many creeklets. Our winding route, now largely on barren bedrock, goes from slab to granitic slab as it climbs and gyrates up toward the lake. Were it not for a superabundance of blazes and ducks, many hikers would get lost. This climb is broken into two distinct, equally long ascents, the first one trending southeast up and around a secondary ridge, the second one trending southwest and passing a trailside pond before it reaches Bull Run Lake's outlet creek and follows it up to the lake's bedrock dam. Finally, the trail descends east past large red firs to the lake's northeast corner.

Although not large by Sierra standards, this popular lake can accommodate dozens of campers, particularly on the spacious flats beneath large red firs. Swimming in the lake is good in early August, and fishing is often good for brook trout.

3rd Hiking Day (**Bull Run Lake** to **Stanislaus Meadow**, 3.5 miles—5.6 km): After backtracking to the trail junction just

west of Heiser Lake's outlet, our route stays on the Bull Run
Trail as it winds, steeply at times, 350 vertical feet down rock
slabs covered with juniper trees and huckleberry oak bushes,
almost touching the outlet creek from both lakes before it
eases off in a shady flat. A short forest traverse brings us to a
crossing of this creek, which in early season can entail a cold,
wide, knee-deep ford. Beyond the ford we follow the creek a
shady, long ⅓ mile to a refording of it, which will give
early-season hikers another challenge. The trail west from the
ford is not very distinct, particularly if you're hiking in the
opposite direction, but essentially it maintains a westbound
course 100 yards to an even wider ford: the headwaters of the
North Fork Stanislaus River. As usual, look for logs across the
stream, which may make fording much drier and perhaps
quicker.

Beyond the North Fork, we cut across a seasonally dry wash
before turning north and roughly paralleling the North Fork
upstream. A wide path leads up this moderate grade, and, near
its top, we may be greeted by a chorus of cow bells, which
incessantly ring as their wearers munch away in grassy
Stanislaus Meadow. A fence keeps the cattle in the meadow
and us in the forest, and an easy ½-mile hike along its west
side brings us to the signed Bull Run Lake trailhead.

Bull Run Lake   *Jeff Schaffer*

Wolf Creek Meadows to Soda Springs 10

TRIP   From Wolf Creek Meadows to Soda Springs Guard Station via High Trail, return via East Carson River Trail (semiloop trip). Topo map *Topaz Lake*. Best mid season; 20.5 miles (33 km).

Grade	Trail/layover days	Total recommended days
Leisurely	3/1	4
Moderate	2/0	2
Strenuous	....	....

HILITES   One can acquire a good feeling for eastside Sierra flora and geology on this trip, ideally suited for weekend backpackers. Because the landscape is viewed from a crest route going and a canyon route returning, the hiker sees it from two very different perspectives.

DESCRIPTION (Moderate trip)

1st Hiking Day (**Wolf Creek Meadows** to **Soda Springs Guard Station**, 9.5 miles—15.3 km): At the edge of a volcanic slope covered with sagebrush, mule ears and bitterbrush, the High Trail climbs upward into an open forest of Jeffrey pine and white fir. With the brief views of Wolf Creek Meadows behind us, we now enjoy the shade that the forest provides on this steep climb. Beyond a large split boulder and its surrounding mountain mahogany bushes, the High Trail parallels the ridge up to a level crest, then climbs steeply to a small, grassy flat. Just beyond this flat, we start an uphill traverse across a grassy, gentle slope that contains a curious combination of water-loving, white-barked aspens almost next to drought-resistant, mangy-barked junipers. Jeffrey pines, white firs, willows, mule ears and sagebrush complete the cast of principal plants. Here, taking a break, one can easily fall asleep to the soothing sounds of rustling aspen leaves.

Up these shady slopes we climb, and about ½ mile beyond the meadow, the steep trail eases up and then levels off as it comes to an open slope. Here the trail provides a momentary view of the Vaquero Camp buildings in the east, down in Silver King Valley, and more enduring views of the granitic Freel Peak area, in the northwest, beyond whose summits lies Lake Tahoe. Along our short, open traverse we find a good exposure of a type of blocky volcanic rock that is common to this "land of fire and ice." It is called an *autobrecciated* ("self-broken") lava flow. From the middle Miocene epoch through the late Pliocene epoch (roughly from 18 to 5 million years ago), thick andesitic lava flows poured from summits that probably resembled today's Oregon Cascades, and they covered an area of the Sierra Nevada that extended from Sonora Pass north to Lassen Park and from east of the present Sierra crest westward to beneath the Central Valley. When the thick lava flows cooled as they flowed along their downward paths, they became less and less able to move, particularly along their rapidly cooling edges, and eventually these edges solidified. But then the pressure of the still-flowing internal material fractured the edges, creating the broken-up texture we see here.

At the base of an autobrecciated flow decorated with vine maples, we enter a shady white-fir forest and encounter a refreshing, flowery, mossy, spring-fed creeklet. Beyond it our trail climbs moderately eastward, then descends slightly to a low knoll covered with ragged mountain mahogany. Leaving the knoll, we pass through a forest of pines and firs, and descend steeply south into two seasonal, parallel creeklets that drain Snowslide Canyon. Volcanic rocks give way to granitic ones as we leave this broad, brushy canyon, descend through a shady forest, round a jagged, granitic ridge, and then reach another seasonal creek.

One-fourth mile beyond this creek, our trail tops out at a bedrock saddle on a ridge above the East Carson canyon. From it, short switchbacks lead steeply down a brushy slope covered with huckleberry oak and manzanita; then our trail diagonals southwest down to a gentle slope on which we cross an unsigned east-west trail. Soon we reach a bubbling creek, and cross it only 90 yards before arriving at the East Fork Carson River. If you don't like river fords, you can camp along or near the riverbank, and later backtrack 1/5 mile to the east-west trail and follow it east 1/4 mile to another river ford. (Those who ford the East Carson southbound on this trip will reford it here.) Before mid-July, the river is usually waist-deep, about 50°F at most, and swift, but by Labor Day it has dropped to knee depth. A rope helps in an early-season traverse across the river's bouldery bottom, but it is unnecessary for the experienced backpacker, since there are no dangerous rapids downstream.

For those who fish this river, a likely catch is the mountain whitefish, which looks like a cross between a trout and a sucker. A small mouth on the lower part of its head is the sucker characteristic, but the presence of an adipose fin on the lower back identifies it as a close relative of trout and salmon. Like these fish, it is good to eat. This river also contains the Tahoe sucker, whose protractile mouth, on the bottom of its head, is ideally suited for scavenging the river bottom. Although bony, it is tasty.

Across the river, the High Trail ends in 80 yards at a signed junction with the East Carson River Trail—an old jeep road closed to motor vehicles. On this gravelly road we parallel the river ⅓ mile upstream to the north edge of a sagebrush flat. Here the river angles west, but our tracks head south through dense sagebrush. Reaching a dry wash debouching from a small, very bouldery gorge, we climb up it to a low bedrock saddle. From the saddle we make a short descent past a small, steep cliff, on the right, then reach a larger, longer, steeper one, on the left. This cliff we parallel southeast, then continue to three close-spaced Jeffrey pines in a sagebrush flat. From between the west and south pines, the main route goes 200 yards southwest to a ford of the East Carson, then south along jeep tracks through a shady forest to a refording of the East Carson one mile later. This refording takes place at the

Bagley Valley (autobrecciated rock in foreground)   *Schaffer*

"bottom" (south) curve of a large meander, whose west half
dries up late in the summer, when the lower river shoots
directly east 150 yards to the ford (see the accompanying map).
Eventually, the meander will disappear as the river estab-
lishes a more efficient, more direct course. About 250 yards

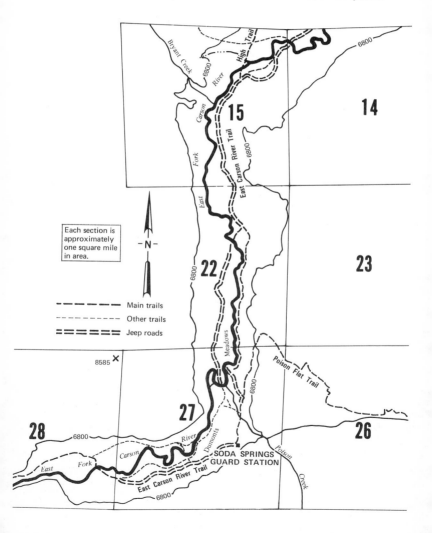

south of this ford, in a field of granitic boulders left by a glacier, an indistinct trail heads east-southeast through the grass another 250 yards to Poison Creek, just beyond whose east bank is a path that leads south 300 yards to the Soda Springs Guard Station.

Most hikers, when they arrive at the three Jeffrey pines, will prefer not to ford and reford the East Carson, even though these two fords are considerably easier than the High Trail ford. For them there is a dry route to the Soda Springs Guard Station. After leaving between the south and east pines, follow a path south-southeast for 100 yards. If you're on the right path—there are many cow paths—it will bend south and soon reach a granitic cliff that plunges down to the East Carson only ¼ mile due south of the three pines. Once around the bouldery base of this small cliff, you have an easy, open walk southward that parallels the East Carson. About ¾ mile beyond, the river bends west and you follow it on a faint trail through sagebrush to the northeast corner of the large meander mentioned in the alternate route. From this corner a set of jeep tracks leads southeast ⅕ mile across a flat to a signed junction with the Poison Flat Trail, just within forest cover. Trip 13 heads north along this trail, and trips 15 and 16 head south along it to this junction. We turn south, up-canyon, and follow the jeep tracks, which quickly reduce to a path in the 100 yards it takes to reach the first of as many as half a dozen distributaries of Poison Creek. Between two of them, the alternate route—a footpath from the west-northwest—ends at our broad path. In a few minutes' walk, we arrive at shady Soda Springs Campground, equipped with a table and an outhouse, beside the guard station. Cool, bubbling water, diverted by a small canal from Poison Creek, adds to the charm of this conifer-clad campsite.

2nd Hiking Day (**Soda Springs Guard Station** to **Wolf Creek Meadows,** 11 miles—17.7 km): First, retrace your steps 2¾ miles to the signed High Trail junction. This day's route continues on a jeep road going northeast from the junction, then quickly curves right as it rounds an open flat. In 0.4 mile from the High Trail junction, we arrive at an East Carson ford which is almost as difficult as the High Trail ford. Our next segment of jeep road starts northeast up a flat and crosses it, then is almost cut in two by a river's meander that has eroded deeply into the flat. Beyond the meander, a traverse across an equally long flat ends at the East Carson one mile below the High Trail junction.

Here, look for two large Jeffrey pines just north of you, between which a barbed-wire gate marks the start of a trail.

From the gate this trail stays on the west side of the East
Carson, paralleling the river at first, but gradually veering
away from it. We cross two long, but not high, moraines—
those bouldery, sandy ridges left by a glacier before it
retreated back up the East Carson canyon and into extinction.
Beyond the second moraine is a seasonal creeklet which we
cross only 70 yards west of the East Carson. The trail now
parallels the river to a junction with some jeep tracks.

We follow these north almost ½ mile up to a low ridgecrest of
a rocky moraine that marks the northernmost extent of a
former glacier in Silver King Valley. Atop this moraine is a
barbed-wire fence across the jeep tracks. Motor vehicles are
allowed on the north side of the gate, and to avoid them our
route goes through an impressive gorge of the East Carson.
This challenging route leaves the jeep tracks atop the
moraine, follows the fence west about 300 yards to a gate,
descends to the entrance of the gorge, and follows the river's
west side 2½ miles. The difficulty of this gorge route varies,
the hardest part occurring in the scenic first half. When the
water is low—after Labor Day—you can walk along the river's
edge, but in early season you'll have to climb above it many
times. Nevertheless, a rope is not necessary. At first, you'll
pass by impressive, deeply cut cliffs of autobrecciated lava
flows. Farther down, you're likely to see columnar flows in
addition. Campsites in this isolated gorge are plentiful, but
unfortunately the best ones are on the opposite bank. Midway
down the gorge campsites are replaced by talus slopes whose
boulders came down from the loose, pinkish-brown cliffs
above. This route ends at the official trail, which fords the East
Carson at Gray's Crossing, directly west of a low gap.

From the crossing, the East Carson River Trail heads west,
then climbs steeply up to gentler slopes above the river. Soon
we reach a gate, pass through it, and gradually curve
westward into Railroad Canyon. Up this canyon we hike,
seemingly too long to be on the right route, and then we cross
its creeklet. From here, the last permanent source of fresh
water, our trail climbs north out of the canyon, circles along
the edge of a flat-topped autobrecciated lava flow, then
traverses ⅓ mile northwest to the south tip of shallow Wolf
Creek Lake (not the larger, better known Wolf Creek Lake at
the east base of Sonora Peak).

From the lake's southeast corner, our trail climbs west up to
the base of steep volcanic slopes, then ascends to the ridge
above the trailhead, along which runs a fence. On the other
side of its gate, we meet the end of a jeep road, and on it walk

west a short distance to a saddle, recognizing that the large, scattered granitic boulders resting on the volcanic bedrock are "erratics"—boulders carried here by a large glacier that once flowed north down Wolf Creek canyon. From the saddle we can look up-canyon and imagine how impressive this canyon would have appeared about 6,000 years ago, when a river of ice, hundreds of feet thick, slowly flowed past this spot, quite likely reaching, and occasionally damming, the East Fork Carson River. After a moment's reflection on this subject, we leave the saddle and descend 100 steep yards to our trailhead, which is beside the trailhead of the High Trail.

East Fork Carson River　　　　　　　　　　　*Jeff Schaffer*

11 Wolf Creek Meadows to Wolf Creek

TRIP From Wolf Creek Meadows to Wolf Creek via Soda Springs Guard Station, Murray Canyon and Wolf Creek canyon (shuttle trip). Topo maps *Topaz Lake, Sonora Pass*. Best mid or late season; 24 miles (38.6 km).

Grade	Trail/layover days	Total recommended days
Leisurely	3/0	3
Moderate	2/0	2
Strenuous	....	....

HILITES Like trip 2, this trip starts as a scenic crest route, then it proceeds through parts of three glaciated canyons. Plenty of creekside campsites await anglers who would like to try their skill at trout fishing.

DESCRIPTION (Moderate trip)

1st Hiking Day (**Wolf Creek Meadows** to **Murray Canyon Trail junction,** 12 miles—19.3 km): First, follow trip 10 to Soda Springs Guard Station, 9.5 miles (15.3 km). Leaving the shady campground at the guard station, we hike west on a jeep trail and after ⅓ mile cross a spring-fed creeklet. Just beyond this creeklet is a well-used campsite under lodgepole pines, only 20 yards downslope. Immediately below it is a trail coming from the larger meander mentioned in Trip 10 (see the map in Trip 10). Westward, this trail parallels our jeep trail, dying out in a grassy meadow. Our easy route through sagebrush reaches this meadow in ½ mile and the jeep tracks, like the trail, die out in it. They quickly reappear at the northwest end of the meadow and lead us 200 yards northwest to a wide ford of the East Carson.

Continuing northwest from the bank on a hiking trail, we arrive at an unsigned trail junction only 20 yards east of a large, trailside Jeffrey pine that is marked with a conspicuous blaze. From here, our comfortable trail goes west through a meadow and gradually curves south, crossing one permanent and several seasonal creeklets before reaching a trail junction only 50 yards beyond a crossing of wide, refreshing Murray Canyon creek. Several campsites are found here, the best one being under large cottonwoods alongside the creek midway between the crossing and the trail junction.

2nd Hiking Day (**Murray Canyon Trail junction** to **Upper Wolf Creek Meadows**, 12 miles—19.3 km): At the signed trail junction, we leave the gentle gradient of the East Fork Carson River Trail and climb, steeply at times, up 15 switchback legs that lead high on a brushy, open-forested slope and then into Murray Canyon. Like virtually every tributary canyon of the East Carson above Soda Springs, this one usually had a glacier in it when there was one in the main canyon. Being much smaller, however, the Murray Canyon glacier was unable to keep pace with the tremendous excavating power of the East Carson glacier, which in this area was sometimes more than 800 feet thick. As a result, the East Carson glacier cut down faster, leaving Murray Canyon as a hanging valley—which we have just entered at the top of the switchbacks.

From the top of these switchbacks we go another 200 yards to the verdant banks of clear Murray Canyon creek. After 100 steep yards, the trail resumes a moderate grade and takes us past the first of many flower-lined creeklets. One-third mile up from the creek crossing, we pass through the gate of a cattle fence, then continue up the flowery path. At a trail junction where Murray Canyon splits in two, our trail, the main one, bends right and climbs steeply west up the canyon.

About ¼ mile above the junction is a permanent creek, lined with willows and alders; then in another ¼ mile the trail crosses a second creek. Beyond it the route steepens, on a few short switchbacks up a granitic slope. Talus that has fallen from volcanic formations above has buried much of the granitic bedrock, and it becomes very widespread as the grade eases and the trail enters a small gully flowered with mule ears. Beyond this gully, we climb steadily north ½ mile to a crest saddle, where, a few yards northwest of the actual crest, is a junction with a fairly new trail. Trip 15, which has coincided with this hiking day up to this saddle, departs south along this crest path.

As we switchback northwest down rather open volcanic slopes, ahead is a flat-topped ridge composed of several thick, horizontal lava flows, below which lies a huge talus slope. This rocky slope was built up after the last glacier retreated up-canyon when water, freezing and expanding in the flows' cracks, pried off countless blocks.

At the bottom of the descent into deep, long Wolf Creek Canyon, we encounter a cattle fence, pass through its gate, and follow the trail as it widens to a jeep road. Joining this short stretch is a jeep spur from the south and, merged together, they head 100 yards northwest to a signed junction, near a conspicuous snow-depth marker, with the Asa Creek Trail. Our route, a jeep road for the remainder of this hike, starts north and quickly reaches a ford—usually a wet one—of Wolf Creek. Across the creek, we amble along an easy path ⅓ mile to a meadow and a signed junction.

Continuing northeast on the jeep road around the fenced meadow, we descend to a creeklet and then parallel Wolf Creek at a short distance, staying above the small gorge it has cut through volcanic rock. Small, tempting pools can be seen in the creek, particularly just before a gate on a low, descending ridge. Beyond the ridge gate, our route descends very steeply to a crossing of Bull Canyon creek, a wet ford except in late season. At this alder-lined crossing, granitic bedrock once again is and it becomes more abundant down-canyon.

Strolling down-canyon to Dixon Creek, we approach and veer away from Wolf Creek several times. A long, wide, rocky stream bed has formed behind a constriction in the canyon created by a prominent granitic ridge on the east side and by Dixon Creek's alluvial fan on the west. Since the *Topaz Lake* topo was made, Dixon Creek has shifted its course to a more northern position down across this fan. For most of the summer Dixon Creek runs too high to ford without getting wet feet. Once across it, though, you'll keep your feet dry the rest of the way. The jeep road first parallels the creek, then veers northwest away from it, skirts a grove of aspens and cottonwoods, and curves east around a well-weathered granitic knob. From here it is an easy 1 mile stroll to the trailhead, the Wolf Creek Meadows Undeveloped Camping Area.

Wolf Creek Meadows to Sonora Pass **12**

TRIP   From Wolf Creek Meadows to Sonora Pass via
Soda Springs, White Canyon and Wolf Creek Lake
(shuttle trip). Topo maps *Topaz Lake, Sonora Pass*.
Best mid season; 30 miles (48.5 km).

	Grade	Trail/layover days	Total recom- mended days
	Leisurely	5/1	6
	Moderate	4/0	4
	Strenuous	3/0	3

HILITES   One of the longest and deepest canyons east of the
Sierra crest, the East Fork Carson River canyon at
times contained glaciers up to 19 miles long. Our
trip heads south up this spectacular canyon, stops
at scenic Wolf Creek Lake, then passes through a
sculptured volcanic "badland" on the south slope
of Sonora Peak. This peak—the highest summit
between State Highway 108 and Mt. Shasta—is
easily climbed in a short side trip.

DESCRIPTION (Strenuous trip)

1st Hiking Day: Follow Trip 11 to **Murray Canyon Trail junction**,
12 miles (19.3 km).

2nd Hiking Day **Murray Canyon Trail junction** to **Wolf Creek
Lake,** 13 miles—20.9 km): Next to granitic bedrock just south
of the Murray Canyon Trail junction is a fair campsite. At this
campsite Murray Canyon creek blocks our path in early and
mid season. During these seasons you may have to wade
several yards downstream before you can resume your brief

walk along the west side of this creek. In about 200 yards, Murray Canyon creek bends east and joins the meadering East Fork Carson River. Immediately south of the creek's bend, we join the main path from our starting point. This path, obvious to northbound hikers, makes four fords of Murray Canyon creek and, due to willows and grass, is difficult for southbound hikers to locate. Staying along the East Carson canyon's meadowy west edge, we now hike about ½ mile south to a usually flowing creek, cross a very low ridge, and make a very steep but short ascent, 200 yards to a junction. Here, a ¼-mile-long alternate route leads east to Carson Falls before turning south and rejoining the main route. Since both routes are equally strenuous, the more scenic Carson Falls Trail is certainly recommended. Midway along this short trail you'll descend briefly to almost level granitic slabs near the lip of the river's gorge. Take your pack off here and then *cautiously* explore the falls and pools of the gorge. Over a period of thousands of years large potholes have been drilled into the bedrock as strong currents have swirled large boulders round and round. When the river's water is low, some potholes make brisk, invigorating swimming holes. If you climb to the top of an almost isolated granitic mass just downstream, you can get the best view of the main falls.

After the Carson Falls Trail rejoins the main trail, we walk through a flat that is being "logged out" by beavers. Entering an aspen grove at the edge of this flat, we curve southeast along a granitic base just above the sometimes swampy flat, and soon reach a ford of the East Carson. If you don't find any dry logs, cross at a wide, shallow place just downstream. A short ½-mile farther, where the river—trapped in a small gorge—turns abruptly west, we leave its company and hike up-canyon to a junction with the Golden Canyon Trail. From the junction our route curves southeast and quickly becomes a steep, brushy climb 400 vertical feet to the top of a granitic mass that has withstood repeated efforts of past glaciers to eradicate it. Leaving its southeast end, our route rollercoasters for ½ mile and touches upon a river meander just before it starts a fairly long climb.

This winding climb crosses a few creek beds before going south up the gully of a north-flowing seasonal creek. Beyond the top of the gully, junipers together with Jeffrey, lodgepole and silver pines are momentarily left behind as we descend into a shady red-fir forest, home of the red squirrel, or chickaree. Our path levels off at a year-round creek and beyond it we parallel the East Carson—usually at a small distance—for 3 miles upstream. The shady path crosses many creeklets as it progresses gently to moderately up-canyon, and along the way one has glimpses of the high cliffs along the canyon's east side.

At the south end of the cliffs, a descending ridge forces our route across the East Carson, which can be a slippery and wet ford in early and mid season. On the west bank, we hike south and in about 150 yards arrive at a junction with the Pacific Crest Trail. One mile from the PCT junction we cross the path of a recent avalanche which built up so much force on its descent of the west slope that it swept across the snow-covered East Carson River and knocked down trees on the east slope.

Beyond a second avalanche path we enter a forest of mature lodgepole pines and in it see more evidence of glaciation. Here, erratics—boulders transported by a glacier—were left behind as the glacier melted back some 12,000 years ago. The glacier that left these erratics was perhaps only 2½ miles long, a midget compared with the massive giant that flowed 19 miles down-canyon perhaps 60,000 years ago. The granitic bedrock over which the more recent one flowed is polished smooth and remains little changed from the day the glacier left it.

A ⅔-mile walk leads to a crossing of a permanent stream, tricky in early season. Then the trail's gradient increases noticeably. Unfortunately, when we sight the windswept saddle we're puffing up to, there is still ⅔ mile of climbing—now up a steep gradient—ahead. Whitebark pines and even late-season snow patches become evident as we make the final push. Finally struggling up to the 10,240-foot-high saddle, we take a well earned rest to pause and admire the view down the glaciated, U-shaped canyon of the East Fork Carson River.

From the saddle, the Pacific Crest Trail leads southwest along Sonora Peak's northeast slopes, but this day's hike ends by descending ⅓ mile south to campsites at the west edge of the grassy, frog-inhabited meadow that contains shallow Wolf Creek Lake. A post marks the start of the ducked path down to the lake. In 200 yards along it you'll see the lake, and can take one of several ducked routes down a moderately steep slope to it. At 10,090 feet, the lake is usually pretty cold for swimming, and fishing would yield only frogs. The lake's serene setting however, renews one's spirit, and while relaxing, you may be fortunate enough to see a large marsh hawk glide across the meadow.

3rd Hiking Day (**Wolf Creek Lake** to **Sonora Pass,** 5 miles—8.1 km): After retracing the steps back to the saddle, we follow the Pacific Crest Trail south. Winding among fractured granitic blocks, we reach a steep, conspicuous ramp up which a new trail segment has been built. The ramp, unfortunately, is narrow, leaving the trail pitifully small latitude to switchback up it, and snow can obscure parts of this climb well into August. Emerging from it, we encounter two creeklets on a slope covered with wind-cropped willows. View-seekers wishing to climb Sonora Peak can leave the trail here for a stiff but technically easy 1000-foot climb up to its lofty, dark summit.

Granitic bedrock gives way to volcanic rocks and talus as we now traverse south along the east slopes of Sonora Peak. Along this easy stretch one can see how the whitebark pines have been reduced to shrub height by winter's freezing winds. To the east, the effects of glaciation are evident in Wolf Creek canyon, but they are negligible in the distant Sweetwater Mountains. At times, you may see camouflaged U.S. Marines from the nearby Mountain Warfare Training Center. In the field from May through October, these troops participate in war games in an area that includes the Sonora Peak environs, Wolf Creek canyon and Silver Meadows canyon. From the saddle southeast of Sonora Peak, the high peaks on the Yosemite border are seen on the distant southeast horizon.

Our trail, now well graded, winds in and out of bleak gullies before coming to the tops of a conspicuous group of volcanic pinnacles that sit right on the Alpine-Mono county line. A 30-yard scramble south to one of their summits permits a sweeping panorama, north-to-east-to-south, of the Pacific Crest Trail and the slopes it traverses, and it also provides a panorama of the Sierra peak summits in the south.

More gullies lie ahead as we descend west. In ½ mile we reach a ridge and double back eastward. Then, hiking south near the crest, we again cross many gullies, so typical of this eroded volcanic landscape. Several of them have good water all year. The sunny slopes between are coated with sagebrush, mule ears, creambush, and a scattering of lodgepole and whitebark pines. Overhead, Clark nutcrackers flap and caw, and red-tailed hawks wheel and soar. Finally, we descend gently to signed Sonora Pass and a small parking area. (Northbound hikers can park 100 yards west of the pass and walk 70 yards up a closed jeep road to intercept the trail.)

Wolf Creek Meadows to Poison Lake 13

TRIP From Wolf Creek Meadows to Poison Lake via Soda Springs and Poison Flat, return via East Fork Carson River (semiloop trip). Topo maps *Topaz Lake, Sonora Pass*. Best mid season; 36.5 miles (58.8 km).

Grade	Trail/layover days	Total recommended days
Leisurely	5/1	6
Moderate	4/0	4
Strenuous	2/0	2

HILITES Good fishing and swimming await hikers who backpack into Poison Lake. Along the way, they'll obtain numerous panoramas of large, glaciated canyons and visit several carbonate and soda springs.

DESCRIPTION (Moderate trip)

1st Hiking Day: Follow Trip 10 to **Soda Springs Guard Station**, 9.5 miles (15.3 km).

2nd Hiking Day (**Soda Springs Guard Station** to **Poison Lake**, 8 miles—12.9 km): From the campground at Soda Springs Guard Station, we head north on the trail we hiked in on. In ¼ mile we arrive at a signed junction with the Poison Flat Trail. This trail we follow north as it hugs the east edge of Dumonts Meadows and then begins to climb above the canyon floor. As we climb higher, we pass a large, white terrace built up by carbonate molecules that precipitated out of spring water. Behind us, the west wall of the East Carson canyon becomes ever more impressive as we climb moderately to steeply up to a ridge just north of Poison Flat creek. From the ridge, we head east up toward a small exfoliating dome that at first resembles those of Yosemite, but closer up is seen to be volcanic. Our trail's gradient eases off as it passes the dome and comes to a signed spur trail to Soda Cone, about 100 yards away on the south bank of Poison Flat creek.

The conifer-lined meadow that we follow beyond the Soda Cone Trail junction is often inhabited by cattle, which give Poison Flat creek a disagreeable taste and odor. The hike through the meadow is an easy one up to a low, shady divide. Then, under the canopy of the forest's edge, we parallel the south side of the meadow eastward, cross an aspen-lined gully, and come to a barbed-wire gate, then another. Immediately beyond, we reach the signed Poison Lake Trail. Travelers who are hiking this trip at a very leisurely pace may want to descend 100 yards on the Silver King Trail to a junction with the Driveway Trail, near Silver King Creek. From this junction to a crossing 300 yards upstream you can find many good, shady, creekside campsites beneath lodgepole pines. Along this creekside route Trip 14 descends before turning east up the Driveway Trail.

Our trail up to Poison Lake starts steeply, then eases as it climbs up to a ridgecrest. It stays on or near the ridge for about a mile, where shade is provided by an open forest of Jeffrey pines and red firs. Where the ridge ends at the base of a steep slope, we climb steeply southwest to a minor ridge that provides a major, sweeping view of rounded hills in the north, granitic cliffs in the east, Silver King canyon in the south, and the ragged Sierra crest in the southwest. From the ridge our trail continues to climb through thick brush, which at times includes shiny-leaved, aromatic tobacco brush. Soon, short, very steep switchbacks lead up into the forest's shade once again, and the gradient becomes pleasant.

Another climb leads to a small, rocky flat, dense with sagebrush and bitterbrush, from whose south end we can look up-canyon into Lower Fish Valley, Upper Fish Valley and Fourmile Canyon. From the flat our trail makes an undulating traverse west toward a small canyon and nearly reaches it at its top. Here the trail turns northwest and goes past several meadows before leveling off on a broad ridge above Poison Lake. A short, steep descent down this ridge leads to the lake's willow-clad south shore. Good campsites lie under lodgepoles and hemlocks on its northwest shore and fishing is good for brook trout.

3rd Hiking Day: Retrace your steps to **Soda Springs Guard Station**, 8 miles (12.9 km).

4th Hiking Day: Follow the 2nd hiking day of Trip 10, 11 miles (17.7 km).

Rodriguez Flat to Lower Fish Valley **14**

TRIP
From Rodriguez Flat to Upper Fish Valley via Corral and Coyote valleys, return via Lower Fish and Long valleys (semiloop trip). Topo maps *Topaz Lake, Sonora Pass*. Best mid or late season; 14 miles (22.6 km).

Grade	Trail/layover days	Total recommended days
Leisurely	2/1	2
Moderate	....	....
Strenuous	....	....

HILITES
A fine weekend selection, this two-day trip visits five subalpine valleys. The country traversed contains some of the largest Sierra junipers to be found anywhere. In addition, over half a dozen side trips can be made from the Silver King Trail.

DESCRIPTION

1st Hiking Day (**Rodriguez Flat** to **Lower Fish Valley**, 7.5 miles—12.1 km): Our trail, the Snodgrass Canyon-Fish Valley Trail, makes a moderate climb southwest and shortly passes two trails from the Little Antelope Pack Station. A forest cover of white fir, silver pine and lodgepole pine persists for the next ⅓ mile of steep ascent, then yields to sagebrush as the old, metamorphosed sediments of Rodriguez Flat give way to much younger volcanic rocks. The view here is quite spectacular, and on a clear day you can see desert ranges northeast well beyond broad, open Rodriguez Flat.

The short, open ascent soon curves around the base of a volcanic hill and gives us new views—of Slinkard Valley below in the north, and the Sierra crest in the northwest. A traverse across broad, gentle, sagebrush-covered slopes leads to a signed junction, at which the Driveway Trail—our returning route—forks right (southwest). Our trail, the smaller of the two, soon passes through a fence gate and descends moderately past sagebrush and bitterbrush to the well-used grazing lands of spacious Corral Valley. On the valley floor, we cross two branches of Corral Valley Creek. The north branch, which drains the area most used by cattle, tends to be muddy, but the south branch, which drains more-forested slopes, looks and is drinkable. In it you'll see piute trout, which, like those in Coyote Valley and upper Silver King Creek, are an endangered and protected species. Please, no fishing here!

Beyond Corral Valley Creek, our southbound trail goes into the forest, curves west, parallels the valley a short distance, and then climbs an ever-increasing slope up to a dry saddle. From here the descent into Coyote Valley is a steep one, but it is made easy by the cushioning effect of the deep gravel. Near the bottom of a gully, the trail crosses a seasonal creek and goes but a short distance southeast before coming to an enormous, two-trunked juniper. With a diameter of 12 feet and a girth of 36, this specimen just might be the largest juniper in the Sierra. Beyond it, our trail winds south down toward Coyote Valley, reaching its sagebrush-covered floor beside a large, five-foot-diameter lodgepole (the key landmark to look for if you're hiking this trail in the opposite direction).

On the valley floor we walk a level ¼ mile to an easy ford of Coyote Valley Creek. Beyond the ford, the trail veers away from the creek and gradually climbs south. Near the crest above Upper Fish Valley, the forest becomes more dense and the aspens more dominant. At the crest's broad saddle a fence greets us, and from its gate we descend, usually past grazing cattle, steeply down to Upper Fish Valley. On the valley floor, a signed trail junction lies near a tall, orange snow-depth marker. Our trip proceeds north about 300 yards beyond the junction to a meeting of three fences, each with its own gate. Go through the north gate and follow the path that parallels the west side of the north-northeast-heading fence. Our trail soon starts to curve northwest, climbs over a low moraine left by a retreating glacier, and then comes to within hearing range of unseen Llewellyn Falls, just southwest of us. Let your ears direct you to this significant 20-foot-high cascade.

Llewellyn Falls creates a barrier trout cannot get over. As a giant glacier slowly retreated up Silver King Canyon, perhaps 50,000 years ago, cutthroat trout followed its path. They were able to swim into Upper Fish Valley and higher valleys before Silver King Creek eroded away bedrock to form the falls. Once isolated. they evolved into a subspecies known as the piute cutthroat trout (*Salmo clarki seleniris*), or simply piute trout. These trout became endangered not through overfishing but rather through the introduction of Lahontan cutthroats and rainbows, which then bred with the piutes to form hybrids. Once this miscegenation was discovered, Fish and Game workers removed purebreds and in 1964 treated Silver King Creek with rotenone to kill the hybrids. After the purebreds were reintroduced above the falls, their numbers grew from about 150 in the late 1960s to about 600 in the early 1970s. By 1975 the population had changed very little more, and it appears to be stable. Fishing, nevertheless, is strictly prohibited, for the piute trout could be easily fished out of existence.

Beyond the Llewellyn Falls gorge, our trail descends briefly northwest into Lower Fish Valley, approaches Silver King Creek, and reaches a white carbonate spring just before leaving the creek. Not far past the spring, the trail again approaches Silver King Creek and follows it about 150 yards. Where the creek veers west away from the trail, you can follow the creek to its merger with Tamarack Lake's outlet creek. (On the *Sonora Pass* topo, this is the unnamed lake about 1 mile southwest of Lower Fish Valley.) A large packer's campsite, once known as Governor's Camp, lies on the flat under the pines between these two creeks. It was named after Edmund G. Brown, Sr. who liked to stay there while deer hunting each year. His successor, Ronald Reagan, never visited it, and the camp's name was eventually changed to Commissioner's Camp. From this camp an extremely steep trail climbs 2 miles up to beautiful, cliff-bound Tamarack Lake. Determined backpackers and climbers can look for this trail behind the camp and on the north side of the lake's creek. Others may wish to stay at the camp and fish for legal rainbow trout.

2nd Hiking Day (**Lower Fish Valley** to **Rodriguez Flat**, 6.5 miles—10.5 km): Continuing downstream, we walk northwest toward a low ridge that hides the forested, little-visited valley of Tamarack Creek. Our path leaves Lower Fish Valley, turns northeast and climbs a low granitic saddle before entering the south end of Long Valley. To avoid springs and boggy meadows, take the trail that circles around the valley's east side. Part way down the flat valley, the trails join and then approach Silver King Creek. This creek meanders lazily through the glacial sediments that long ago buried its canyon's bedrock floor, and our trail approaches several of these meanders before leaving the valley's north end.

Hugging the creek, our trail follows it northwest to its union with Tamarack Creek. After a short ½ mile of easy, shaded walking, we're forced to make a wet ford of Silver King Creek where a photogenic granitic pinnacle and its adjacent cliffs block progress along the east bank. Grassy banks on both sides help make the knee-deep ford a pleasant one. What follows is 300 yards of grassy, shaded creekside campsites—among the best you'll find anywhere. Our trail stays above these campsites, and, near the last of them, meets the signed Driveway Trail.

Our route follows the Driveway Trail 70 yards to a second wet ford of grass-lined Silver King Creek. Across the creek is a sunny, steep climb where scattered junipers growing on the volcanic ridge provide convenient, shady rest spots for the first few hundred yards, and after that the trail's gradient eases to a comfortable angle. Views up Silver King canyon improve, and, 2¼ miles from the creek, we again reach the Snodgrass Canyon-Fish Valley Trail. Before hiking the last mile along this familiar trail back to the trailhead, stop and look at the oversized cairn just before this junction. Built seven feet high by careful hands, this cairn stands as a monument to the loneliness of the Basque shepherds who once tended flocks in this area. Called *arri mutillak*, or "stone boys," monuments like this were built by lonely shepherds for lack of any other way to pass the time. Today, hikers *seek* to be alone and *look* for places of solitude in this east Sierra landscape.

an arri mutillak   *Jeff Schaffer*

Rodriguez Flat to Ebbetts Pass **15**

TRIP From Rodriguez Flat to Ebbetts Pass via Corral Valley, Coyote Valley, Silver King Creek, Soda Springs Guard Station, Murray Canyon, Asa Lake and Nobel Lake (shuttle trip). Topo maps *Topaz Lake, Sonora Pass, Dardanelles Cone, Markleeville*. Best mid season; 34 miles (54.8 km).

Grade	Trail/layover days	Total recommended days
Leisurely	5/1	6
Moderate	4/0	4
Strenuous	3/0	3

HILITES Ridges and canyons east of the Sierra crest wait to be explored along this scenic route. You'll encounter mammoth junipers, a rare trout, soda and carbonate springs, diverse scenery and good fishing. The last 11 miles are along the famous, ridge-hugging Pacific Crest Trail.

DESCRIPTION (Moderate trip)

1st Hiking Day: Follow Trip 14 to **Lower Fish Valley**, 7.5 miles (12.1 km).

2nd Hiking Day (**Lower Fish Valley** to **Murray Canyon Trail junction**. 9.5 miles—15.3 km): Follow the 2nd hiking day, Trip 14, to the Driveway Trail junction and walk 100 yards up the Silver King Trail to the Poison Lake Trail junction. From it, reverse the steps of the first half of the 2nd hiking day, Trip 13, to Soda Springs Guard Station, and then follow the 1st hiking day, Trip 11, to the Murray Canyon Trail junction.

3rd Hiking Day (**Murray Canyon Trail junction** to **Asa Lake**, 10 miles—16.1 km): Follow the first part of the 2nd hiking day, Trip 11, up Murray Canyon to the crest junction. Our trail starts southeast from the crest, crosses a pebbly flat, and then returns to the crest to follow it a short distance. Through the thinning forest we see Highland Peak and other volcanic summits to the northwest, and in the southwest are the volcanic cliffs of Arnot Peak. Our trail soon leaves the crest and contours ½ mile south across a brushy slope to a saddle just north of a low knoll. We cross the saddle, descend southeast, and gradually curve southwest through lodgepole forest over toward a grassy meadow south of the knoll. At the east end of this meadow our trail disappears, but you'll find it again at the west end. From here, you can look down across a large, open bowl. Our route, very vague, starts southwest down into the bowl, contours south just below the forest's edge, and then climbs southeast toward a saddle on the southwest side of a very prominent summit of highly broken volcanic rock. Just before the saddle, you'll reach a new segment of the Pacific Crest Trail.

Choosing the Pacific Crest Trail at the junction, we descend northwest along the west side of the bowl. As the bowl gives way to steeper slopes, the PCT circles west around a ridge, descends southwest and momentarily enters and then leaves a small but deep side canyon before reaching the slightly cloudy east fork of Wolf Creek, flowing down a wide, rocky wash. The cloudy color is due to fine volcanic sediments suspended in the water. In your drinking cup, these harmless sediments will settle out quite fast. A ⅓-mile traverse west past caves and fingers of a cliff of deeply eroded volcanic deposits gets us to the wide, silty middle fork of Wolf Creek.

Leaving this stream, we curve west briefly, then climb steadily northwest up to several branches of the west fork of Wolf Creek. The Pacific Crest Trail climbs north up a slope just beyond the main, east-flowing branch, switchbacks west, and climbs more steeply through a thinning forest. Rather than traversing west to a forested saddle, our trail continues to climb northwest above its east end—a route designed to avoid cattle-grazing lands on the other side. On reaching the west slopes of summit 8960+, we diagonal northwest down them, then curve north down to a small, flat saddle that lies at the base of the summit's northwest ridge. Here, it is important that you not continue north and cross the saddle. Rather, head west down a small gully, then parallel a low ridge, staying on its southwest side. A large cow meadow will quickly appear below you, and you'll almost touch it just before reaching a small gorge. The meadow's creek joyfully cascades down the resistant, volcanic end of the gorge, then flows out into Lower

Gardner Meadow. The Pacific Crest Trail descends to a jeep road at the east end of this meadow, and on this road Trip 14 parallels the creek westward. At this junction, situated on a broad, low ridge known as Wolf Creek Pass, the road curves north immediately into a grassy, boggy meadow.

From the jeep road, the Pacific Crest Trail climbs northwest up a low ridge crest, then curves north above the boggy meadow. The trail crosses the old Asa Creek Trail, then in ¼ mile arrives at a small pond just southeast of unseen Asa Lake. A minute's walk upstream off trail from the pond leads to the lake's east shore, where it is apparent why this small lake stays full and clear even in late summer: refreshing springs gush from the volcanic rocks above its east shore, and with the aid of a canal, their water is continually channeled into the lake. Under shady red firs above its northeast shore are some good campsites, and brook trout await the skillfull—or lucky—angler.

4th Hiking Day (**Asa Lake** to **Ebbetts Pass**, 7 miles—11.3 km): Get back on the Pacific Crest Trail by walking about 150 yards up-slope from Asa Lake's northeast corner. Once on the trail, follow it moderately to steeply up around a ridge, then through a small cove shaded by red firs. On the climb out of the cove, the forest of hemlocks and pines gives way to sagebrush as the trail traverses northwest toward a saddle. Tryon Peak looms ahead, and in the southwest, the large popular Highland Lakes stand out clearly in their broad, glaciated canyon. At the often windy saddle we encounter whitebark pines, which, better than any other conifer in this area, thrive in the harsh winter climate of this high elevation (9300′).

We cross a crest-line fence, then follow a descending path that diagonals through tight clusters of whitebark pines and mountain hemlocks before crossing the willow-lined head-waters of Nobel Creek to intersect the faint Nobel Canyon Trail. Beyond this intersection the Pacific Crest Trail skirts above the east edge of a meadow and descends gradually southwest. Then our route curves north to a low saddle above the southwest corner of Nobel Lake. Staying high above the lake, the route curves northwest across a low ridge. The trail here is vague over the next hundred yards. It quickly dies out, but can be found again on the east side of the small gully immediately below. From the gully, the trail curves east to Nobel Lake's outlet creek, crossing it about 200 yards below the lake. Now the obvious trail heads north and soon switchbacks down a bizarre landscape of eroded, broken-up, *autobrecciated* lava flows (see Trip 10) that support only a few hardy junipers. We recross Nobel Lake's creek, head west briefly to a ridge of glacial sediments, and follow it north ¼ mile to a fork. Here, just east of the ridge crest, the Nobel Canyon Trail leaves the PCT.

The PCT rounds the ridge, descends to the bouldery main arm of Nobel Creek, and begins a traverse northwest. After ⅓ mile it starts climbing in earnest and momentarily leaves volcanic rock behind as it approaches granitic knobs atop a northeast-trending ridge. Our trail climbs north to the ridge's crest, curves around one knob back to the crest again, and then starts southeast around a second knob. At its south side we cross the crest for good and commence a winding traverse west along the base of some impressive, deeply eroded, volcanic cliffs. Northeast across Nobel Canyon is Silver Peak (10,774'), site of hectic mining activity beginning in 1863.

A brief climb north leads to the top of another northeast-trending ridge, this one just east of State Highway 4. Then a ¼-mile descent southwest from it brings the hiker to a junction, from which the PCT winds ⅓ mile southwest to a crossing of State Highway 4 only 200 yards north of Ebbetts Pass. From the junction, our route leads north and descends a spur trail ¼ mile to the Pacific Crest Trail parking lot.

Nobel Canyon from above Nobel Lake   *Jeff Schaffer*

Rodriguez Flat to Lake Alpine 16

TRIP From Rodriguez Flat to Lake Alpine via Corral, Coyote and Fish valleys, Soda Springs Guard Station, White Canyon, Highland Lakes, Hiram Meadow and Rock Lake (shuttle trip). Topo maps *Topaz Lake, Sonora Pass, Dardanelles Cone* (*Markleeville* optional for Asa Lake). Best mid or late season; 49 miles (78.9 km).

Grade	Trail/layover days	Total recommended days
Leisurely	8/2	10
Moderate	6/1	7
Strenuous	4/0	4

HILITES This exciting route traverses several major Sierra ridges along its westward course. As you progress west, the vegetation changes dramatically, sagebrush and juniper giving way to dense forests of pine and fir. Sections of two famous trails are hiked along this route: first, the 2600-mile-long Pacific Crest Trail, then later, the 180-mile-long Tahoe-Yosemite Trail.

DESCRIPTION (Moderate trip)

1st, 2nd and 3rd Hiking Days: Follow Trip 15 to **Asa Lake**, 27 miles (43.5 km).

4th Hiking Day (**Asa Lake** to **Hiram Meadow, 9 miles—14.5 km**): From Asa Lake, retrace your steps ½ mile south down the Pacific Crest Trail to the jeep road at Wolf Creek Pass. This road we take ½ mile west, following a creek through spacious, cow-inhabited Lower Gardner Meadow. Leaving the creek, we traverse southwest across undulating country for another ½ mile to a north-flowing creek. In 150 yards we reach a signed fork, turn northwest, and wind ¼ mile up to a gap, 100 yards beyond which our road is joined by a faint trail from Upper Gardner Meadow. In another 80 yards, this trail resumes its course, veering left. We follow it northwest ¼ mile up to a low crest, on which we cross a north-leading jeep road. From this junction the hiker will follow the trail about 200 yards to a reunion with the road 70 yards before a creek crossing. Draining lower Highland Lake, this creek can be a wet ford in early season. A trailhead parking lot is seen just above the west bank, and from it our road curves west 100 yards to the Highland Lake Road.

Wide, level Highland Lake Road contours around the west shore of lower Highland Lake, popular with fishermen for its population of brook trout. Beyond the lake, our road climbs gradually to Highland Lakes Campground, just north of the upper lake, which is divided into two camps. Backpackers will usually find quieter sites in the camp at the end of a short, eastbound spur road.

At the far end of upper Highland Lake the road ends and the well-signed Highland Creek Trail to Lake Alpine begins with a steep descent along the lake's outlet creek, then bends more westward away from it. Beyond a small knoll on the left, we descend west ½ mile down a steep, winding trail, passing a small gorge before we reach upper Highland Lake's outlet creek. In early season large boulders just downstream will make the crossing a dry one. Heading south, we pass through two small meadows, each with an abundant garden of corn lilies, then in ¼ mile approach a creek that drains what the map calls "Poison Canyon." (Poison Canyon is incorrectly called "Champion Canyon" on the topo map. All the canyon labels on the topo map from "Poison Canyon" to "Slaughter Canyon" should be moved one canyon to the southwest; the canyon labeled "Poison" on the map is actually unnamed.)

We follow the creek ¼ mile downstream, cross it near its union with Highland Creek, and in another ¼ mile come to a good campsite, under large cottonwoods, on the east bank of Highland Creek. At times, logs placed by hikers make this wide-creek crossing a dry one, but if you are here before mid-July, you can expect to wade. Two paths start from the west bank, one following Highland Creek downstream, the other staying farther west. They quickly re-unite at a barbed-wire fence. Then we round the base of a granitic ridge, enter a lodgepole flat, traverse the west side of a damp meadow, and return to forest cover as the trail and the nearby creek both bend south. In this part of the canyon, Highland Creek has several shallow pools that are ideal for a quick bath.

Our trail soon reaches a second ford of Highland Creek—just as wide and a little deeper than the first. Once across, we veer away from the creek on a minor climb, then descend to the stream that drains Champion Canyon ("Hiram Canyon" on the topo map). Its ford is an easy one, and on a moderately descending trail we head down to the sunny flats of Hiram Meadow. Only 80 yards south of Highland Creek's union with Weiser Creek is a third usually wet ford of the former.

Late-season hikers will note that this ford is a wet ford long after most Sierra snow has melted. This is because Highland Creek canyon and its tributary canyons have abundant volcanic sediments that act as a reservoir to hold water well into September. Good campsites lie across the ford on the west bank.

5th Hiking Day (**Hiram Meadow** to **Rock Lake,** 8.5 miles—13.7 km): About 100 yards west of the Highland Creek ford is a junction with the Weiser Trail. At the start of the deer-hunting season on the last weekend of September, hunters will descend this trail on motorcycles, bringing noise and pollution with them. Plan accordingly. From the junction we hike west across wide, flat Hiram Meadow, re-enter lodgepole cover, and quickly arrive at a cabin. Our path turns southwest, soon reaches willow-lined Highland Creek, and then crosses some low knolls of highly fractured, fine-grained igneous rock. One mile southwest of Hiram Meadow the Highland Creek Trail briefly climbs away from the creek just before it turns south and cascades down a sizable gorge. Our trail parallels the watercourse at a distance as we descend steeply to a junction with the Woods Gulch Trail. This trail east—part of the Tahoe-Yosemite Trail—crosses Highland Creek in 60 yards, just north of its union with the creek from Jenkins Canyon ("Slaughter Canyon" on the topo). Westward, the next 13-mile stretch of the Tahoe-Yosemite Trail coincides with the Highland Creek Trail.

Leaving the junction, our route turns west and in a few minutes brings us beside some small, lovely Highland Creek pools. We follow the creek only momentarily, then gradually veer away and climb up a brushy, granitic slope to an open forest of Jeffrey pines. In it, we descend quickly to a shady flat from which our trail descends moderately to the canyon bottom, where we cross a usually trickling creek that originates in a small, shallow lake northwest of Hiram Meadow. Traversing around the east shore of this lake is the Bull Run Creek Trail, which we meet only ¼ mile west of the trickling creek. Although motor vehicles are allowed on this trail, few successfully make it up or down due to its excessively steep, very sandy nature. In 100 yards we cross refreshing Bull Run Creek, shaded by cottonwoods and white firs.

Reaching Gabbot Meadow we hike briefly alongside Highland Creek, then leave it and parallel the northwest side of a southwest-running fence. In ½ mile is a gate, and in another ¼ mile a second gate. From this second gate the level trail follows the fence line 300 yards, then turns abruptly up-slope. During the summer of 1975 the Highland Creek Trail was rebuilt and/or relocated from this point west to the saddle above Lake Alpine. The trail climbs steeply northwest, but then turns southwest and almost levels off, giving one a chance to catch one's breath on the traverse through a shady forest of white fir and Jeffrey pine. Emerging from the forest, we begin to climb steeply again, this time up brushy slopes to a small gap in the granitic bedrock. Almost immediately, we pass through a second gap, then start a short traverse southwest, from which we can admire the dark, volcanic formations called the Dardanelles. This monumental ridge, composed of lava hundreds of feet thick, is only a small remnant of a long lava flow that originated near Bridgeport, California, about nine million years ago. From that source it flowed about *100 miles* down-canyon, stopping at the western edge of the Sierra foothills. In the ensuing millions of years, the walls of the canyon it flowed down were eroded away while the canyon bottom it buried was preserved beneath the flow. Two million years of glacial attacks further eroded the Dardanelles landscape until the granitic floor of Highland Creek lay a good 1000 feet below the base of the Dardanelles. We can expect future glaciers to excavate Highland Creek's canyon even more. Visible up-canyon are Iceberg, Airola and Hiram peaks—all with volcanic summits but none of them related to the Dardanelles flow.

Crossing the crest, which stands 550 feet above Highland Creek, we hike southwest just west of the crest. That the last Highland Creek glacier was *at least* as thick as the crest is high is obvious from the fresh polish it gave the granitic bedrock here. The glacier was, in fact, about 1300 feet thick. At a point where one could head south cross-country 1 mile down to Highland Creek, our trail turns northwest and climbs to a glaciated saddle. Then, midway along the mile-long rollercoaster path to Wilderness Creek, we cross one of its tributaries. The ford of Wilderness Creek is difficult in early season, but the stream disappears in late season. Beyond this creek our trail passes the Sand Flat Trail, climbs north to a gravelly, barren flat, and then briefly parallels Wilderness Creek. Continuing a moderate-to-easy climb north, we reach the east end of Rock Lake in ¾ mile. Grassy and unappealing at this end, Rock Lake provides good swimming and fishing (brook trout) near its southwest end. Along its south shore are several forested campsites.

6th Hiking Day (**Rock Lake** to **Lake Alpine**, 4.5 miles—7.2 km): From the lake's east end, our route starts northwest along the old Highland Lake Trail, and then, just out of sight of the lake, turns northeast and follows a new tread ¼ mile up a granitic ridge. Then, from the slightly higher main ridge, we curve north, cross a small, dry wash, and descend to a flat ¼ mile east of the North Fork Stanislaus River. From it, a short climb north and then a steep descent bring us to the river (difficult ford in early season).

Beyond this ford we climb steeply northwest to cross a ridge, and then wind ½ mile down glacier-polished slabs to a large, forested flat with a trail junction. From here the old trail goes 1¼ miles west past the south shore of Duck Lake to a cabin-side junction with a jeep road. Through July and part of August the mosquitoes along this swampy route are almost unbearable. Turning right on the new trail, we immediately cross a creek, and wind west along the north edge of this forested flat. When the trail reaches a point about 200 yards north of Duck Lake, it abruptly turns north and climbs up a ridge. After 300 yards it turns abruptly west and then climbs more moderately ⅓ mile west up to a switchback in the jeep road that ascends northward from the Duck Lake basin. On this closed road we climb west briefly up to a saddle, pass through a gate, follow the crest southwest, and then descend ½ mile to the trailhead at the east end of Lake Alpine's Silver Valley Campground.

17   Sonora Pass to Clark Fork

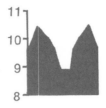

TRIP   From West Sonora Pass Trailhead to Clark Fork
Meadow (round trip, part cross country). Topo map
Sonora Pass. Best mid season; 7 miles (11.2 km).

Grade	Trail/layover days	Total recom- mended days
Leisurely	2/0	2
Moderate	....	....
Strenuous	....	....

HILITES   Clark Fork Meadow is secluded by the steep sides
of the deep bowl which protects it, and here—only
two airline miles from a state highway—one can
get away from it all even on a short weekend. On
the way, the views from the pass are among the
most sweeping in the entire Sierra.

DESCRIPTION

1st Hiking Day (**Sonora Pass Trailhead** to **Clark Fork Meadow,** 3.5
miles—5.6 km.): The trailhead is located at the foot of a
barred road which leads north from Highway 108 about 0.85
mile west of Sonora Pass. From a parking area (9760′) we
walk up the jeep road toward timberline, through sparse
lodgepole and whitebark pine understoried by considerable
sagebrush. The pinkish soil here slowly and steadily gives off
its stored winter water, and these slopes are dotted with a
pleasant variety of high-elevation wildflowers throughout the
season. Beyond a small runoff stream that flows all summer,
the road becomes trail, and after a short level section we veer
eastward and ascend steadily. A breather stop here allows us
to look south and see the great peaks of the Emigrant Basin
and northern Yosemite. Below us is the threadlike highway
curving up to Sonora Pass, and beyond the pass we see unnamed Peak 11245. West of this imposing if nameless height,
the long chocolate-brown west ridge of Leavitt Peak shows its

snowy north slope, and even a few tiny glaciers.

The crest of this little climb (10440') is called St. Marys Pass. Here we obtain a view far to the north—on clear days, as far as the peaks west of Lake Tahoe. Looking north and south, we realize we are standing right on the boundary between the rugged High Sierra of Yosemite and beyond, and the lower, less rugged northern Sierra. Immediately below us to the north, the bowl that contains Clark Fork Meadow is so deep that we cannot see the bottom of it.

From the pass we turn southwest and follow a sporadically ducked route near the top of a granite ridge for about one mile, dipping slightly to cross several runoff streams not shown on the topo map. In midseason these seemingly bare slopes boast a profusion of blue flax, lavender phlox and yellow woolly sunflower. Once past the billowy granite outcroppings that line most of the route for the first mile from St. Marys Pass, we veer north and start down the valley of a little stream not shown on the topo map. We follow the ridge that lies east of the upper basin of this stream until, at about timberline, we drop down next to the stream and parallel it, on its east side, into thick hemlock forest, where we may find occasional ducks. This route passes close under the west face of the cliffs that are ½ mile southeast of the meadow.

At the bottom of the steep ascent we ford the infant Clark Fork on a log, turn west, and soon ford a tributary on boulders. Half a mile of level walking under a moderate forest cover of silver, lodgepole and whitebark pine and some hemlock brings us to the good campsite at the northwest edge of the meadow (8875') beside a clear stream. Fishing in the Clark Fork is good for eastern brook (to 9").

2nd Hiking Day: Retrace your steps, 3.5 miles (5.6 km).

South from St. Marys Pass

18   Sonora Pass to Iceberg Meadow

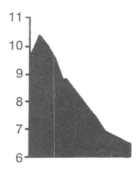

TRIP   From West Sonora Pass Trailhead to Iceberg
               Meadow (shuttle trip, part cross country). Topo
               map *Sonora Pass*. Best mid season; 11.5 miles
               (18.5 km).

Grade	Trail/layover days	Total recommended days
Leisurely	2/1	3
Moderate	2/0	2
Strenuous	....	....

HILITES   Few trips are downhill most of the way, but this
               one ascends only 800 feet and then descends 4000
               feet. The descent follows the canyon of Clark Fork
               Stanislaus River from its wellsprings above
               timberline through meadows and down granite
               gorges to a thickly forested, gently flowing section
               of the river.

DESCRIPTION

1st Hiking Day: Follow Trip 17 to **Clark Fork Meadow,** 3.5 miles
(5.6 km).

2nd Hiking Day (**Clark Fork Meadow** to **Iceberg Meadow,** 8
miles—12.9 km): From the campsite, we walk to the foot of the
meadow and cross the Clark Fork on boulders. On the west
side, a few yards downstream, we encounter ducks, and this
ducked route soon becomes a trail—although none is shown on
the topo map. The trail passes a stock-drift fence (close the
gate) and makes a short, steep descent under a moderate forest
cover of hemlock, silver pine and lodgepole. At the foot of the

descent we enter red-fir forest, and this superb conifer is frequent for the rest of the hiking day. A short mile from Clark Fork Meadow is a boulder ford to the east side of the stream, and several fair-to-good campsites lie just beyond it. After the ford, the sandy trail veers away from the stream and descends gently to moderately, fording a small runoff stream every half mile or so.

After paralleling and then fording a larger tributary, the trail enters a sloping meadow considerably marred by the hooves of grazing cattle. The route across the slope is indistinct, but we find the trail again in granite sand under red firs near the Clark Fork. After crossing another tree-shaded meadow with fair campsites, we begin a steep, switchbacking descent on a rocky dusty trail down to an almost level valley, where the Clark Fork swings west. At the foot of the descent, the trail crosses Boulder Creek and meets a trail up the creek. From this junction the route descends along a shaded sand-and-duff trail, close to the alder-lined Clark Fork, now big enough to call a river. Numerous good campsites line this shaded canyon, with its dense forest cover of white fir, alder and Jeffrey pine. Nearing Iceberg Meadow the trail makes a short, steady-to-steep descent and then parallels the river on pleasant, sandy underfooting to the roadend (6460').

Clark Fork Meadow

19 Kennedy Meadow to Summit Creek

TRIP From Kennedy Meadow to Summit Creek (round trip). Topo maps *Sonora Pass, Tower Peak*. Best early-to-mid season; 13.6 miles (21.8 km).

Grade	Trail/layover days	Total recommended days
Leisurely	2/0	2
Moderate	....	....
Strenuous	....	....

HILITES A part of this route follows the historic Emigrant Trail used by the pioneers in crossing the Sierra from the area around Bridgeport to Columbia and points west. Relief Peak was a major landmark for these early travelers, and the terminus of this trip, lies in this unusual formation's shadow. The scenery along the way is an absorbing study in glacial and volcanic terrain.

DESCRIPTION

1st Hiking Day (**Kennedy Meadow** to **Summit Creek**, 6.8 miles—10.9 km): The trailhead (6400') is located alongside Middle Fork Stanislaus River at Kennedy Meadow resort. Amid a dense forest cover of Jeffrey pine, incense-cedar, sugar pine, juniper and white fir, the trail crosses a small ridge to Kennedy Meadow itself and skirts the east side of the meadow, offering sweeping views of the lush grasslands. Beyond the meadow, the trail crosses the river via a bridge and immediately veers west onto a new trail section. This trail section ascends gently past the foot of a small granite dome and then switchbacks up a steeper grade between this dome and its larger neighbor. Under a sparse-to-moderate forest cover of mixed conifers, the route ascends steadily up a little canyon to a saddle, where it turns eastward to descend a sandy, multi-tracked slope to Summit Creek. After paralleling the creek for a few steps, the trail crosses it on a bridge and meets the old, abandoned trail a few yards south of the Kennedy Lake Trail junction, near the PG&E dam-maintenance station.

Our route then contours high above the east side of Relief Reservoir. The trail section paralleling the shore offers excellent views to the south and west before it descends to the timbered shallow at the Grouse Creek ford. From Grouse Creek the trail ascends steadily over a series of rocky switchbacks, and then veers southeast to pass the Lower Relief Valley Trail after one mile. Then our trail begins a steady-to-steep uphill climb as it leaves the shaded riparian zone and enters the brush-covered volcanic rubble above Summit Creek. Along the rock-strewn trail one can compare varieties of penstemon flowers in various hues. This steady ascent is relieved when the trail drops into the little pocket encompassing Saucer Meadow. The gravesite indicated on the topo and Forest Service maps was that of a passing immigrant, but all that remains of this last resting place of a would-be immigrant is a small, vandalized sign on a tree.

The section of trail beyond this point was part of a major trans-Sierra route, used during the middle of the 19th century—the Emigrant Trail. With the many-hued volcanic rock of Relief Peak on the left, and white, glaciated granite on the right, the trail climbs along Summit Creek to several fair campsites. Fishing along the creek is poor.

2nd Hiking Day: Retrace your steps, 6.8 miles (10.9 km).

South of Grouse Creek

20 Kennedy Meadow to Emigrant Meadow

TRIP
From Kennedy Meadow to Emigrant Meadow Lake via Brown Bear Pass (round trip). Topo maps *Sonora Pass, Tower Peak*. Best mid or late season; 25.2 miles (40.4 km).

Grade	Trail/layover days	Total recommended days
Leisurely	4/0	4
Moderate	3/0	3
Strenuous	2/0	2

HILITES
A good portion of this trail follows the historic Emigrant Trail, and travelers today have an excellent opportunity to identify with these hardy pioneers. Scenically, this route splits the terrain into two distinctly different parts: To the north, the basaltic and pumice slopes vividly disclose the vulcan overlay that gives the country its colorful reds and blacks. To the south, mirrorlike stretches of glacially polished granite add contrast and interest.

DESCRIPTION (Leisurely trip)

1st Hiking Day: Follow Trip 19 to **Summit Creek**, 6.8 miles (10.9 km).

2nd Hiking Day (**Summit Creek** to **Emigrant Meadow Lake**, 5.8 miles—9.3 km): Our level trail continues up-canyon on red-fir-dotted slopes for a mile, then makes a rocky 400-foot ascent to a little saddle which is the portal of the camping area called Sheep Camp, a very overused area. Winding above Summit Creek beyond Sheep Camp, the trail soon leaves timber cover, and crosses a pumice slope above Lunch Meadow. This large meadow is subalpine, dotted with sparse stands of lodgepole and mountain hemlock. At the east end of Lunch Meadow our route passes the trail to Emigrant Lake. North of our trail, red and black volcanic columns thrust up from the otherwise smooth, red, pumice slopes, and punctuate the skyline with their tortured shapes. Directly to the east the traveler can discern the shallow saddle that is Brown Bear Pass. The trail to the pass is a gradual but steady ascent offering colorfully contrasting views of Granite Dome and Relief Peak to the west. It is easy to see why the emigrants who used this same route relied upon the distinctive outline of Relief Peak as a landmark. At the summit of Brown Bear Pass (9700'), the grassy expanses of historic Emigrant Meadow present themselves, and the serenity of this pioneer waystop is enhanced by the placid blue waters of Emigrant Meadow Lake.

As the trail descends from Brown Bear Pass on a long traverse, the visitor cannot help being impressed by the gigantic scale of this grassy, granite-walled basin. It seems a fitting stage for the enactment of the "great move westward," and it doesn't take a great deal of imagination to hear boisterous shouts, the creaking of wagons, the barking of dogs, and the tired, hungry lowing of trail-weary stock. This great meadow saw the frenzied summertime travel of thousands of pioneers headed for the western slope, but of their passing all that remains is an echo in the wind. Fair campsites may be found along the west side of Emigrant Meadow Lake (9400'). Fishing for rainbow (8-13") is good, with a midseason slowdown.

3rd and 4th Hiking Days: Retrace your steps, 12.6 miles (20.2 km).

Author at Brown Bear Pass   *Jason Winnett*

21 Kennedy Meadow to Emigrant Lake

TRIP From Kennedy Meadow to Emigrant Lake (round trip). Topo maps *Sonora Pass, Tower Peak*. Best mid-to-late season; 26.8 miles (43 km).

Grade	Trail/layover days	Total recommended days
Leisurely	4/1	5
Moderate	3/1	4
Strenuous	3/0	3

HILITES A long-time favorite of anglers, Emigrant Lake is often used as a base camp for short fishing trips to the surrounding lakes. This route to Emigrant Lake allows the traveler to take in the geological variety of the country. Alpine meadows surrounding isolated melt-off tarns compete for attention with vast slopes of red pumice and fields of polished granite.

DESCRIPTION (Leisurely trip)

1st Hiking Day: Follow Trip 19 to **Summit Creek,** 6.8 miles (10.9 km).

2nd Hiking Day (**Summit Creek** to **Emigrant Lake,** 6.6 miles—10.6 km): First follow Trip 20 to the trail junction at the east end of Lunch Meadow. Here our route branches right (south), fords Summit Creek, and ascends through a sparse mountain-hemlock cover to a long, low saddle. Views along this segment of trail present a wide range of colors. The superimposed vulcanism of Relief Peak and the ridge to the east are a potpourri of pastel shades of reds, blacks, yellows and ochres. Black Hawk Mountain to the west is granite in varying shades of dun, gray, and buff-brown.

The long saddle through which our trail winds is a series of granite fields that are delightfully broken by tiny, wildflower-filled meadows. Many of these meadows are further enhanced by one or two small melt-off tarns. The long, shallow valley on the other side of the saddle contains a tributary of North Fork Cherry Creek, and from it there are excellent views across the Cherry Creek watershed south to Michie and Haystack peaks. The trail descends on the east side of this tributary for ½ mile and then fords to the west side. This ford is the correct place from which to head east cross country to reach Mosquito Lake, which has pink-fleshed rainbow trout. Continuing down the east bank, we ford a little tributary and then recross the main stream to the west side. From here our trail descends to the large meadow at the inlet to large (230-acre) Emigrant Lake (8800′). There are several good-to-excellent campsites at the inlet, on the north side, and at the outlet. This popular lake is glacial in character, with a sparse forest cover, and fishing for rainbow (8-18′) is good (excellent in early and late season).

3rd and 4th Hiking Days: Retrace your steps, 13.4 miles (21.6 km).

near Lunch Meadow

22   Kennedy Meadow to Emigrant Lake

TRIP   From Kennedy Meadow to Emigrant Lake via
                    Middle Emigrant and Emigrant Meadow lakes
                    (semi-loop trip). Topo maps *Sonora Pass; Tower
                    Peak*. Best mid or late season; 30.4 miles (48.9 km).

Grade	Trail/layover days	Total recom- mended days
Leisurely	5/2	7
Moderate	4/2	6
Strenuous	3/2	5

HILITES   Like the previous trip this route tours a part of the
                    historic Emigrant Trail and visits large Emigrant
                    Lake. In addition, linking Emigrant Lake with
                    Emigrant Meadow Lake, this route makes a good
                    fisherman's loop and takes in more scenic variety.

DESCRIPTION (Leisurely trip)

1st and 2nd Hiking Days: Follow Trip 21 to **Emigrant Lake**, 13.4
miles (21.6 km).

3rd Hiking Day (**Emigrant Lake** to **Emigrant Meadow Lake**, 4.4
miles—7.1 km): Beginning at the trail junction above the
inlet to Emigrant Lake, this route crosses a log bridge over
North Fork Cherry Creek and ascends a moderately forested
slope to Blackbird Lake (9000') and a junction with a trail to
Middle Emigrant Lake, where we turn left and follow part of
the 5th hiking day, Trip 23.

4th and 5th Hiking Days: Reverse the steps of the 2nd and 1st
hiking days, Trip 20, 12.6 miles (20.2 km).

Kennedy Meadow to Cow Meadow Lake 23

TRIP From Kennedy Meadow to Cow Meadow Lake via Emigrant Lake and Buck Lakes (loop trip). Topo maps *Sonora Pass, Tower Peak*. Best mid or late season; 45 miles (72.5 km).

Grade	Trail/layover days	Total recommended days
Leisurely	7/2	9
Moderate	5/2	7
Strenuous	4/2	6

HILITES This is a fine choice for a midseason fishing trip, as it circles the lake-dotted Cherry Creek watershed. A day's walking from one or another base camp will permit the fisherman to sample almost 100 lakes. The route also tours some of the finest scenery in the Emigrant Wilderness, which should provide adequate incentive for the nonfisherman as well.

DESCRIPTION (Leisurely trip)

1st and 2nd Hiking Days: Follow Trip 21 to **Emigrant Lake**, 13.4 miles (21.5 km).

3rd Hiking Day (**Emigrant Lake** to **Cow Meadow Lake**, 6 miles—9.7 km): From the trail junction at the inlet to Emigrant Lake, our route traverses the long, timbered north side of the lake, and passes a junction with a poorly maintained trail to Cow Meadow Lake via North Fork Cherry Creek. It then crosses a low, forest-covered saddle and descends to ford Buck Meadow Creek. After crossing the long meadow at the north end of upper Buck Lake, the trail circles the west side of upper Buck Lake, passing a trail to Deer Lake, crosses the isthmus separating the two lakes, and follows the east side of lower Buck Lake, often being back in the trees away from the lakeside. Upper Buck Lake is a good-sized

(50-acre) glacial lake with numerous good campsites around
the shore. Fishing for rainbow (to 18') is good. Lower Buck
Lake is somewhat deeper and rockier, though about the same
size, and fishing is usually about the same as at the upper lake.
About ¼ mile beyond the south end of Lower Buck Lake, the
trail passes the Wood Lake lateral, and amid a nice forest
cover of lodgepole descends steeply (600') to the Emigrant
Lake Trail junction and lovely Cow Meadow Lake (7840').
There are excellent campsites along the north edge of the lake.
This 55-acre lake is connected by lagoons with overhanging
banks. A DF&G dam at the south end keeps the water level
fairly constant, and fishing for rainbow and some brook is
excellent (8-18'). Angling on the stream above the lake is good.

4th Hiking Day (**Cow Meadow Lake** to **Maxwell Lake**, 7.5
miles—12.1 km): From the east side of Cow Meadow Lake,
the trail ascends 560 feet via a frequently blasted, usually
cobbled trail to the bench containing rocky, deep Lertora Lake
(8400'), passing a trail to the west and Huckleberry Lake
before arriving at Lertora. This 25-acre lake offers only fair
angling for brook and rainbow (7-13"). From the west end of
Lertora Lake this route veers east along the south side of the
lake, and descends over a very rough trail to the northeast end
of large (200-acre) Huckleberry Lake (8000'). This subalpine
lake provides good fishing for brook and rainbow (8-18"), and
East Fork Cherry Creek above the lake often provides
excellent angling. From the meadows at the northeast end of
Huckleberry, the trail heads upstream and soon fords East
Fork Cherry Creek as it ascends the canyon. Views of the
unusual granite island known as Sachse Monument dominate
the northern skyline as the trail passes a tungsten mine. At
this point the trail joins the mining road, and then it refords
the stream before passing the Twin Lakes Trail lateral. At the
south end of Horse Meadow our trail branches northwest up a
timbered slope to Maxwell Lake (8700'). Maxwell Lake (46
acres), an emerald-green gem with a tufty meadow fringe,
affords excellent angling for brook trout (8-14"). The polished
granite of Sachse Monument towers over the south side of this
charming lake, and the choice campsites on the north side of
the lake have an uninterrupted view of both the lake and the
peak.

5th Hiking Day (**Maxwell Lake** to **Emigrant Meadow Lake**, 5.5
miles—8.9 km): From Maxwell Lake the trail climbs by a
series of switchbacks through a moderate forest cover of
lodgepole pine and then winds through a long, rock-lined
meadow past several beautiful lakelets to Blackbird Lake and

a junction with a trail to Emigrant Meadow Lake. Here our route branches right (north) past several small tarns that are usually dry by late season. The trail soon becomes faint, since this lateral is unmaintained, and one must keep a sharp eye out for ducks and blazes. This footpath ascends along the south side of the wandering North Fork Cherry Creek for about 1½ miles, and then fords the creek. From the ford onward, the trail is rutted into meadowy turf, but has become overgrown due to lack of maintenance. The trail becomes a little steeper just south of Middle Emigrant Lake, and then levels out at the wet meadows at the foot of the lake. Anglers who wish to try their luck on this fair-sized, granitic lake will find the fishing fair-to-good for rainbow (7-10″). The trail rounds the west side of the lake, fords the inlet stream, and crosses a low, rocky ridge to the Emigrant Meadow Lake basin (9400′). This huge meadow was the traditional stopping place for emigrant trains on the first leg of their Sierra crossing. This hiking day terminates at the open and exposed fair campsites on the west side of the lake. Fishing in Emigrant Meadow Lake is good for rainbow (8-13″).

6th and 7th Hiking Days: Reverse the steps of the 2nd and 1st hiking days of Trip 20, 12.6 miles (20.3 km).

Maxwell Lake

24   **Kennedy Meadow to Hetch Hetchy**

TRIP   From Kennedy Meadow to O'Shaughnessy Dam (Hetch Hetchy Reservoir) via Brown Bear Pass and Jack Main Canyon (shuttle trip). Topo maps *Sonora Pass, Tower Peak, Pinecrest, Lake Eleanor*. Best mid or late season; 44 miles (70.9 km).

Grade	Trail/layover days	Total recom- mended days
Leisurely	7/2	9
Moderate	5/1	6
Strenuous	4/0	4

HILITES   This is a trip of contrasts. The route begins by bisecting the volcanic and glacial terrain north of Bond Pass. This terrain is, as one writer aptly described it, "a land born of fire and ice." As beautiful as the terrain is northwest of Bond Pass, the primitive, unspoiled beauty of Jack Main Canyon has to be the high point of this trip. Glacial, subalpine meadows like those around Emigrant Meadow Lake impress the visitor, but it remains for the lower grasslands of Grace Meadow, with its meandering Falls Creek, to claim the heart. This is an excellent trip for the intermediate as well as the seasoned wilderness traveler.

DESCRIPTION (Leisurely trip)

1st and 2nd Hiking Days: Follow Trip 20 to **Emigrant Meadow Lake**, 12.6 miles (20.3 km).

3rd Hiking Day (**Emigrant Meadow Lake** to **Dorothy Lake**, 5 miles—8.1 km): From Emigrant Meadow the route climbs over a rocky ridge to Grizzly Meadow (9700') and two unnamed lakes. Fishing here is fair-to-good for rainbow (to 10"). This area is subject to the Forest Service's Multiple-Use land program; hence the traveler may encounter summer-grazing steers. Further evidences of this program mar the serenity of this wilderness just beyond the lakes, where the trail encounters a mining road. Our route follows this road as it descends to the Summit Meadow "trail" junction, a distance of about 2 miles. From here our route follows another mining road across the northern fringe of the meadow, and then ascends by a series of switchbacks to the gentle saddle called Bond Pass (9700'). Amidst a clump of red fir marking the summit, the trail leaves the dirt road and crosses into Yosemite National Park. There are excellent views, east from the summit, of Saurian Crest and Tower Peak.

The descent on the east side winds through dense lodgepole and fir to a junction of the trail to Dorothy Lake (9440'). After turning north on it, a ½-mile gentle ascent brings the traveler to the scattered campsites on the west shore. Anglers should ready their tackle for the good-to-excellent fishing for brook and rainbow (8-15"). Dorothy Lake, with its pleasant meadow fringes and bunched stands of lodgepole, makes an excellent base camp from which to explore the surrounding lakes and terrain. Of particular interest is the "rock glacier" beneath nearby Forsyth Peak. A discovery side trip to the lake just south of Dorothy Lake provides excellent views of this geologic wonder. Like their ice counterparts, rock glaciers are moving masses.

4th Hiking Day (**Dorothy Lake** to **Grace Meadow,** 3.2 miles—5.2 km): First, retrace your steps ½ mile to the first junction, then continue down-canyon. Jack Main Canyon begins at Dorothy Lake, and from the start it is a great hiker's route. A whole spectrum of wildlife may be found along this trail, and the abundance of the wildlife is testimony to the effectiveness of the National Park system. In the meadowed fringes of Dorothy Lake, the piping of the Belding ground squirrel ushers the traveler past the marmot-inhabited opposite slopes. If one is on the trail early enough, deer still out grazing will keep him entranced with their graceful movements. Ample signs of the black bears that roam this section of the park will be found along the trail—particularly during gooseberry season. Scenically, this short stretch of trail is an idyllic series of tiny meadows alongside murmuring Falls Creek. To the east, somber Forsyth Peak and abruptly divided Keyes Peak (juxtaposed black gabbro and white granite) cap the canyon walls. The trail gradually descends through a dense forest

cover to the north end of long, rolling Grace Meadow (8620′).
In contrast to the wide-open, windy stretch of Emigrant
Meadow, Grace Meadow has a soft, intimate feel that makes it
a favorite base camp. Anglers should be ready for excellent
brook and rainbow (to 13″) along Falls Creek.

5th Hiking Day (**Grace Meadow** to **Paradise Valley,** 8 miles—12.9
km): From the lower end of Grace Meadow the route
stepladders down through smaller meadows on a well-
maintained trail paralleling aptly named Falls Creek.
Directly to the south there are excellent views of the massive
granitic upthrust named Chittenden Peak, and as the trail
descends alongside this landmark the terrain becomes
rougher. Our route passes the trail to Tilden Lake and
continues to descend through rocky terrain that shows
increasing signs of glacial action. Chittenden Peak, at a
higher elevation and greater exposure, shows signs of
progressive erosion on its exfoliating dome. Lower down in the
canyon, by contrast, the smooth, polished surfaces of the rock
look as though they had just emerged from their glacial sleep.

Two miles south of the Tilden Lake lateral, the trail passes
sheltered Wilmer Lake (called "Wilma Lake" on the topo map)
and a lateral trail going east to Tilden Canyon and Benson
Lake. Set off to the side of our trail, this blue mountain jewel is
fringed with meadows and lodgepole and mountain hemlock.
There are good campsites and good fishing for rainbow and
brook (8-13″). In late season swimming is excellent in the
potholes along Falls Creek and in some of the shallower
nearby lakes. From Wilmer Lake the trail crosses a small
rocky ridge and descends through a narrow canyon. Here the
surroundings change dramatically. Quaking aspen groves are
more frequent, and the previously dashing Falls Creek has
become a series of tranquil, lakelike, turgid lagoons. The trail
now winds through dense ferns and willows until it arrives at
a trail junction in Paradise Valley (7680′). Just before this
junction, the trail passes an unnamed, charming, picturebook
lake, perfectly flanked by a towering granite cliff across the
lake from the trail. There are several campsites on the long
meadow. Fishing on the lake and in Falls Creek is fair for
brook and rainbow (to 9″).

6th Hiking Day (**Paradise Valley** to **Beehive,** 8 miles—12.9 km.):
From the meadow, the trail goes past granite-domed Andrews
Peak, and passes several small, unnamed lakes before
ascending the steep, rocky "Golden Stairs" to Moraine Ridge.
At the foot of this rocky ascent, the trail veers away from Falls
Creek, and travelers get an excellent view down to the
meadowed flats surrounding Lake Vernon. The ascent to the

crown of Moraine Ridge is marked by a magnificent stand of red fir and lodgepole pine. The panorama from the top of the ridge includes Tiltill Mountain and Andrews Peak in the east, Bailey Ridge and Mahan Peak farther north, and Forsyth Peak, Saurian Crest, Tower Peak, Pettit Peak and Mt. Conness on the skyline, northeast to east. The trail across the crest of Moraine Ridge becomes very sandy as it descends past a junction to Lake Vernon and on to Beehive (6500'). Beehive is a charming meadow campsite set in a classic red-fir forest. At one end of the meadow is a fenced-off, coldwater spring. Even in the driest years, this meadow is a splash of wildflower color. On the negative side, the area has been rather littered and bears are assiduous here.

7th Hiking Day (**Beehive** to **O'Shaughnessy Dam,** 7.2 miles—11.5 km.): At Beehive this route passes a trail to Laurel Lake, and continues south on a duff path that winds through dense stands of fir alternating with small wildflower-filled meadows. As this route descends gradually past a second lateral to Laurel Lake, it becomes rockier, and finally it drops via steep, rocky switchbacks. The forest cover changes with the advent of incense-cedar and black oak. One final grove of mature sugar pine, red fir, and incense-cedar marks the end of the trail as it joins the Forest Service road from Lake Eleanor to O'Shaughnessy Dam. This arterial winds down by long, dusty switchbacks over a steep slope covered with black oak and lilac. From this 4-mile stretch of road, views are excellent of the Grand Canyon of the Tuolumne, Kolana Rock and LeConte Point. Shortly before arriving at the dam (3796') the hiker passes through a long, cool, dripping tunnel blasted through a solid granite wall on the north side of the dam.

Sign near O'Shaughnessy Dam

25   Gianelli Cabin to Y Meadow Lake

TRIP   From Gianelli Cabin to Y Meadow Lake (round
               trip). Topo map *Pinecrest*. Best mid or late season;
               10 miles (16.2 km).

Grade	Trail/layover days	Total recommended days
Leisurely	2/0	2
Moderate	....	....
Strenuous	....	....

HILITES   Except for the short distance from Gianelli Cabin
               to Burst Rock, this trip is within beautiful
               Emigrant Wilderness, and the route parallels a
               segment of the historic Emigrant Trail. En route
               to Y Meadow Lake, anglers can try their luck on
               two small but fairly productive lakes, and early-
               trip views, from Burst Rock, are panoramic.

DESCRIPTION

1st Hiking Day (**Gianelli Cabin** to **Y Meadow Lake,** 5 miles—8.1
km): At Gianelli Cabin (8560')—now only part of the log
cabin's base remains—the trail begins in a meadow and
ascends a steep slope covered with red fir and silver and
lodgepole pine. This segment has been used as a jeep trail, so it
is somewhat eroded. The trail tops the ridge at Burst Rock
(9161'), a landmark for the old Emigrant Trail, and crosses the
Emigrant Wilderness boundary (no motorized vehicles allowed). This vantage point offers excellent views to the north
of Liberty Hill, Elephant Rock, the Dardanelles, Castle Rock,
and the Three Chimneys. You can see as far as Mt. Lyell on the
southeast border of Yosemite Park. As the trail bears east
along the ridge, the traveler also has excellent views of the
Stanislaus River watershed to the north and the Tuolomne
River watershed to the south.

   The trail descends gradually to a low saddle overlooking
granitic Powell Lake. This small lake offers fair fishing for
brook trout in early and late season, and the fine views to the

northeast makes this an attractive spot for a lunch break. The trail then crosses a small ridge, descends through a forest of lodgepole, fir, and mountain hemlock, and arrives at the open stretches of meadowy Lake Valley. A faint fisherman's trail (0.7 miles) to Chewing Gum Lake turns south through the meadow. Anglers with a yen will want to try the fair-to-good fishing for brook on this small (5-acre) lake before continuing. From Lake Valley it is 1½ miles across another broad ridge to the turnoff to Y Meadow Lake. Here our route turns south for one winding mile to the fair campsites at the north end of Y Meadow Lake (8600'). Unfortunately, the water level fluctuates so much that the lake cannot support fish life. However, anglers accustomed to cross-country walking may elect to try the waters of Granite Lake (0.7 mile south) for the good fishing for brook (8-13"). There are some poor-to-fair campsites at Granite Lake.

2nd Hiking Day: Retrace your steps, 5 miles (8.1 km).

Gianelli Cabin

26   Gianelli Cabin to Wire Lakes

TRIP   From Gianelli Cabin to Wire Lakes (round trip).
             Topo map *Pinecrest*. Best mid or late season; 24.8
             miles (40 km).

Grade	Trail/layover days	Total recom- mended days
Leisurely	4/1	5
Moderate	4/0	4
Strenuous	2/1	3

HILITES   This round trip penetrates the heart of the
             Emigrant Wilderness as it wends through a
             delightful series of meadows and over high, open
             ridges. Wire Lakes, the destination for this trip, is
             a stepladder set of three memorable high-
             mountain lakes that afford excellent angling and
             several fine choices for secluded camping.

DESCRIPTION (Leisurely trip)

1st Hiking Day: Follow Trip 25 to **Y Meadow Lake,** 5 miles (8.1
km).

2nd Hiking Day (**Y Meadow Lake** to **Upper Wire Lake,** 7.4
miles—11.9 km): First retrace your steps from Y Meadow
Lake to the trail junction of the Gianelli Cabin/Whitesides
Meadow Trail. Here our route turns right (northeast) toward
very large Whitesides Meadow. Travelers should be prepared
for the probability of seeing summer-grazing cattle on these
broad expanses (Forest Service Multiple-Use land program)
but these bovine occupants should not detract too much from
an appreciation of this subalpine grassland. At the east end of
the meadow our route passes the Eagle Pass Trail, and then
ascends the moderately timbered slope at the northeast end.
On this ascent our rough path passes a trail to Upper Relief
Valley and Kennedy Meadow, and another one after 1½ miles
of descent. Then it dips down to ford West Fork Cherry Creek
(sometimes dry in late season) at Salt Lick Meadow (8520′).
From here the trail climbs to a tarn-dotted bench and then

descends past several picturesque tarns to Spring Meadow. Tiny lakes sprinkle the green expanse of the meadow, and early-to-mid season trailpounders will find the grassland areas spiced with lupine, paintbrush and buttercup. Fishermen will find the fishing for brook trout fair-to-good along the tributary (Spring Creek) flowing through Post Corral Canyon. A short mile farther southeast, a signed trail leaves the main trail and winds the remaining 0.4 mile along a ridge to the excellent campsites on the northwest side of upper Wire Lake (8800'). Equally good campsites may also be found at Banana Lake (middle Wire Lake), 0.3 miles southwest on a cross-country route. Fishing on the Wire Lakes is good-to-excellent (with a midseason slowdown) for brook (8-14"). Campers will find any of the several secluded campsites on these high montane lakes an idyllic setting for a base camp.

3rd & 4th Hiking Days: Retrace your steps, 12.4 miles (20 km.).

Marmot

Caroline Winnett

27   Crabtree Camp to Bear Lake

TRIP   From Crabtree Camp to Bear Lake (round trip)
               Topo map *Pinecrest.* Best early-to-mid season; 8
               miles (12.8 km).

Grade	Trail/layover days	Total recom- mended days
Leisurely	2/0	2
Moderate	....	....
Strenuous	....	....

HILITES   Bear Lake usually is a good bet for an early-season
               trip, when fishing for the rainbow trout that
               inhabit the lake waters is best.

DESCRIPTION

1st Hiking Day (**Crabtree Camp** to **Bear Lake,** 4 miles—6.4 km):
Leaving the moderately forested flats of Crabtree Camp, we
hop Bell Creek, making sure that our canteens are full for the
waterless climb to Camp Lake, and quickly come to a junction
with the Chewing Gum Lake Trail on a sandy bench. Our
route ascends dustily through open mixed conifers, then
contours, undulating gently, south to reach a segment of older
trail. Here we assault a steep, much abused path, fortunately
well-shaded, which levels out under aspen and lodgepole at a
lateral trail to Pine Valley. Open stands of mature Jeffrey
pine, lodgepole pine, black oak, red fir, and Sierra juniper
allow a viewful traverse above deeply forested Pine Valley;
then the trees close in as we follow a red-fir corridor around a
grassy pond and gently ascend to the Emigrant Wilderness
boundary. Four hundred yards later we reach the west end of
shallow, green Camp Lake. This sparsely forested, sorely
trampled lakelet supports a harried population of brook trout.
At a saddle just past Camp Lake, we branch left and go 1 mile
to granitic Bear Lake (7700'). Campsites on the west of this
high, mountain lake have been somewhat vandalized but they
are the best to be had. Swimming in late season is invigor-
atingly good, and fishing on this 30-acre lake is fair for rainbow and brook (7-13").
2nd Hiking Day: Retrace your steps, 4 miles (6.4 km).

Crabtree Camp to Deer Lake 28

TRIP From Crabtree Camp to Deer Lake (round trip). Topo map *Pinecrest*. Best mid or late season, 24.8 miles (40 km).

Grade	Trail/layover days	Total Recommended days
Leisurely	6/2	8
Moderate	5/2	7
Strenuous	4/2	6

HILITES Fine fishing and the protected beauty of the Emigrant Wilderness highlight this round trip. A variety of wildlife is present along this route through three life zones, and the higher ridges offer impressive views of the glaciated terrain.

DESCRIPTION (Leisurely trip)

1st Hiking Day: Follow Trip 27 to **Bear Lake**, 4 miles (6.4 km).
2nd Hiking Day (**Bear Lake** to **Piute Lake**, 5.4 miles—8.8 km): First, retrace your steps to the Crabtree Camp/Deer Lake Trail, where our route turns left (east). From the junction, the steep, dusty trail switchbacks down on deep sand flanked by dense manzanita and ceanothus to an easy ford of Lily Creek. Swinging southeast through a meadow sporting corn lilies, lungwort and groundsel, our path soon comes to a granite headwall, and makes a steep, rocky ascent. Now above most of the trees, we see, in the south, Pine Valley and the chaos of white domes in the Chain Lakes region. A parade of switchbacks leads to a lengthy traverse that passes through meadows south of black-streaked granite outcrops, and we soon reach a pretty lakelet, much larger than shown on the topo map, speckled with Indian pond lilies and backdropped by dancing aspens and lichen-dappled granite. Its clear, shallow waters support a thriving population of yellow-legged frogs.

After a short climb east of this tarn, we survey large Piute Meadow in the east, dome-guarded Toms Canyon in the north, Groundhog Meadow below in the southeast, and, on the east-

ern horizon, Bigelow Peak and the jutting prominence of Tower Peak. Bone-jarring dynamited switchbacks, esthetically
ameliorated by a profusion of wildflowers, lead down to a
sidehill traverse in glacial boulders west of Piute Meadow.
Keeping to the trees south of the willowed west arm of Piute
Meadow, we pass a small campsite; then, where our route
bends south to easily cross Piute Creek, there is another,
larger site. Only yards after Piute Creek the unsigned
Groundhog Meadow spur trail comes in from the south. The
dry slabs and lodgepole pines demarcating the lower margin of
Piute Meadow are left behind when our path bends upward,
switchbacking rockily up the east slope of Piute Creek canyon
to a broad saddle southwest of Piute Lake. The trail then
descends to the meadowed fringes of tiny (2-acre) Piute Lake
(7900′) and the good campsites on the north side. Fishing for
rainbow (8-12″) in this shallow lake is fair to good.

3rd Hiking Day (**Piute Lake** to **Deer Lake,** 3 miles—4.8
km): From Piute Lake the trail drops to ford West Fork
Cherry Creek and then strenuously ascends a steep, rocky,
washed-out section to an overlook just above warm little Gem
Lake. Less steep than the previous climb, the trail from Gem
to Jewelry Lake is nonetheless a rocky ascent. Our route
skirts the north side of the meadow fringes surrounding
Jewelry Lake, and anglers will want to try their luck for the
fair-to-good fishing for rainbow (to 10″) in the lake and the
lagoons around the inlet. From the east end of Jewelry Lake, it
is a short mile by rocky, gently ascending trail to the excellent
campsites on the north side of Deer Lake (8540′). This long,
granite-bound lake has nice meadow fringes on the north side.
The forested campsites look out over the lake's island- and
rock-dotted surface. Fishing for nice-sized rainbow (8-16″) is
good-to-excellent on both the lake and the inlet stream.

4th, 5th and 6th Hiking Days: Retrace your steps, 12.4 miles
(20 km).

Gianelli Cabin to Crabtree Camp 29

TRIP   From Gianelli Cabin to Crabtree Camp via Wire and Deer Lakes (shuttle trip). Topo map *Pinecrest*. Best mid or late season, 27.3 miles (44 km).

Grade	Trail/layover days	Total recommended days
Leisurely	5/2	7
Moderate	4/2	6
Strenuous	3/2	5

HILITES   This route has proved popular with angler, naturalist, photographer and hiker alike. High, coldwater lakes and streams vie with deep fir forests and alpine meadows for the attention of the visitor. The shortness of the shuttle for this trip makes it a near-loop.

DESCRIPTION (Leisurely trip)

1st and 2nd Hiking Days: Follow Trip 26 to **Upper Wire Lake**, 12.4 miles (20 km).

3rd Hiking Day (**Upper Wire Lake** to **Piute Lake**, 5.5 miles—8.9 km): From upper Wire Lake the traveler has the option of circling to Deer Lake by the longer trail route or descending through the Wire Lakes basin and going cross country to the west end of Deer Lake. The trail route, after retracing the short fisherman's lateral, rejoins the Spring Meadow/Deer Lake main trail and turns south. After a slight climb, the remaining distance to Deer Lake is a steady descent over a forested streamcourse that passes several small, unnamed lakes. At Deer Lake this route passes the Buck Lakes trail and turns right (southwest) toward Jewelry Lake.

The cross-country route from upper Wire Lake to this point first leads southwest to Banana Lake (middle Wire Lake), where all semblance of trail vanishes. The easiest descent from here is to take the clear route through the meadowed area east of Banana Lake and then descend via the usually dry streamcourse to the Jewelry Lake/Deer Lake Trail about 0.3 mile west of Deer Lake. The trail from Deer Lake to Jewelry Lake is a ½-mile rocky descent that brings the traveler to the pleasant meadow fringes surrounding Jewelry Lake. This lake has placid lagoons forming its inlet which provide fair-to-good fishing for rainbow (to 10″). Crossing the inlet stream, the route descends a rocky trail to warm little Gem Lake (8240′). From this viewpoint the trail descends steeply to a ford of West Fork Cherry Creek and then climbs gently to tiny Piute Lake. Fishing for rainbow (8-12″) in this shallow lake is fair-to-good.

4th and 5th Hiking Days: Reverse the steps of the 1st and 2nd hiking days, Trip 28, 9.4 miles (15.1 km).

Gianelli Cabin to Kennedy Meadow **30**

TRIP   From Gianelli Cabin to Kennedy Meadow via
Deer and Emigrant Lakes (shuttle trip). Topo
maps *Pinecrest, Tower Peak, Sonora Pass*. Best
mid or late season; 33.3 miles (53.7 km).

Grade	Trail/layover days	Total recom-mended days
Leisurely	5/2	7
Moderate	4/2	6
Strenuous	3/2	5

HILITES   This trip journeys through a cross section of the
Emigrant Wilderness. The route touches some
justly popular base-camping lakes, and from these
points the traveler has access to the unusual and
exciting surrounding country. Taken at Leisurely
pace, this route affords one of the best possible
week-long excursions in the region.

DESCRIPTION (Leisurely trip)

1st and 2nd Hiking Days: Follow Trip 26 to **Upper Wire Lake**,
12.4 miles (20 km).

3rd Hiking Day (**Upper Wire Lake** to **Emigrant Lake** via Deer and
Buck Lakes, 7.5 miles—12.1 km): The traveler going to Deer
Lake has a choice of going by trail or cross country. The trail
route entails retracing the short fisherman's trail to its
junction with the main trail from Spring Meadow. There our
route turns right (south), and descends gently past several
unnamed tarns to Deer Lake. The cross-country route goes
south through the Wire Lakes basin to Banana Lake (middle
Wire Lake), and then veers east a short distance through a
meadowed basin. At the end of this meadow a long, usually dry
streamcourse descending to the south gives access to the trail

0.3 mile west of Deer Lake (8540'). This is a large, granitoid, meadow-fringed lake offering good-to-excellent fishing for nice-sized rainbow (to 16"), and anglers who have had an early start will want to try these waters.

The trail to Buck Lakes continues east over a low rocky ridge, and then descends steeply to join the Emigrant Lake/Cow Meadow Lake Trail on the west shore of Buck Lakes. At this junction our route turns left (north) along the west side of upper Buck Lake, and follows Buck Meadow Creek as it crosses the long meadow at the lake's north end. Our route then veers east, fords Buck Meadow Creek, and crosses the steep, low ridge separating the Emigrant Lake and Buck Lakes basins. At Emigrant Lake (8800') the trail follows the long north shore to the several good-to-excellent campsites near the inlet. Emigrant Lake is the largest lake (230 acres) in the Wilderness, and is a long-time favorite of fishermen because of the good-to-excellent rainbow fishing (8-18") in its deep waters. Those who prefer stream fishing will find the lagoons near the inlet exciting sport, but the fish are smaller.

4th and 5th Hiking Days: Reverse the steps of the 2nd and 1st hiking days, Trip 21, 13.4 miles (21.6 km).

Lower Buck Lake *Luther Linkhart*

Kennedy Meadow to Gianelli Cabin

31

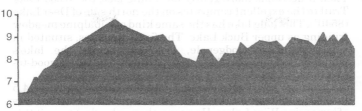

TRIP   From Kennedy Meadow to Gianelli Cabin via
Brown Bear Pass and Emigrant Meadow, Maxwell, Buck, Wire, and Y Meadow lakes (shuttle
trip). Topo maps *Sonora Pass, Tower Peak,
Pinecrest*. Best mid or late season, 43.1 miles (69.5
km).

Grade	Trail/layover days	Total recom-mended days
Leisurely	7/3	10
Moderate	5/2	7
Strenuous	4/2	6

HILITES   After visiting the north side of the Emigrant
Wilderness, this route turns south and traverses
the beautiful, lake-dotted country of the Cherry
Creek watershed. At Emigrant Meadow the trail
joints the old Emigrant Trail, and history buffs
will have the opportunity of seeing this historic
crossing as the pioneers did.

DESCRIPTION (Leisurely trip)

1st and 2nd Hiking Days: Follow Trip 20 to **Emigrant Meadow
Lake**, 12.6 miles (20.3 km).

3rd and 4th Hiking Days: Reverse the steps of the 5th and 4th
hiking days, Trip 23, 13 miles (21 km).

5th Hiking Day (**Cow Meadow Lake** to **Deer Lake**, 3.5 miles—5.6
km): Leaving Cow Meadow Lake, the trail passes a junction
with a trail from East Fork Cherry Creek and then ascends
steeply 600 feet amid a dense, predominantly lodgepole forest
cover to a junction with the Wood Lake lateral. Lower Buck
Lake (42 acres) is a rocky, deep, glacial lake that is separated
from upper Buck Lake by a narrow isthmus. Fishing on both
lakes for rainbow (to 18″) is good. Our route crosses the
isthmus and turns north, where it strikes the Deer Lake Trail.

Here our route turns left (west) and climbs steeply for ½ mile. Then it descends more gently for a mile past the Wood Lake Trail to the excellent campsites on the north side of Deer Lake (8540'). This long lake has the same kind of subalpine meadow fringing as upper Buck Lake. The fine campsites, situated in small stands of lodgepole, look out across the lake's island-dotted surface. Fishing for rainbow (to 16") is good-to-excellent.

6th Hiking Day (**Deer Lake** to **Y Meadow Lake**, 9 miles—14.5 km): The mileage for this hiking day is calculated on the basis of bypassing Wire Lakes. However, those who elect to visit this charming lake chain (good fishing) should examine the alternative route offered in the description of the 3rd hiking day, Trip 29. From the trail junction at the middle of Deer Lake's north shore, our route climbs north beside an unnamed stream and past a series of inviting tarns. About 1.7 miles from Deer Lake we pass the Wire Lakes Trail going left (west) and then descend a densely forested slope to the east end of Spring Meadow. This meadow is a vast, lakelet-dotted grassland that is lush with buttercups, lupine and paintbrush. One frequently sees cattle grazing here, allowed by the National Forest multiple-use land program. From Spring Meadow the trail crosses a small ridge containing more tarns and then descends moderately-to-steeply through a wooded section to Salt Lick Meadow, where it crosses tiny West Fork Cherry Creek (sometimes dry in late season). Then the route ascend through lodgepole pine and mountain hemlock, passing the first of two trails leading north to Upper Relief Valley and Kennedy Meadow and, 0.6 mile later, an unsigned trail leading south to secluded Toejam Lake. Our trail tops the ridge and then descends to sprawling Whitesides Meadow. At its head we pass another trail to Upper Relief Valley and, soon after, a trail to Cooper Meadow, both leading north. The green expanse of this meadow is broken by the flow of an unnamed tributary of South Fork Stanislaus River. Our trail touches this stream at the meadow's west end, then veers away southwest to the Y Meadow Lake Trail junction. Here we branch left and walk one winding mile to the fair campsites in the timber fringe at the north end of Y Meadow Lake (8600').

7th Hiking Day: Reverse the steps of the 1st hiking day, Trip 25, 5 miles (8.1 km).

The North Boundary Experience

Wherever Sierra mountaineers gather there is sure to be talk of the fabulous "North Boundary Country," and there is just cause for this preoccupation. Here Yosemite boasts its least-visited and wildest backcountry. In these glaciated canyons and on these granite crests, five generations of hikers, climbers and horsemen have found the solitude, beauty and challenge they sought. Lying between the Tioga Road (State Highway 120) and the northern edge of the Park, it is a heavily glaciated region of uniform drainage pattern and rounded slopes that appeals to the cross-country wanderer. It is remote because it is large, and because it is isolated by the main Sierra crest on the east and north, and by the Grand Canyon of the Tuolumne on the south.

The topography of this region also contributes to the feeling of solitude that attends trips taken through it. The terrain is split by no fewer than 11 ridge-valley sequences, all running northeast to southwest. A group of hikers can be in one drainage and totally oblivious of another group only one mile away, with a natural wall of glaciated granite in between. Travelers on the famed Pacific Crest Trail are aware of another, equally desirable quality that accrues to the ridge-valley sequence: each ridge encountered and surmounted is sure to reveal a fresh, new valley full of different claims on the visitor's attention.

With the exception of the volcanic and metamorphic rock along much of the eastern escarpment, this is all granite country. Time and evolution are at work here, and mountains are being leveled. You might be misled into thinking that these things are occurring too slowly to be noticed, but the joyous instant a wildflower frantically bursts into bloom is an integral part of the juggernaut process, and the spreading of its petals is as inexorable as the sun's rise, and, in its context, more powerful than an earthquake. One writer put it this way: "Time is the factor. If a butterfly were to brush a wing against the great granite wall of Half Dome in a daily pilgrimage, it would eventually level the mountain." The valleys of the northern part of the Park are full of life that is moving mountains, and if you watch closely you *can* see it happen.

Aside from the remoteness, perhaps the most appealing things about the North Boundary Country is the variety of the plant life. The elevation spread of nearly 9000 feet encompasses almost every kind of Sierran ecological niche. From the digger-pine belt near Hetch Hetchy Reservoir to the whitebark-pined summits of Burro Pass, almost every tree to be seen in the Sierra is represented. Early-summer wildflower displays are nowhere more abundant nor varied, and it is not at all unusual to come across the sunburst yellow of golden brodiaea and the delicate blossom of the alpine-dwelling yellow columbine in the same hiking day. On every hand the hiker sees a vital urgency for life—a living claim for one's right to the sun. Perhaps it is this intense process of life frantically renewing itself in a high alpine meadow that man returns time and again to witness. Both a wildflower and a backpacker cram a lot of living into an all-too-short summer. In all cases it is an affirmative celebration of life, and the backpacker, by his personal witness, is a celebrant.

Trails through the North Boundary Country are, understandably, not as well maintained as trails more heavily used and closer to roads in the Park. However, these neglected paths are ways of solitude where one is sometimes able to walk for long distances without encountering another living soul. Best-known among the North Boundary trails is the Tahoe-to-Yosemite route, which is also a segment of the Pacific Crest Trail. This trail receives the brunt of the traffic. Most of the routes described in this section begin on the east side of the Sierra. The weekend trips flirt with the Sierra crest, but one should plan at least a three-day trip for any serious penetration of the North Boundary Country.

All kinds of reasons are given for trips into wilderness, but the most commonly given is fishing. For the angler who measures any and all wilderness experiences in terms of the fishing opportunities, the North Boundary Country is a frustrating area to consider—frustrating because the options are so many, the fishery so varied, and the scenery so distracting. Living in the waters of this region are eastern brook, rainbow, brown, golden and some cutthroat trout. The most consistent fish-producing streams are Falls Creek in Jack Main Canyon, Rancheria Creek in Kerrick Canyon, Matterhorn Creek in Matterhorn Canyon and Return Creek in Virginia Canyon. Lakes that are annual "hotspots" include Benson, Smedberg, Peeler, the McCabes, and the lakes above Saddlebag Lake. A state fishing license is required within the Park for all persons over 16.

A word about bears

Since the first edition of this book, more and more people have taken up backpacking. One result has been more and more unnatural food for bears—the food brought in by backpackers. Since this food is attractive to bears, and all too often easily available, the animals have developed a habit of seeking it and eating it. They patrol popular campsites nightly. As the bears have become more knowledgeable and persistent, backpackers have escalated their food-protecting methods. From merely putting it in one's pack by one's bed at night, and chasing away any bear that came, backcountry travelers switched to hanging the food over a branch of a tree. But bears can climb trees, and they can gnaw or scratch through the nylon line that you tie around a tree trunk. When they sever the line, the food hanging from the other end of the line of course falls to the ground. This happens all too often in Yosemite Park.

To avoid food loss due to line severance, you can learn the *counterbalance* method of "bearbagging." First, tie a small stone to the end of a 30-foot length of nylon line (⅛" or so in diameter) as a weight to hurl up and over a likely branch. The branch should be at least 16 feet up, and long enough that the line can rest securely at a point at least 6 feet from the tree trunk. When you have the line over the branch, tie a rock that weighs about the same as the food bag to one end of the line. (Instead of a rock, you could tie a bag containing half the food, if you have two appropriate bags.) Now pull the rock up to the branch that the line passes over. Then tie your food bag to the other end of the line, as high as you can conveniently reach, and stuff any extra line into the mouth of the food bag. Now push up on the food bag with just enough force—you hope—that the system will come to rest with the rock and the bag equally high. If they aren't equally high, take a long enough stick, preferably forked, and push up the lower of the two until they are even. If you can reach them standing on tiptoes, they are too low. Try again. Next morning, push up either rock or bag until one descends enough that you can reach it.

REMEMBER: If a bear does get your food, he will then consider it his, and he will fight any attempts you make to retrieve it. Don't try! Remember also never to leave your food unprotected even for a short while during the daytime.

The Trailheads

O'Shaughnessy Dam (Hetch Hetchy Reservoir). Go east on State Highway 120 4 miles beyond Buck Meadows and turn left at a signed junction. Go 6 miles to another signed junction, turn right and go 6½ miles to Camp Mather and then 9½ more miles to the roadend.

Leavitt Meadow. Go 8 miles east from Sonora Pass on State Highway 108, or 7 miles west from U.S. 395 on the same highway.

Buckeye Roadend. Go 7 miles west from Bridgeport on the Twin Lakes road and turn north for 4 dirt-road miles at the junction signed **Buckeye Campground**. Just beyond Buckeye Creek, turn left and go 1.1 miles, passing through a Forest Service Campground, to the end of the road. Alternatively, leave U.S. 395 3.8 miles north of Bridgeport and drive 6.0 miles to the same roadend.

Twin Lakes. Drive to the end of the paved 13½-mile road marked *Twin Lakes* that branches west from U.S. 395 in downtown Bridgeport.

Green Creek Roadend. Take the dusty dirt road signed *Green Lakes Pack Station* which leaves U.S. 395 4.7 miles south of Bridgeport and 21 miles north of Lee Vining. Go 9½ miles west to the roadend.

Saddlebag Lake. Go 2 miles up a gravel road that branches northwest from State Highway 120 2 miles north of the Tioga Pass entrance to Yosemite.

Glen Aulin Trailhead. From State Highway 120 in Tuolumne Meadows, just east of the bridge over the Tuolumne River, turn west on a dirt road and go 0.3 mile to a parking area near the stables. On crowded days you may have to park immediately off the highway at the Dog Lake trailhead parking lot.

Leavitt Meadow to Fremont Lake   **32**

TRIP   From Leavitt Meadow Campground to Fremont
Lake (round trip). Topo map *Sonora Pass*. Best
mid or late season; 18 miles (29 km).

Grade	Trail/layover days	Total recom- mended days
Leisurely	2/1	3
Moderate	2/0	2
Strenuous	....	....

HILITES   Along this well-traveled route the traveler is
introduced to the contrasts of the North Boundary
Country. Here the dark rock thrown up by
volcanoes meets the lighter, more typical Sierra
batholith granite. Cameras for the photo-bug are a
must, and the angler can look forward to good
rainbow-trout fishing at Fremont Lake.

DESCRIPTION

1st Hiking Day (**Leavitt Meadow Campground** to **Fremont Lake**, 9
miles—14.5 km): There are two ways to begin this hiking day.
The first is shorter and quicker, but it requires fording the
West Walker River in an area where the river is formidable in
early season. You should take the longer trail, described
second, until about mid-July of a typical year.

The short trail begins on State Highway 108 about 200
yards west of the pack station, 45 feet above a big yellow
sign *Gate 500 feet ahead*. (This sign is sometimes turned
parallel to the highway, and so hard to see.) From the
highway, the trail skirts above a 40-acre plot of private
property that has several structures on it and a fence around
it. At first you descend toward Leavitt Creek under a moderate
canopy of black cottonwoods, Jeffrey pines and junipers. In
about 100 yards is a boulder ford of a branch of the creek, and
in another 100 yards a second boulder-hop. Where the trail
dips close to the property fence, it meets and joins a dirt road
and then soon comes to the edge of large Leavitt Meadow.

After skirting the grassland for ½ mile, the road rises over a small saddle on a granite shoulder and then returns to the meadow. At its upper end, the route turns east and soon reaches road's end under a large Jeffrey pine. From this handsome tree, walk 125 steps northeast, crossing a small branch of the West Walker River, to meet the main river at a point where a fallen tree probably will allow a dry crossing in mid and late season. Across the ford, immediately veer right, into a grove of lodgepole and aspen trees with a campsite, and on the far side of the grove you will find the packer trail that has come up the center of Leavitt Meadow. This dusty trail switchbacks up a moderate grade for ½ mile to meet the foot trail from the campground.

The longer foot trail leaves the Leavitt Meadow Campground (7120') via a metal bridge across the West Walker River. Beyond the bridge our trail ascends stiffly in several stages to reach the top of a long, undulating volcanic ridge that looks down on the broad green expanses of the meadow and the oxbows of the meandering river. Looking down, it does not take a great deal of imagination to picture emigrant wagons working their way southwest toward Emigrant Pass, at the headwaters of this river. Close beside the trail are many tall specimens of a bush-tree called mountain mahogany. Despite its dry, tough appearance, the foliage of this desert plant is relished by the local mule-deer population. The plant is particularly striking in the early fall when the styles of the flowers are white, silky, 3-inch-long plumes growing by the hundreds on each bush.

At the highest point on this ridge east of Leavitt Meadow, views are excellent of the Marine Corps Cold Weather Camp in Pickel Meadow to the northeast and of the bone-white-topped Sweetwater Mountains on the eastern horizon. Below in the east is large, sandy-shored Poore Lake and directly south up-canyon rugged Forsyth Peak dominates the visible Sierra crest. From this viewpoint the trail descends to Secret Lake (7440'), which has a few good campsites scattered around its partly reedy shores. One-half mile farther we reach a junction with a trail to Poore Lake and, about ⅛ mile from there, the junction with the packer trail described above. Now one merged trail, our route rises slightly and then descends gently to the north shore of algae-bottomed Roosevelt Lake, ringed with a sparse fringe of Jeffrey pines. There are some undistinguished campsites on the west side of the lake, and sometimes fishing is good for brook trout to 13".

Then our trail leads over a granite shoulder and down to the
outlet of Lane Lake, nearly a twin of Roosevelt and only a few
yards from it. This outlet usually dries up by midsummer, but
the dead lodgepole pines southwest of the ford are testimony to
flooding earlier in the season. From the ford, the trail ascends
briefly southeast and then levels off as it passes several
lovely aspen groves, some with lush grass floors even into
late season. Just over a mile from Lane Lake we pass a junction with the old trail, no longer maintained, which runs
north from Lane Lake near the West Walker River. Past the
junction, our trail soon descends to the willow-lined banks of
the river, crossing a small but vigorous tributary ⅛ mile
before reaching the main stream. We ascend gently near the
riverside for ¼ mile through a cool forest of mixed conifers,
aspens and cottonwoods, then veer away on a steeper ascent
that fords another tributary. The rocky-dusty trail then
steepens to surmount a saddle crested with junipers and Jeffrey pines, which offers fine views up the West Walker valley
to Forsyth Peak and the Sierra crest. Descending over a
sandy trail, our route passes the marked turnoff to Hidden
and Red Top lakes, and then resumes its moderate ascent
along the east bank of the West Walker River. The rocky
stretch of trail alongside the river gives access to many
pleasant, granite-bottomed potholes. Here the river tumbles
along in a series of small falls and cascades that have carved
a narrows through the white granite which typifies the middle of the West Walker River Valley. The upper walls are of
barren, metavolcanic rock that ranges the color spectrum
from black to reds and yellows.

Where the narrows opens out onto a forest flat, rife with
mosquitoes in early season, we come to a junction with the
Fremont Lake Trail, just off the Sonora Pass topo map. Turning right, we follow this trail to the riverbank and find a good
log crossing less than 100 yards downstream. Across the river
are many well-used campsites, and we stroll downstream
past several to reach the signed Fremont Lake trail continua-
tion. This we follow westward and ascend steeply to cross a
saddle topped with juniper and Jeffrey pine. This saddle offers V'd views south to Tower Peak. The trail then descends
gently, passes the trail to Chain of Lakes, and in 100 yards
reaches Fremont Lake (8240'). The forest cover around this
generous-sized lake is moderate-to-dense lodgepole and
juniper, most of it around the south end of the lake. Here in
the timber are fair campsites, and fishing for rainbow (to
12") and eastern brook (to 10") is good.

2nd Hiking Day: Retrace your steps, 9 miles (14.5 km).

33   Leavitt Meadow to Cinko Lake

TRIP   From Leavitt Meadow Campground to Cinko Lake (round trip). Topo maps *Sonora Pass, Tower Peak*. Best mid or late season; 28 miles (45.2 km).

Grade	Trail/layover days	Total recommended days
Leisurely	3/1	4
Moderate	3/0	3
Strenuous	2/0	2

HILITES   This interesting route traces West Fork West Walker River to its headwaters cirque beneath the Sierra crestline. From the sagebrush and Jeffrey pine belt it ascends to the Boreal belt, passing through three ecological zones. Of the several trips in this drainage, this offers one of the best exposures to the geological, topographical and biological features of the country.

DESCRIPTION (Leisurely trip)

1st Hiking Day: Follow Trip 32, to **Fremont Lake**, 9 miles (14.5 km).

2nd Hiking Day (**Fremont Lake** to **Cinko Lake**, 5 miles—8.1 km): After retracing our steps back to the Chain of Lakes junction described in Trip 32, we turn right (south) and ascend steadily near, but out of sight of, Fremont Lake. This ascent steepens as it crosses open, granite-sand slopes with only a few junipers and pines for shade. Near the top of this ascent one has uninterrupted views to the south of Forsyth and Tower peaks, and one encounters his first silver pines of this trip. The first of three large granite domes that tower over the east side of Chain of Lakes comes into view, and the trail crosses to the north of it. Then, on a gently descending path through an increasingly dense forest cover, we pass the marked trail to Walker Meadows and arrive at the first of several tiny, green, lily-padded lakes. These lakes reflect the verdant forest cover that extends to their willow-lined shores, and by late summer their shallow depths teem with the biota that typifies near-stagnant waters. Fair campsites for early and mid season, usable when the water is moving, dot the west sides of all three lakes.

The trail leaves the last and largest of the Chain of Lakes and ascends gently over sand and duff through a moderate forest cover of lodgepole and silver pine past a small, unnamed lake north of Lower Long Lake. A few yards past this lily-padded lake, the trail veers right, around the north side of Lower Long Lake. The "blancoed" rock in the center of the lake is a favorite midday resting place for the sandpipers that inhabit the area. Fishermen seeking the pan-sized rainbow here will enjoy the sandpiper's low, skimming flight, which seems to trim the fringe of rushes. Fair-to-good campsites dot the north and west sides of the lake. More extensive campsites are found a few yards farther up the trail, at Upper Long Lake. The trail jogs around the lower end of Upper Long Lake, fords the intermittent outlet stream and meets the Piute Meadows lateral, going left. Our route turns right past a picturesque tarn to the banks of West Fork West Walker River. Here at another junction our route branches left alongside this tumbling stream. Good campsites dot both sides of the West Fork near the junction, marred only by the cowflops incident to the Multiple-Use grazing permit for nearby Walker Meadows. Occasional hemlocks with their gracefully bowed tops occur along the pleasant, granite-ledged, timber-pocketed ascent from the campsites. Many wildflowers, including shooting star, penstemon, bush lupine, aster, pennyroyal, columbine, goldenrod, heather, false Solomon's seal, Mariposa lily, wallflower, woolly sunflower and fleabane, decorate the stream's edge and complement the cheerful splashing of the nearby stream. This gentle-to-moderate climb continues along the southeast side of the stream to the foot of a large, white granite dome (Peak 10010), where it fords via boulders to the northwest side of the creek. Contrasts of the dark volcanic rock and the white granite underlayment of this part of the Sierra are nowhere more marked than in this valley, and the viewer is assailed with dark battlements of multihued basalt, and sheer escarpments of glacially smoothed batholithic granite. William H. Brewer, head of the Brewer Survey party that passed near here in July 1863, took note of the volcanic surroundings, saying ". . . in the higher Sierra, along our line of travel, all our highest points were capped with lava, often worn into strange and fantastic forms—rounded hills of granite, capped by rugged masses of lava, sometimes looking like old castles with their towers and buttresses and walls, sometimes like old churches with their pinnacles, all on a gigantic scale, and then again shooting up in curious forms that defy description."

This ascent takes the traveler to timberline and to alpine climes as the surrounding forest cover becomes stunted and includes occasional altitude-loving whitebark pines. At a signed junction our route turns southeast along a clear trail to Cinko Lake. This trail fords West Fork West Walker River and passes a charming meadow with a tiny tarn in its upper reaches. Then it makes a brief moderate ascent to the intermittent north outlet of arrowhead-shaped Cinko Lake. There is another outlet on the south side of the lake. The trail emerges at the lake's edge (9200'), adjacent to the north outlet, where there are several good campsites. Fishing for rainbow and eastern brook (to 12") is good.

3rd Hiking Day: Retrace your steps, 14 miles (22.6 km).

Crown Point over Barney Lake

Leavitt Meadow to Dorothy Lake   **34**

TRIP From Leavitt Meadow Campground to Dorothy Lake (semiloop trip). Topo maps *Sonora Pass, Tower Peak*. Best mid or late seaon; 34 miles (54.7 km).

Grade	Trail/layover days	Total recommended days
Leisurely	6/1	7
Moderate	4/1	5
Strenuous	3/1	4

HILITES Touring the headwaters of the West Fork West Walker River and the headwaters of Cascade Creek and Falls Creek would be an ambitious undertaking in any one trip, but this trip boasts more. Near Dorothy Lake, the culmination of the trip, the visitor can take in the unusual Forsyth Peak "rock glacier."

DESCRIPTION (Moderate trip)

1st and 2nd Hiking Days: (**Leavitt Meadow** to **Dorothy Lake**, 18 miles—29 km). First follow Trip 33 to **Cinko Lake**, 14 miles (22.6 km). From the southeast side of Cinko Lake our trail winds down a lodgepole- and hemlock-clothed hillside to the unpopulated banks of an unnamed stream. Then it climbs slightly, veering east away from the water. A very short, steep descent then takes the hiker to a beautiful lakelet. About ⅛ mile past the lake, we reapproach the stream and then veer away again eastward. In another ⅛ mile the trail crosses this persistent tributary on a wooden bridge, then ascends for a moment, levels off, and passes three snowmelt tarns on the right. Continuing level through a tarn-filled saddle here, our southbound trail soon meets the Dorothy Lake Trail. Here we turn right (south), following the trail on a gentle ascent through a thinning forest cover of lodgepole, hemlock and whitebark pine. The trail then boulder-fords, first, Cascade

Creek, and then, in ⅓ mile, the outlet of Lake Harriet. After this ford the trail ascends more steeply, and becomes rocky after passing island-dotted Lake Harriet. This ascent levels through a meadowy section and fords the stream joining Stella and Bonnie lakes. Ahead, the low profile of Dorothy Lake Pass is fronted by another moderate, rocky ascent, and the trail then levels past the grassy north arm of Stella Lake. At the northeast end of this arm, a ducked cross-country route to Lake Ruth and Lake Helen departs from our route.

The long, low saddle on which Stella Lake sits terminates at Dorothy Lake Pass, where there is an excellent view of Dorothy Lake (9400′). To the southeast, the hiker has **V**-notched views of Tower Peak, and to the south, the granite grenadiers of multi-turreted Forsyth Peak dominate the landscape. From the pass, the trail descends steadily over a rocky slope that is the territory of numerous conies and marmots. As the trail skirts the north side of this beautiful lake, it winds through lush grass and willow patches with spots of color provided by bush lupine, shooting star, elephant heads, goldenrod, paintbrush, whorled penstemon, aster, fleabane, pussy paws and false Solomon's seal. This stretch of the north shore was not so lush when the first recorded explorer of this lake walked here. Lt. N. F. McClure, of the 4th Cavalry, came this way in 1894 noting, "Grazing here was poor, and there had evidently been thousands of sheep about." The trail passes three windy campsites along the north shore before arriving at the good campsites at the west end of the lake. Fishing for rainbow and occasional eastern brook is good-to-excellent except during a midsummer slowdown. This lake makes an excellent base-camp location for exploring and fishing the surrounding lakes in the upper Cascade Creek basin, and for viewing the Forsyth Peak "rock glacier."

This phenomenon can be viewed from the unnamed lake south of Dorothy Lake. Seen from here, it is a prominent "river" of rock flowing in a long northwest-curving arc. This arc begins on the northeast face of Forsyth Peak, then curves down the easternmost ravine and points its moving head toward Dorothy Lake. Composed of coarse rock that tumbled from Forsyth Peak's fractured face, it hides an underlayment of silt, sand and fine gravel, and it depends upon ice caught between larger boulders for its mobility. Other rock glaciers are found in the Alps, Alaska and the Andes.

3rd Hiking Day (**Dorothy Lake** to **Fremont Lake Trail Junction**, 8 miles—12.9 km): First retrace the steps of the previous hiking day as far as the Cinko Lake Trail. Then continue to descend on the north side of tumbling Cascade Creek. Switchbacks are needed to convey the hiker down past the cascades of this namesake creek. Near the bottom of this descent the forest, now including stately red firs, becomes thicker. As the trail nears the West Walker River, the moderate descent levels, and then the route fords near an old corral. Beyond the wading ford is a **Y** junction, and here our route turns left (downstream). The trail continues north along the east side of the West Walker River, fords an unnamed tributary of the river, and skirts a large meadow before beginning a gentle-to-moderate ascent. The sand-and-duff trail then crosses a saddle and descends to ford Long Canyon Creek. About ¼ mile beyond this stream is the Fremont Lake Trail junction, and we take this trail across the river to the campsites passed on the first hiking day. Alternatively, one may continue downstream on the east side of the river to other good campsites. Fishing in the deeper holes of this section of the river is good for rainbow (to 11″).

4th Hiking Day: Reverse the steps of most of the 1st hiking day, Trip 32, 8 miles (12.9 km). (If your car is above the pack station, turn left on the trail that goes west through a grassy flat just before the final small descent to the campground, and wade the river to reach the highway.)

Dorothy Lake and "rock glacier" on Forsyth Peak

35 Leavitt Meadow to Tower Lake

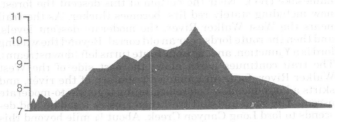

TRIP   From Leavitt Meadow Campground to Tower Lake (semiloop trip, part cross country). Topo maps *Sonora Pass, Tower Peak*. Best mid or late season; 40 miles (64.4 km).

Grade	Trail/layover days	Total recommended days
Leisurely	7/2	9
Moderate	5/2	7
Strenuous	4/2	6

HILITES   The cross-country segment of this trip makes it a choice for experienced backpackers only. The strenuousness of the route guarantees the walker a proportionate measure of solitude, and views of the alpine crestal country seldom seen by anyone except the cross-countryer.

DESCRIPTION (Moderate trip)

1st and 2nd Hiking Days: Follow Trip 34 to **Dorothy Lake**, 18 miles (29 km).

3rd Hiking Day (**Dorothy Lake** to **Tower Lake**, 5 miles—8.1 km): From the campsites at the west end of Dorothy Lake, retrace the steps of the previous hiking day to Stella Lake, where the ducked cross-country route to Lake Ruth rounds the northeast end of the lake. This route ascends over a rock-and-grass ledge system along the east side of the intermittent stream joining Stella Lake and Lake Ruth, and arrives at the outlet end of Lake Ruth. Here, nestled in the sparse whitebark-pine fringe of the lake, are good campsites that make a fine alternative to the more crowded environs of Dorothy Lake. The route from the outlet skirts the east side of the lake for a short distance and then ascends a long, gentle swale to the southeast. Several small melt-off tarns mark the crossover point to the Lake Helen drainage. Keeping to the south side of this large, granitic, circular lake, the route fords the tiny but noisy southwest inlet, and then crosses the rocky slope directly south of the lake.

At the southeast inlet our route fords and ascends moderately to a lovely grass bench. The remaining ascent to the obvious saddle in the southeast crosses steeper sections, and route-picking is best accomplished on the left (north) side of the cirque wall. This steep pitch brings one to a sparsely dotted whitebark-pine saddle offering incomparable views. Included in the views to the north and west are, from north to west, Wells Peak, White Mountain, Sonora Peak, Stanislaus Peak, Leavitt Peak, Kennedy Peak, Relief Peak and Forsyth Peak. To the east and southeast the view encompasses, from east to south, Flatiron Butte, Walker Peak, Buckeye Ridge, the Kirkwood Creek drainage, Grouse Mountain, Hunewill Peak, Hawksbeak Peak, Kettle Peak, Cirque Mountain and Tower Peak. From the summit of this saddle one can also see most of the lakes of the Cascade Creek drainage, as well as Tower Lake at the foot of Tower Peak. Tower Peak, the most spectacular peak of the North Boundary Country but not the tallest, is the goal of most climbers in this region. Visible from most of the drainages to the south, it has served mountaineers as a landmark for more than a hundred years.

Descending from the saddle on the southeast side entails crossing rock and scree to a rocky bench, and thence a grass-and-ledge system to a small lakelet just north of Tower Lake. The route then rounds the south nose of a granite ridge to the willowed outlet of Tower Lake, where it fords to the fair campsites, centered in the only stand of timber found here on the east side of the outlet (9600'). There is fair-to-good fishing for the golden trout (to 11") that inhabit this lake. Good alternative campsites can be found ½ mile down the outlet stream.

4th Hiking Day (**Tower Lake** to **Fremont Lake Trail Junction**, 9 miles—14.4 km): From Tower Lake the trail descends over a rocky slope close to the north side of the outlet stream from Tower Lake. This steep, rocky descent affords a view of a dramatic avalanche chute that slices the slope on the northeast side of Kirkwood Creek canyon. To be rear, back toward Tower Peak, the view is dominated by the climactic, phalluslike northern extension of Tower Peak. This classic white-granite pinnacle soon obliterates views of Tower Peak itself, and it stands as mute testimony to the obdurate granite's resistance to glacial erosion. The rocky descent soon reaches timberline, where hemlock and lodgepole pine appear, and then refords the outlet stream in a willowed section at the confluence of the Tower Lake outlet and the tiny stream draining the glacier at the foot of the granite column to the south. This new section of trail from Tower Lake keeps to the east side of the creek as it descends gently over duff and rock, and fords an unnamed tributary.

Beyond the ford, the new trail rejoins the old trail, winding through a dense forest cover of lodgepole and hemlock. Then the trail refords Tower Lake's outlet stream and ascends above the narrowing canyon. These narrows show almost vertical granite walls, between which the stream becomes a plummeting ribbon. Ahead, the valley of the West Walker River can be seen through the trees, and a short, easy descent over a duff trail soon brings us to a trail junction just north of the confluence of the Tower Lake outlet and Kirkwood Creek. Our route turns right, fords the West Walker River, and then skirts the oxbows of the river where it serpentines through Upper Piute Meadows. At the north end of the meadows the sandy trail passes a turnoff to Piute Cabin, a Forest Service trail-maintenance station, and then veers away from the river as it continues to descend gently. The cattle in Upper Piute Meadows are part of the Forest Service's "Multiple Use" administrative concept. Cowflops have been reported as far away as the head of Thompson Canyon—and it may be logically assumed that they were a result of allowing grazing here. After jogging around a marshy section, the trail again comes within sight of the river, and then joins the trail from Dorothy Lake. From the junction we proceed as described in the 3rd hiking day, Trip 34.

5th Hiking Day: Reverse the steps of most of the 1st hiking day, Trip 32, 8 miles (12.9 km).

Upper Piute Meadows

Jason Winnett

Leavitt Meadow to Buckeye Creek   **36**

TRIP   From Leavitt Meadow Campground to Buckeye
Roadend (shuttle trip). Topo maps *Sonora Pass,
Tower Peak, Matterhorn Peak*. Best early or mid
season, 39.9 miles (64.2 km).

Grade	Trail/layover days	Total recom- mended days
Leisurely	7/2	9
Moderate	5/2	7
Strenuous	4/1	5

HILITES   Using two major eastside drainages this trip cir-
cumnavigates Walker Mountain and Flatiron
Ridge, and is about evenly split between high
country and lower, forested areas. This is a superlative choice for the novice who has a couple of
shorter trips behind him, and who is looking for a
longer trip with some of the challenge of cross-
countrying.

DESCRIPTION (Moderate trip)

1st, 2nd and 3rd Hiking Days: Follow Trip 35 to **Tower Lake**, 23
miles (37.0 km).

4th Hiking Day (**Tower Lake** to **Buckeye Forks**, 7.5
miles—12.1 km): First, descend to Upper Piute Meadows as
described in the 4th hiking day, Trip 35. Just below the
confluence of Kirkwood Creek and the creek draining Tower
Lake, ford to the northeast side of the stream and turn right,
up Kirkwood Creek. Here at the southernmost extension of
Upper Piute Meadows our route ascends moderately through a
dense forest cover of lodgepole and occasional silver pine that
sees the inclusion of hemlock near the top of the climb. This
route passes below the spectacular avalanche chute noted on
the previous hiking day. On a moderate ascent that steepens

as it turns east and then northeast, the trail rises to the saddle marking the divide between the Walker River and Buckeye Creek. The startling eminence of Hawksbeak Peak to the south vies for the traveler's attention with the rich volcanic reds and blacks of the slopes to the north. After reaching a small pond at the headwaters of Kirkwood Creek, the trail descends moderately on duff and rocky surfaces to the head of North Fork Buckeye Creek. This descent through a sparse-to-moderate forest cover of lodgepole, hemlock, and occasional whitebark and silver pine crosses back and forth over the splashing creek. Then, in a final steep descent, the trail drops to "Buckeye Forks," where it meets the trail descending from Buckeye Pass to the south.

Here at the forks is a meadow-set snow-survey cabin of log-tenon construction. It is believed that this well-made cabin was constructed in 1928, and is the oldest U. S. Snow Survey shelter. When built, the cabin was surrounded by open meadow, which has since been overgrown with the ubiquitous lodgepole and willow. This dense growth is undoubtedly due to the strong evolutionary contribution of the nearby colony of beavers. As is clearly seen just downstream, these beavers have repeatedly flooded this section between Buckeye Forks and The Roughs, and the consequent buildup of sediments and high water table were conducive to forest reproduction. However, what the beaver giveth he also taketh away. Were this dense forest to be flooded again, these healthy trees would be drowned. That happened downstream, where the bleached white ghost snags make skeletal reminders of the beaver's potent niche in the evolutionary web. Of the mammals, excepting man, the beaver is far and away the greatest single alterer of the natural environment.

There are good campsites near the old cabin, and fishing in Buckeye Creek is good for rainbow and eastern brook (to 9″). *5th Hiking Day* (**Buckeye Forks** to **Buckeye Roadend**, 9.4 miles—15.1 km): From the cabin, the trail continues to descend steadily over alternating duff, sand and rock. On each side, gnawed and fallen aspen show the beaver's dietary preferences, but despite this rodent's industrious efforts (some naturalists would say "because of it") the forest cover along the creek is dense, and it serves as a foraging grounds for all manner of birdlife, including flickers, chickadees, juncos, robins, Williamson's sapsuckers, hummingbirds and nuthatches.

As the canyon narrows between high, glacially polished granite walls, the trail enters the section known as The

Roughs. Here the sometimes swampy trail winds along the left bank of Buckeye Creek, overshadowed by sheer, rounded granite to the north and polished spires to the south. Good campsites can be found in The Roughs. The first one is one mile from the forks, and there is another ¼ mile farther. Then, ¼ beyond, we make a steep 200-yard ascent over black medasedimentary shale to a juniper-topped saddle and the boundary of the Hoover Wilderness. From just beyond the saddle views down Buckeye Canyon are spectacular. The lush grasslands of Big Meadow provide a soft counterpoint to the ruggedness of Flatiron and Buckeye ridges.

A few hundred steep yards down beyond the saddle, we ford the vigorous creek that drains the basin between Ink Rocks and Hanna Mountain, and the tumultuous sounds of the cascades above and below the ford furnish soul-satisfying background music for a fine rest stop. From this viewpoint the trail descends over a rocky, exposed slope on a long traverse to rejoin the trail shown on the topo map just upstream from the confluence of Buckeye Creek and the tributaries draining the slopes of Hunewill and Victoria peaks. This steady descent is the last of the precipitous terrain, and the remainder of the walk is over long, gradual slopes covered with sagebrush, mountain mahogany, bitterbrush and mule ears. Occasional clumps of aspen occur where the trail crosses a tributary or where it veers close to Buckeye Creek, and they provide welcome shade on a hot mid-summer afternoon. In these well-watered sections the traveler also encounters colorful clumps of monkey flower, goldenrod, lupine, shooting star, paintbrush and penstemon.

Big Meadow itself is a charming two-mile-long grassland replete with Belding ground squirrels and morning-feeding deer. At one time, around 1870, this meadow rang with the sounds of axes and the whirring of a sawmill blade. Here the Upper Hunewill mill operated to provide mining timber. Near the fence at the bottom of the meadow, the observant passerby can make out the signs of an abortive effort to construct a flume to carry water from Buckeye Creek to Bodie.

We pass through a gate in this fence and immediately head right, downhill, for the ford of Buckeye Creek, marked by two posts about 6 feet tall, about 30 yards downstream from the fence. This ford can be difficult in early season. From the creek our trail leads up a small ridge and then undulates over several more ridges, generally within sight of the stream. Beyond a viewpoint for seeing a beaverdam, the trail traverses along a hillside clothed by many head-high aspen

trees and many flowers (in season), including scarlet gilia,
with its red, trumpet-form blossoms. After crossing two little
runoff rills, we can look through the trees down upon a large
meadow, which we skirt on a level trail under aspen, juniper,
red-fir and lodgepole-pine trees. About ½ mile farther we cross
the tip of a tongue of that meadow, and an unmapped stream
that flows late into the summer. Soon the trail becomes a
two-track abandoned vehicle way, and we stroll through a
sagebrush field squeezed between the lodgepole pines that
border the creek and a large stand of aspen trees on the nose of
a ridge that protrudes onto the canyon bottom.

The next section of trail passes through alternating green
meadows and gray sagebrush fields, with constant good views
of the towering north and south walls of Buckeye Canyon.
Past one last, fairly large meadow we come to a fence with both
a hiker's gate and a stock gate, where we begin the last mile of
this 5-day journey under the shade of Jeffrey and ponderosa
pines, red firs and quaking aspens. This last mile is a gentle
downhill stroll that ends at a parking area just up-canyon
from a Forest Service campground.

37   Twin Lakes to Peeler Lake

TRIP   From Twin Lakes to Peeler Lake (round trip).
               Topo map *Matterhorn Peak*. Best mid or late
               season; 16 miles (25.8 km).

Grade	Trail/layover days	Total recommended days
Leisurely	....	....
Moderate	2/1	3
Strenuous	....	....

HILITES   Despite a stiff 2500-foot climb, this trip makes a
               fine choice for the city-weary hiker with a "long
               weekender" trip-selection problem. An early start

will allow the hiker to enjoy the morning freshness on the steeper uphill parts, and to be in camp soon enough for a pleasurable swim or some afternoon angling. Peeler Lake, as a destination, is a delightfully unique Sierra experience in that one camps literally on top of the mountain chain, for this lake pours its waters down both sides of the Sierra.

DESCRIPTION

1st Hiking Day (**Twin Lakes** to **Peeler Lake**, 8 miles—12.9 km): This trip begins in the Mono Village Campground at the west end of Twin Lakes. (There is a fee for parking on the private property here.) First, follow signs saying *Barney Lake* through the campground to find the wide, level, shaded trail. Travelers setting out in the fall season should take a few minutes at the outset for a side trip to view the colorful Kokanee salmon spawning in the shallows of Robinson Creek south of the campground.

Beyond the campground our sandy trail winds through a moderate-to-dense forest of Jeffrey pine, juniper, lodgepole pine, aspen and cottonwood along Robinson Creek. In late summer, cottony catkins from the cottonwood trees here litter the initial section of trail, leaving the ground surface the gray-white of spring snow. Crossing several small tributaries, the trail then ascends gently, and within ¾ mile encounters the first fir trees, but the forest cover soon gives way to a sagebrush-covered, gently sloping bench, from where one can see the great headwall of the valley in the west. As one makes his way up this open bench through thigh-high sagebrush, rabbitbrush, chamise and mule ears, one has unobstructed views of Victoria, Hunewill and Robinson peaks on the right, and some ragged teeth of the Sawtooth Ridge on the left. About halfway up this bench the trail passes a "ghost forest" of drowned trees caused by beaver dams downstream. Beavers still share this fine Sierra stream with us. On the right, somnolent marmots are likely to be seen dozing among piles of scree that flow from the feet of the avalanche chutes scarring Victoria Peak; on the left, the dramatic, unbroken granite wall of Blacksmith Peak at the top of Little Slide Canyon dominated the view. A sign here proclaims this area as part of the Hoover Wilderness. On the left, Robinson Creek becomes a willow-lined cascade that is frequently heard but seldom seen. About ½ mile into the wilderness, the ascent resolves into switchbacks that ford several small tributaries. In their moist banks one encounters monkey flower, monkshood, red colum-

bine, swamp onion and shooting star scattered among clumps
of bracken fern. Along the drier stretches of trail the severity
of the rock is alleviated by colorful patches of Indian
paintbrush, Mariposa lily, scarlet gilia, yarrow milfoil,
whorled penstemon, pussy paws, streptanthus and goldenrod.

After the ascent levels out, the trail veers south, fords
another tributary, and arrives at the outlet point of arrow-
shaped Barney Lake. Anglers wishing an interlude of fair-to-
good fishing for eastern brook and a rainbow trout will want to
tarry around the deeper east and northeast shores of this
9-acre gem. The alternatives for the nonfisherman are equally
attractive. He may elect to take a cool, quick dip, or merely to
lie on the sandy beach and watch the play of the local water
ouzels. (If you camp here, you must camp at least 200 feet from
the lake.)

The remainder of the trail to the top of the watershed is not
marked on the topo map, but is patently clear on the scene.
This trail skirts the west side of the lake in a steady, long, hot
ascent that takes one onto the canyon wall well above the
"ghost forested" delta inlet of Barney Lake. Once above the
wetter sections of the delta, the trail descends to a
wildflower-decorated ford of Robinson Creek. Here amid the
willows can be found lavendar swamp onion, red columbine,
orange tiger lily and yellow monkey flower. The moderate
forest cover now shows the transition to higher climes with the
introduction of hemlock and some silver pine. About ¼ mile
upstream the trail refords Robinson Creek, and after fording
the outlet creek from Peeler Lake just above its confluence
with Robinson Creek, it rises abruptly by steep, rocky
switchbacks. Leveling off somewhat, it then comes to a bench
junction with the Crown Lake Trail. This junction is ¼ mile
northwest of Robinson Lakes (the two tiny lakes downstream
from Crown Lake). Here our route turns right and ascends
moderately for about ½ mile near the south outlet from Peeler
Lake, and then steeply up the draw just northeast of the lake,
to reach this outlet. Beautiful Peeler Lake (9500') sits astride
the Sierra crest, contributing water to Robinson Creek on the
east and Rancheria Creek on the west. Large (about 60 acres),
it has abrupt, rocky shores, and the deep-blue color characteristic of deeper Sierra lakes. There are good-to-excellent
campsites almost all around the lake, though some are within
200 feet of the lake, where camping is now forbidden. The best
campsites lie on the east shore, reached by leaving the trail
where it starts to descend to cross the south outlet. Fishing for
eastern brook and rainbow trout (to 14") is sometimes good.
2nd Hiking Day: Retrace your steps, 8 miles (12.9 km).

Twin Lakes to Crown Lake   38

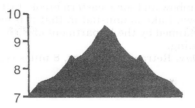

TRIP   From Twin Lakes to Crown Lake (round trip). Topo map *Matterhorn Peak*. Best early, mid or late season; 16 miles (25.8 km).

Grade	Trail/layover days	Total recommended days
Leisurely	....	....
Moderate	2/1	3
Strenuous	....	....

HILITES   Like the previous trip, this one entails considerable "up," but it is still a good two-day trip selection. This route follows Robinson Creek all the way to Crown Lake, and in its course exposes the traveler to some of the finest east-side scenery available anywhere along the Sierra. Crown Lake itself is set in the heart of the Sierra crest, and consonant with its name, it forms a royal diadem of blue in a regal setting of forest greens.

DESCRIPTION

1st Hiking Day (**Twin Lakes** to **Crown Lake**, 8 miles—12.9 km.): First follow Trip 37 to the junction of the Peeler and Crown Lake trails. From this junction our route leads south, undulating gently between large outcroppings of glacially polished granite. As the trail ascends moderately below Robinson Lakes (unlabeled on the topo map; they are the lakes downstream from Crown Lake) it winds through one near-pure stand of hemlock—unusual for this part of the Sierra. Robinson Lakes are two small, shallow, placid lakes with a sparse forest cover of lodgepole pine, silver pine and hemlock, separated by an isthmus. The trail rounds the south side of the larger Robinson Lake, fords Robinson Creek, and turns south on a steady ascent. Just below Crown Lake we reford the creek and then switchback up to the good campsites

(9500′) just downstream from the lake along the outlet, where there are excellent views of Kettle Peak and Crown Point. Fishing for rainbow and some eastern brook (to 9″) is fair. The fishery of Crown Lake is unusual in that it is one of the few Sierra lakes claimed by the Department of Fish and Game to be self-sustaining.

2nd Hiking Day: Retrace your steps, 8 miles (12.9 km.).

Sierra Crest over Crown Lake

Twin Lakes to Upper Piute Creek **39**

TRIP
From Twin Lakes to Campsites, Upper Piute Creek (round trip). Topo map *Matterhorn Peak*. Best mid or late season; 23 miles (37.1 km).

Grade	Trail/layover days	Total recommended days
Leisurely	....	....
Moderate	4/1	5
Strenuous	3/1	4

HILITES
This trip is a satisfying one for the hiker who has viewed the Sawtooth Ridge from the north side only. Following Robinson Creek nearly to the crest of the Sierra, this route circles the west end of the Sawtooth Ridge, and then drops down into the scenic upper reaches of Piute Creek. For those who appreciate spectacular mountain scenery of alpine character, this trip is a must.

DESCRIPTION (Moderate trip)

1st Hiking Day: Follow Trip 38 to **Crown Lake**, 8 miles (12.9 km).

2nd Hiking Day (**Crown Lake** to **Campsites, Upper Piute Creek,** 3.5 miles—5.6 km.): From Crown Lake's outlet the trail ascends along the west side, offering fine views of the meadowed inlet. The ascent soon steepens as the trail begins a series of short, rocky switchbacks that terminate just east of Crown Point, Here the trail levels out in a willowed meadowy area with several small lakelets, and meets the Snow Lake Trail just beyond. Our route turns left (south), fords the stream draining Snow Lake, and climbs over an easy talus-and-scree pile. This rocky ascent levels briefly within sight of another small lakelet; then the trail cuts across a bench and ascends steeply by rocky switchbacks. In most years there is a large snowbank across this slope well into summer, and one should exercise some caution here. After one more bench this ascent terminates at a tundra-topped saddle on the divide north of Slide Mountain. Here sparse whitebark pine and hemlock stoop to alpine climes, and the traveler taking a breather at this unnamed pass is likely to hear the scolding of a disturbed cony.

From this pass the trail stepladders down through a series of sandy tundra pockets, serpenting its way north and then east before beginning the long traverse down to Piute Creek. This traverse strikes timberline just below the cross-country turnoff to Ice and Maltby lakes, which is at the ford of the stream draining the swale that gives access to Ice Lake. Fishermen will find the excellent fishing for eastern brook in these two lakes worth the side trip. On the lodgepole and hemlock that line the trail, one will encounter the historic T blaze typical of the older trails in Yosemite National Park—a sign emblazoned on these trails by the U.S. Cavalry in the early part of the century, when it was their responsibility to patrol the Park.

This hiking day terminates at the campsites upstream from the signed turnoff to the cross-country route down Slide Canyon, located on Piute Creek (9600') along the first ½ mile after the trail comes within sight of the creek. Fishing for eastern brook (to 8") is fair. This location makes a fine base-camp location for exploratory trips down Slide Canyon or over into Matterhorn Canyon, and it is a traditional base camp for climbers making ascents of Matterhorn Peak and other climbs along the Sawtooth Ridge.

3rd and 4th Hiking Days: Retrace your steps, 11.5 miles (18.6 km.).

Switchbacks on Crown Lake Trail

Twin Lakes to Buckeye Creek

40

TRIP
From Twin Lakes to Buckeye Roadend (shuttle trip via Peeler Lake and Buckeye Pass). Topo map *Matterhorn Peak*. Best mid or late season; 22.4 miles (36.0 km).

Grade	Trail/layover days	Total recommended days
Leisurely	4/1	5
Moderate	3/1	4
Strenuous	3/0	3

HILITES
This circle trip around Buckeye Ridge visits nearly the entire gamut of Sierran ecology, from the sagebrush-scrub of the east side to the subalpine grassland of Kerrick Meadow. In between, it winds through pure stands of hemlock, past water-loving clumps of quaking aspen and amidst windblown, gnarled whitebark pine. In its ecological variety it is indeed an "everything trip for everyone."

DESCRIPTION (Moderate trip)

1st Hiking Day: Follow Trip 38 to **Peeler Lake**, 8.0 miles (12.9 km).

2nd Hiking Day (**Peeler Lake** to **Buckeye Forks**, 5.0 miles—8.0 km): From Peeler Lake the trail descends along the lake's west outlet, crossing and recrossing this outlet as it flows down into the marshy upper reaches of Rancheria Creek in Kerrick Meadow. In the meadow, we meet the Kerrick Canyon Trail, turn right (north) on it, and ascend a gentle slope above the north end of the meadow. A moderate forest cover of mostly pines lines the rest of the gently ascending sand-and-duff trail to the summit of Buckeye Pass. This pass (9580') in a small, lodgepole-encroached meadow is on the Park boundary.

Then the duff trail drops down the northeast side of the pass, and soon fords the infant rill of Buckeye Creek. From here to the next ford, this descent skirts a series of charmingly meadowed steps on the northwest side of the creek. These pockets of grasslands have rich gardens of flowers whose full, splashy colors invite the passerby to linger and enjoy the aster, goldenrod, paintbrush, penstemon, shooting star, larkspur, lupine, buttercup, columbine and monkey flower. Owls hunt these meadows at night, and the daytime traveler should keep a lookout for large convoctions of agitated birdlife. At the core of such gatherings, frequently, is a large owl seeking protection in dense foliage.

The series of meadows terminates at a ford where the trail crosses to the east side of the creek. About ¼ mile beyond this ford is a snowcourse, and from it an unmaintained trail takes off over the ridge bound for Barney Lake. For the next ½ mile our trail continues to descend moderately through an area where the trees are much avalance-broken, and then we jump across an unnamed tributary that tumbles down from Hunewill Peak. In another ½ mile we reach the first of several fair and good campsites located at places where the trail periodically touches the stream. Then a steep descending section followed by two less steep inclines bring us to the flat where the North and South Forks of Buckeye Creek conjoin. In this quiet flat we cross the South Fork on a log and 200 yards farther on wade the North Fork. There are good campsites in the vicinity of a snow-survey cabin here, and the junction with the main east-west trail is just beyond. Fishing in the forks for rainbow and brook (to 9″) is good.

3rd Hiking Day: Follow the 5th hiking day, Trip 36, 9.4 miles (15.1 km). (Just 1.1 miles down the road toward Bridgeport a side road goes south across Buckeye Creek, but if you go straight ahead 0.4 mile and then park in a used-looking area beside the road, you can walk a few yards downhill to Buckeye Hot Springs. Here, right beside the singing brook, you can soak away the trip's dirt in a natural hot spa.)

Twin Lakes to Kerrick Meadow

41

TRIP
From Twin Lakes to Kerrick Meadow (semiloop trip via Crown and Peeler lakes). Topo map *Matterhorn Peak*. Best mid or late season; 22.5 miles (36.3 km).

Grade	Trail/layover days	Total recommended days
Leisurely	5/1	6
Moderate	3/1	4
Strenuous	3/0	3

HILITES
To use a business metaphor, this trip gives a great return for a minimum investment. From the outset this route is enveloped in magnificent scenery. Along Robinson Creek, the skyline and the immediate surroundings are those of rugged grandeur, consonant with the physical expenditure of effort required on the uphill. As the trip circles Crown Point, it "levels out" both in physical terrain and in emotional impact. The ruggedness gives way to sweeping meadows and rounded summits, providing the traveler an opportunity to absorb some of the impact of this land of contrasts.

DESCRIPTION (Moderate trip)

1st Hiking Day: Follow Trip 38 to **Crown Lake**, 8 miles (12.9 km).

2nd Hiking Day (**Crown Lake** to **Peeler Lake**, 6.5 miles—10.5 km): Rounding the rocky west side of Crown Lake, the trail rises out of the lake basin by steep, rocky switchbacks that offer fine views back of the clear blue lake. This ascent levels out as it crosses a granite-flanked saddle and meets the Rock Island Pass Trail just west of a lakelet in a sandy-meadowed section, with several small lakelets and tarns hidden in willows near the trail. Our route turns right (southwest) and

begins a long, steadily traversing climb toward Snow Lake.
This traverse gives way to switchbacks midway up the hill,
and jogs southwest under Crown Point before resuming its
southward course on more switchbacks by a little stream.
Looking back from the top of this climb, we have fine views to
the east of the soldier-tipped summit of Kettle Peak and the
west end of the Sawtooth Ridge (called Blacksmith Peak).
Snow Lake itself, like Peeler Lake to the north, is a crestal
lake perched atop a divide, but in angling circles it is best
known for its fishery of golden trout. As the trail rounds the
rocky north edge of the lake, we see the meadowy lake fringes,
which are most extensive at the southwest end. Here the
meadows extend from the lake's edge to the low-profiled
saddle called Rock Island Pass (10,150'), a few hundred yards
southwest of the lake.

From Rock Island Pass the trail descends into the Rancheria
Creek drainage. The descent witnesses a change from sparse
whitebark pine to a conglomerate forest of lodgepole, hemlock
and silver pine. After traversing above a sandy meadow, the
T-blazed trail here rises sharply over a sandy ridge and then
drops moderately on switchbacks through dense forest cover to
Kerrick Meadow and a ford of Rancheria Creek.

On the northwest side of the ford, the trail meets the Kerrick
Canyon Trail, where our route turns right and ascends gently
up Kerrick Meadow. Rancheria Creek winds its oxbowing way
through these sandy grasslands, and on the right we can see
large crestal sand accumulations indicating where the living
stream has moved across the meadow floor, leaving its spoor.
The meadow bottlenecks briefly into a canyon narrows, where
the creek tumbles over a silver cascade, and then opens into a
beautiful, open, wetter section near the headwaters. In the
middle of this marshy section the trail fords one arm of the
creek, and then continues on to meet the unsigned Peeler Lake
Trail at the meadow's head, where our route turns right (east).
From this junction the trail crosses the open meadow and
winds through a broken, moderate forest cover of lodgepole.
This route crisscrosses back and forth over the west outlet
stream from Peeler Lake and arrives at the good campsites
along the west shore of this large and beautiful lake (9500').
These campsites offer fine views to the east of Cirque
Mountain, Kettle Peak and Crown Point, and the deep waters
near the west shore offer fine bank fishing for eastern brook
and rainbow (to 14").

3rd Hiking Day: Reverse the steps of the 1st hiking day, Trip
37, 8 miles (12.9 km).

Twin Lakes to Hetch Hetchy

TRIP   From Twin Lakes to O'Shaughnessy Dam via Bear Valley (shuttle trip). Topo maps *Matterhorn Peak, Tower Peak, Hetch Hetchy Reservoir*. Best mid or late season; 43.8 miles (70.7 km).

Grade	Trail/layover days	Total recommended days
Leisurely	8/2	10
Moderate	7/2	9
Strenuous	6/2	8

HILITES   Striking through the heart of the North Boundary Country, this trip crosses the Sierra crest at Peeler Lake and then, with a detour to Pleasant Valley, traces the course of Rancheria Creek from its beginning to the point where it enters the pipeline to San Francisco faucets. This long-trans-Sierra crossing appeals to the solitude-seeker because it is one of the least traveled yet most scenic routes in Yosemite.

DESCRIPTION (Strenuous trip)

1st Hiking Day: Follow Trip 37 to **Peeler Lake,** 8 miles (12.9 km).

2nd Hiking Day (**Peeler Lake** to **Arndt Lake,** 5 miles—8.1 km): Leaving Peeler Lake beside the west outlet, the trail drops down gently as it crosses back and forth over the outlet stream. This descent soon leaves the moderate forest cover and enters the north edge of Kerrick Meadow. At the head of this open, rank grassland the trail meets the Buckeye Pass Trail, where our route turns left (south) and begins a long, gentle descent. The trail on the west side of twisting Rancheria Creek is a narrow, sandy track lined with a wildflower collage of shooting star, penstemon, paintbrush, aster, goldenrod, buttercup, lupine, Douglas phlox, and pussy paws. In a timber-lined bottleneck, the meadows narrow briefly and then reopen. On the left one can see sand banks that were stranded when the oxbowing stream altered course sometime in the geologic past. The broad grasslands are alive with the scurrying and piping of alarmed Belding ground squirrels.

The trail then passes the Rock Island Pass Trail and continues to descend to a second timbered narrows. This brief stretch of lodgepole pine opens to yet another long meadow that is flanked on the southwest by the granite heights of Price Peak. On the descent through this meadow the canyon starts to narrow, and where the trail starts a gentle 200-yard ascent, our route leaves the trail.

Our short cross-country segment strikes out southward, fords Rancheria Creek, and ascends beside the tundra-lined outlet of Arndt Lake. A good route to the north shore of hidden Arndt Lake is via the saddle in the granite just east of where the outlet leaves the lake.

One will find good campsites at the outlet and around the north shore of Arndt Lake (9240'). Those with a tolerance for cool mountain water will enjoy the swimming off the granite that drops into this lake. Views of the polished granite domes flanking the south and east sides of the lake are soul-satisfying, and beckon the explorer to further investigation and discovery.

3rd Hiking Day (**Arndt Lake** to **Upper Bear Valley Lake,** 7 miles—11.3 km): From Arndt Lake our route retraces the cross-country segment of the previous hiking day to the Kerrick Canyon Trail, and then continues down through a narrow, rocky canyon. The unseamed white granite canyon walls in this narrows show the glacial polish, smoothing and sculpting that reflect the geologic history of the canyon. Rancheria Creek on the left bumps and splashes down through a series of fine potholes offering swimming and fishing spots. Like all the older trails in the Park, this one is T-blazed, indicating that it was once a U.S. Cavalry patrol route—a route blazed when the Army was responsible for the integrity of the Park lands.

The sparse-to-moderate forest cover of whitebark, hemlock and lodgepole pine in the narrows gives way to another meadow as the trail continues to descend. This meadow is surrounded by several magnificent examples of glacial domes—all unnamed. The clean, sweeping lines of the dome to the west are particularly impressive, and the passerby cannot help but feel the awesome power of the natural forces that created it. Near the foot of the meadow, the trail fords to the east side of Rancheria Creek, where it hugs the sheer, water-stained granite wall. Both the trail and the creek make an exaggerated **Z** before straightening out on a westward course and reaching the Pacific Crest Trail. Beyond this junction the trail undulates along the south wall of Kerrick Canyon. As it passes below the heavily fractured north facade of Piute Mountain, it is sometimes high above the creek and sometimes on the creek's banks. Many tributaries, varying in size from step-across to jump-across fords, break this route segment into lush gardens of monkey flower, tiger lily, shooting star, bush lupine, corn lily, columbine and goldenrod. As the canyon walls open, the trail descends close to the creek and reaches the Bear Valley Trail, which we turn onto, temporarily heading down-canyon. A short distance past this ford and junction, our route begins a steep switchbacking ascent up the south wall of Kerrick Canyon. Winding back and forth through a moderate forest cover of lodgepole pine, silver pine and hemlock, the trail near the top affords superlative views to the north and northeast. The panorama includes the hallmark of the North Boundary Country, Tower Peak.

These views behind, the trail tops the canyon wall and emerges suddenly to the dramatic setting of upper Bear Valley Lake (9200'). Drama at this alpine gem of a lake is provided by a spectacular granite pinnacle on the south side of the lake that spires upward, 600 feet above the lake's surface. Here excellent camping may be found in the timbered swales between the long granite fingers that slide under the north edge of the lake. Swimming is excellent.

4th Hiking Day (**Upper Bear Valley Lake** to **Pleasant Valley,** 5.5 miles—8.9 km): The trail from upper Bear Valley Lake drops down along the outlet, Breeze Creek, and then fords to the east. The descent through a moderate forest cover of lodgepole pine, hemlock, silver pine and occasional whitebark pine passes a marsh-fringed lake, and then climbs over an easy ridge to Bear Valley. This valley, the headwaters of the south fork of Breeze Creek, is a large, circular, sandy meadow with a beautifully whitened silver-pine snag in its center.

The trail then fords the south fork of Breeze Creek and begins a steep ascent. The tread on this ascent is indistinct in the willowy sections, but the tedium of route-finding is made more tolerable by the fine wildflower displays along this wet slope. Included in these displays are lush stands of red columbine, lupine, aster, fleabane, monkey flower, paintbrush, tiger lily, currant, lilac, forget-me-not, golden brodiaea and shooting star. At the top of this long climb the trail levels out on a long, sandy saddle offering spectacular views to the north. Evidence of the ambitious pocket gopher can be seen on every side in the form of its sand castings.

The sandy trail then makes a long, gradual descent across a meadow filled with brilliant fields of lupine, corn lily, whorled penstemon, elephant heads, lavender paintbrush and golden-rod, and then re-enters dense timber. Views across the rolling country to the south include Colby Mountain and occasional glimpses of Mt. Hoffman.

Our trail then fords one fork of an unnamed tributary of Rancheria Creek, and skirts the edge of the meadowed head of another branch of this same tributary. In midsummer this meadow is filled with shoulder-high corn lily and cow parsnip, making the route sometimes difficult to pick out. After fording this branch, the trail winds through dense stands of red fir and lodgepole pine. Some stands of lodgepole have been struck by the needleminer and are fast becoming ghost forests.

The trail then skirts the west edge of a marshy lake set in dense stands of lodgepole pine, and near the outlet encounters some quaking aspen. Just past this marshy lake one has his first views into the Piute Creek drainage, and these views are impressive in their scope. The steep east wall of the canyon holding Pleasant Valley is deeply scarred with gigantic granite avalanche chutes, while the near wall shows sign of a recent forest fire.

Then, at the crest of a knifelike ridge, our trail comes to a junction with the Pleasant Valley Trail, where we turn left and descend by steep switchbacks into Pleasant Valley. Views along this descent include the Cathedral Range to the southeast and the granite domes up Piute Creek canyon just below Benson Lake and Volunteer Peak. In Pleasant Valley we find a trail that leads up Piute Creek to a packer campsite below a series of cascades. If it's occupied, there are other campsites nearby. (Bears are a threat to food improperly stored here.) These campsites provide an excellent base-camp location for exploratory and fishing excursions to nearby Table, Irwin Bright and Saddle Horse lakes. All three of the lakes in Pleasant Valley hold rainbow, and fishing is good.

5th Hiking Day (**Pleasant Valley** to **Rancheria Creek**, 11.8 miles—19 km): First retrace your steps to the Hetch Hetchy Reservoir Trail, where our route turns left (southwest) toward the dry slopes of Rancheria Mountain. As the first water is five miles from the starting point of this hiking day, it is suggested that the traveler carry a full water bottle. From the junction, the trail ascends moderately through hemlock, red and white fir and occasional lodgepole. This forest cover gives way to open meadow at the rounded crest of Rancheria Mountain, and the trail winds through fields of mule ears. Beyond the meadow, the trail reenters timber, crosses a summit, and begins a moderate descent that fords the stream draining the west shoulder of Rancheria Mountain. Near this ford the wildflower fancier will want to linger in the lush clumps of thigh-high lupine and larkspur, and right on the stream banks quaking aspens shade scarlet patches of columbine and rank clusters of the long-leafed corn lily.

The trail veers south to the next stream before resuming its westward course, and at this second stream it passes an ancient, notched-log cabin built before the turn of the century. Crossing the drainage separating the unnamed creek near the cabin and the creek forded earlier, the trail touches the edge of the same forest-fire scars that were seen en route to Pleasant Valley. Here Jeffrey pine, incense-cedar and fir show blackened trunks from the holocaust that swept the mountain. Since the fire, brush has taken over much of the hillside, and it proves a haven for many coveys of quail. Most of the brush is manzanita, mixed with ceanothus. The descent here reflects the drop in altitude as deciduous forest makes its appearance in the form of black oak and lower-growing conifers, like the sugar pine. Across the reservoir to the south and southwest one can see the perpendicular scars of the avalanche chutes east of Smith Peak, and as the trail nears LeConte Point, Kolana Rock comes into sight.

The trail then ascends gently over the east shoulder of the rounded granite prominence of LeConte Point. On this shoulder the reservoir itself comes into view, and the blue of the water is a cool invitation to the good swimming available at Rancheria Creek. The trail then begins a series of steep, rocky switchbacks down a long slope which terminate at the metal bridge crossing just above Rancheria Falls. Deep potholes above and below the bridge in smooth granite bedrock beckon to the swimmer, and the campsites (4550′) a few yards below the falls are a welcome end to this hiking day. Fishing on Rancheria creek for rainbow (to 13″) is fair. Bears are numerous.

6th Hiking Day: Reverse the steps of the 1st hiking day, Trip 48, 6.5 miles (10.5 km).

43   Twin Lakes to Benson Lake

TRIP   From Twin Lakes to Benson Lake (round trip). Topo maps *Matterhorn Peak, Tower Peak*. Best mid or late season; 37.2 miles (59.8 km).

Grade	Trail/layover days	Total recommended days
Leisurely	9/3	12
Moderate	6/3	9
Strenuous	4/2	6

HILITES   This long trip penetrates to the heart of the North Boundary Country. In its course it surmounts the Sierra crest and traces a westside watershed to the Shangri-la basin of Benson Lake. Because of its moderate climes and its remote location, this lake is a favorite layover spot for parties traversing the Pacific Crest Trail, and its popularity is well founded.

DESCRIPTION (Moderate trip)

1st and 2nd Hiking Days: Follow Trip 42 to **Arndt Lake**, 13 miles (21 km).

3rd Hiking Day (**Arndt Lake** to **Benson Lake,** 5.6 miles—9 km): Proceed to the Kerrick Canyon Trail junction as described in the third hiking day, Trip 42. At this junction our route turns left (south) and ascends steadily by switchbacks through a moderate forest cover of hemlock. At the top of the first rise Piute Mountain comes into sight, and the trail levels briefly as it wends past a tiny snowmelt tarn. The trail then resumes climbing steeply through an increasingly sparse forest cover of lodgepole, hemlock and silver pine to Seavey Pass (9150′).

From the glacially polished granite setting of Seavey Pass the trail drops past another stately rockbound tarn just below the pass, and finally plummets down over steep, eroded pitches alongside a riotous unnamed stream that feeds the Benson Lake alluvial fan. This descent is rocky going, requiring a "grunt and bear it" attitude of the downhill-weary traveler, alleviated only by the fine views of Volunteer Peak across Piute Creek and of the splashing waterfall springing from the ridge south of Piute Mountain.

Where the trail levels out on the valley floor, it crosses the sandy alluvial sediments, and witnesses some drastic changes in the flora. The initial contact with the valley floor, with its solitary-standing specimens of Jeffrey pine towering amid gooseberry, gives the traveler the impression of sandy aridity. But within a few yards, the atmosphere changes as the trail becomes immersed in bracken fern, overflow freshets and dense forest. The trail is sometimes difficult to follow because of the rank growth and quagmire conditions of the valley floor. Two trails cut through this fertile area to Benson Lake. One, unmarked, turns right just after you enter the valley floor. The other departs just before the ford of Piute Creek. This lateral winds along the northwest bank of Piute Creek through fields of corn lily and bracken fern, with occasional clumps of tiger lily and swamp onion, to the good campsites along the east shore of the lake (7600'). Fishermen can look forward to good fishing for rainbow and eastern brook trout (to 14"). Except in mosquito season, this lake makes a fine spot for a layover day.

4th, 5th and 6th Hiking Days: Retrace your steps, 18.6 miles (29.9 km).

Benson Lake

44 Twin Lakes to Smedberg Lake

TRIP   From Twin Lakes to Smedberg Lake (semiloop
               trip via Peeler Lake, Arndt Lake, Benson Lake,
               Smedberg Lake, Matterhorn Canyon and Burro
               Pass). Topo maps *Matterhorn Peak, Tower Peak.*
               Best mid or late season; 49.6 miles (79.8 km).

Grade	Trail/layover days	Total recommended days
Leisurely	11/3	14
Moderate	8/3	11
Strenuous	5/2	7

HILITES   Making a grand loop through the center of the
               North Boundary Country, this trip traces three
               major watersheds, visits six major lakes, and
               views the finest scenery in the region. Layover
               days taken on this long route provide the
               opportunity of visiting any of the nearby lakes,
               over a dozen, or making side trips into any one of
               several other watersheds. It is a long trip with
               many stiff climbs that make it advisable for the
               hiker to first prepare himself by taking one or
               more shorter trips.

DESCRIPTION (Moderate trip)

1st, 2nd and 3rd Hiking Days: Follow Trip 43 to **Benson Lake,**
18.6 miles (29.9 km).
4th Hiking Day (**Benson Lake** to **Smedberg Lake,** 4.5 miles—7.2
km): There is an old saying among those who have visited
Benson Lake, "Everywhere from that hole in the ground is
up," and one contemplating this hiking day must agree.
Retracing our steps over the short lateral to the main trail, the
route then fords Piute Creek and begins a long, steep climb

through a moderate forest cover of lodgepole laced with occasional silver pine. Criss-crossing back and forth over the outlet stream from Smedberg Lake, the trail then circles beneath the steep west facade of Volunteer Peak, and finally crosses over the shoulder of this peak past the first of two trail junctions to Pate Valley. On the north side of Volunteer Peak the trail drops to the south shore of Smedberg Lake (9220'), where excellent campsites may be found all along the south shore and along the southeast inlet about 200 yards from the lake. Fishing for rainbow and occasional eastern brook (to 13") is excellent. As a layover point this picturesque, island-dotted lake makes a fine central location for excursions to nearby Surprise and Sister Lakes.

5th Hiking Day (**Smedberg Lake** to **Matterhorn Canyon**, 6.5 miles—10.5 km): From the narrow valley holding Smedberg Lake, the trail is a steady climb to Benson Pass. It first follows up an inlet of Smedberg Lake on a southeast, meadowed course, then swings east on a stepladdering climb through moderate, then sparse, forest cover to an upper meadow above the main drainage feeding Smedberg Lake. After this brief respite the trail resumes its steep, rocky, upward course to Benson Pass (10,139'). The last climb is over a heavily eroded surface through sparse whitebark pine and hemlock. Excellent views to the northeast present themselves at the pass, and one can see Whorl Mountain, Twin Peaks, some of the pinnacles making up the Sawtooth Ridge, and the granite divide between Matterhorn Creek and Piute Creek.

The trail leaves Benson Pass on a descent that is steep, level and steep again as it drops to Wilson Canyon. Then the downgrade is gradual along the banks of Wilson Creek to the lip of Matterhorn Canyon. In this section the trail winds back and forth over Wilson Creek through an increasingly dense forest cover of lodgepole, with occasional whitebark pine near the top and silver pine near the bottom. Finally, the path is steep again to the floor of Matterhorn Canyon. On the canyon floor, Matterhorn Canyon Creek is a meandering stream flowing alternately through willowed meadows and stands of lodgepole mixed with silver pine. Our trail turns north and follows the stream a mile, then fords it to several campsites 200 yards downstream from the junction with the trail to Tuolumne Meadows. These canyon campsites (8480') boast several fine swimming holes just upstream in granite potholes. Fishing for eastern brook and rainbow trout (to 12") is good.

6th Hiking Day (**Matterhorn Canyon** to **Campsites, Upper Piute**

Creek, 8.5 miles—13.7 km): From these campsites our route goes northeast and leaves the Pacific Crest Trail behind. The route ascends moderately through alternately sandy and rocky sections. On both sides of the canyon, glaciated gray granite shoulders drop to the valley floor, and the black water-staining on their broad surfaces, particularly on Quarry Peak, makes eerie configurations. In a wet, muddy section where the trail fords several small tributary runoffs, it winds through wildflower displays that include false Solomon's seal, lupine, elephant heads, monkey flower, paintbrush, goldenrod, aster, fleabane, buckwheat and Mariposa lily. The trail then fords to the west side of Matterhorn Canyon Creek and then refords to follow the east bank through the latter part of the canyon narrows and well beyond. About ½ mile above a meadow it refords back to the west side.

From this ford the trail keeps to the west side of the creek, winding through meadow and tundra sections on a moderate ascent. Ahead, the pointed tops of Finger Peaks come into view, and later the massive granite of Whorl Mountain and Matterhorn Peak. Scattered lodgepole and hemlock trees dot the trail as it progresses up to the sky-parlor meadows of the upper basin. Some clumps of trees hold campsites (their protected location is testimony to the wind that often sweeps through the canyon), and the tree clumps are interspersed with stretches of grassland laced with sagebrush and willow.

The trail passes the last stand of trees, and ascends steadily on a long traverse below Finger Peaks. Views, across the barren upper basin, of Whorl Mountain are awesome, and its rugged massiveness contrasts sharply with the delicate wildflowers found underfoot as one nears Burro Pass. Here, scattered among sparse whitebark pines, one enjoys the spots of color provided by primrose, scarlet penstemon, wallflower and Douglas phlox. The final climb to the divide is accomplished via rocky switchbacks that terminate on the low saddle of Burro Pass (10,560'). Fine views of both the Matterhorn and Piute Creek canyons are to be had, but overshadowing all are the soldier-topped summits of the Sawtooth Ridge to the north.

The first recorded crossing of this pass was made by Lt. N. F. McClure in 1894. Today's traveler can compare his observations of the pass and its surroundings with those of McClure, who said, "The route now led for five miles through little meadows on each side of the stream, until a comparatively low saddle was seen to the left of us and near the head of the canyon. Investigating this, I found it was a natural pass. The scenery here was truly sublime. I doubt if any part of the main chain of the Sierras presents a greater ruggedness . . ."

As the trail descends on the north side of the pass, it affords fine views of the tiny, barren lakes at the foot of Finger Peaks. The basin of the pass is usually wet, and sometimes covered with snow, thereby making route-picking an instinctive matter. Here Piute Creek is a far cry from what was seen two hiking days ago. A mere stripling of a stream, it tinkles through meadow grass, and the traveler fords to the north side by an easy step. Belding squirrels pipe one's passage through the grassy tundra stretches, and the call of marmots on the nearby scree is a cacophonous accompaniment to the gentle descent into the moderate forest cover of lodgepole and hemlock. This hiking day ends at the good campsites (9600') found along that stretch of Piute Creek where the trail touches the creek banks northeast of Finger Peaks. Here fishing for eastern brook (to 8") is fair.

7th and 8th Hiking Days: Reverse the steps of Trip 39, 11.5 miles (18.5 km).

Up the Robinson Creek Trail

45   Green Creek to East Lake

TRIP   From Green Creek Roadend to East Lake (round
                trip). Topo map *Matterhorn Peak*. Best early, mid
                or late season; 7 miles (11.2 km).

Grade	Trail/layover days	Total recommended days
Leisurely	2/0	2
Moderate	....	....
Strenuous	....	....

HILITES   This is a fine beginner's weekend hike. East Lake
                offers one of the most colorful backdrops for a
                camping scene to be found in any wilderness. The
                trilogy of Gabbro, Page and Epidote peaks is
                composed of rocks varying in hue from vermilion
                reds to ochre, and these colors are set in
                metavolcanic blacks for contrast. Nearby Nutter,
                Gilman and Hoover lakes offer good fishing to
                supplement the angling in East Lake, and the
                general spectrum of scenery along the trail rounds
                out a rich diet indeed.

DESCRIPTION

1st Hiking Day (**Green Creek Roadend** to **East Lake**, 3.5
miles—5.6 km): The trailhead is just beyond the Green Lakes
Pack Station at road's end. Amid moderate-to-dense Jeffrey,
juniper, lodgepole and aspen forest cover, the trail ascends
gently to a small step-across spring runoff. A ground cover of
sagebrush, mule ears, serviceberry, western blueberry, wild
lilac, lupine, wallflower, paintbrush, pennyroyal and
buckwheat lines the trail in the initial drier stretches, and
along the wetter spots one finds tiger lily, penstemon, shooting
star, monkshood, monkey flower, columbine, rein-orchid and
aster. The ascent then becomes steeper as it crosses an easy
rocky ridge, and finally it begins a long series of steady switchbacks.

Crossing several intermittent runoff tributaries coming

down from Monument Ridge, the trail keeps to the northwest side of West Fork Green Creek. While the creek itself is never out of hearing, it is often obscured visually by the sheath of willows that line its bank. Ahead, on the left, one can make out Gabbro Peak, and on the right the stream that falls from the hanging valley containing West Lake. Added to the wildflowers to be seen along the trail here are iris, corn lily, cow parsnip, stickseed, gooseberry, Douglas phlox and pussy paws.

The trail then climbs another dry slope by moderately ascending switchbacks to a junction just before Green Lake where the right fork leads to campsites on Green Lake and to West Lake. Anglers may wish to tarry here for the good fishing for rainbow and eastern brook (to 14″). Green Lake is large (about 50 acres), with a rocky west shore and a steep southeast shore. A mixed timber cover of lodgepole, hemlock and occasional silver pine surrounds most of the lake except for the meadowed inlet delta.

Our route, the left fork, fords West Fork Green Creek just below the lake and makes a long dogleg to the south before turning east to ford the outlet stream from East Lake. This outlet stream is a vigorous watercourse that follows the natural ravine shown on the topo map just north of East Lake. The trail makes a long loop away from the stream and then veers back to a second ford. The ascent is sometimes steep as it continues on to the meadowed outlet of East Lake. Fair-to-good campsites (9440′) can be found around the outlet just below the flood-control dam, and on the north shore. Fishing for rainbow trout on this 75-acre lake is good. This lake makes a fine base-camp location for forays to nearby Nutter, Gilman and Hoover lakes.

2nd Hiking Day: Retrace your steps, 3.5 miles (5.6 km).

46   Green Creek to Tuolumne Meadows

TRIP   From Green Creek Roadend to Tuolumne
              Meadows (shuttle trip). Topo maps *Matterhorn
              Peak, Tuolumne Meadows.* Best mid or late season;
              26.2 miles (42.2 km).

| | Trail/layover | Total recom- |
Grade	days	mended days
Leisurely	4/1	5
Moderate	4/0	4
Strenuous	3/0	3

HILITES   Three quarters of this scenic route travels remote
              sections of Yosemite National Park that are not
              frequented by day walkers. The solitude-seeker
              will find the quiet of upper Virginia Canyon to his
              liking, and the fisherman wanting a variety of
              lake and stream fishing for rainbow and eastern
              brook will pronounce this trip ideal.

DESCRIPTION (Moderate trip)

1st Hiking Day: Follow Trip 45 to **East Lake**, 3.5 miles (5.6 km).
2nd Hiking Day (**East Lake** to **Lower Virginia Canyon**, 9
miles—14.5 km): From the outlet of East Lake the trail
ascends above the lake's waters as it rounds the east shore,
affording superlative views of Gabbro, Page and Epidote
peaks foregrounded by the deep blue of East Lake. The trail
drops briefly across the gentle ridge separating East Lake
from the tiny lakelets to the east, and then veers away from
East Lake on an ascending traverse before descending gently
to the meadow-fringed shores of Nutter Lake. Through a
sparse forest cover of lodgepole and hemlock, the trail then
climbs above the west shore of beautiful Gilman Lake, passing
a lateral trail down to it. Flanked by the steep west face of

Dunderberg Peak, and foregrounded by a meadow and timber cover, this lake is a favorite of photographers. Fishermen may also wish to linger—the better to sample the good fishing for rainbow.

From the Gilman Lake lateral our trail ascends past several small tarns, fords the stream joining Gilman and Hoover lakes, and then rises steeply to the bench holding Hoover Lakes. These two alpine lakes are set between the dark rock of Epidote Peak and the burgundy-red rock of the magnificent unnamed mountain to the southeast (see cover photo). They are considerably colder than the lakes below, and they have been planted with eastern brook trout. The trail skirts the southeast side of the first, fords the stream between them, and passes by the northwest side of the second. After fording the inlet, it ascends steeply along the stream joining Hoover Lakes with Summit Lake. This rocky ascent through a thinning forest cover of lodgepole and occasional hemlock and whitebark pine meets the unsigned Virginia Lakes Trail on a small bench, where our route turns right (northwest). This moderate ascent fords the aforementioned stream and arrives at aptly named Summit Lake (10,160'). Like Peeler Lake to the north, Summit Lake contributes water to both sides of the Sierra. It sits atop the crest in a **V**'d notch between the dark rock of Camiaca Peak and a lighter ridge extending north from Excelsior Mountain.

The trail skirts the north side of Summit Lake to the Sierra crest and then switchbacks steeply down the west slope. Looking back toward Summit Lake, we can see clearly that the glaciers which had their beginnings below Camiaca Peak on both the east and the west sides met at the present site of Summit Lake. Across the cirque basin of upper Virginia Canyon, the rounded eminence of Grey Butte and the sharply nippled tops of Virginia Peak and Stanton Peak dominate the views to the west. The descent levels out before it fords Return Creek and continues down-canyon. Recent avalanches have made obvious incursions into the sparse forest cover of lodgepole, aspen and occasional red fir and hemlock, and have left broken stubs on every hand.

The trail then fords several tributary streams as it keeps to the west side of Return Creek on a long, moderate descent to a junction with the Pacific Crest Trail. At this junction our route turns left, fords Return Creek, and arrives at some good campsites (8600') in the granite ledge system on the east side of the creek. Fishing for eastern brook and rainbow is fair to good.

3rd Hiking Day (**Lower Virginia Canyon** to **Glen Aulin**, 8 miles—12.9 km): The trail from the campsites near the ford continues southwest along the banks of Return Creek and fords McCabe Creek before beginning the steep ascent of the canyon wall. This gentle descent along Return Creek passes the stream's beautiful bedrock-granite cascades. Dropping into deep, clear potholes, the creek has carved and sculpted the bedrock into smooth, mollescent lines that invite the traveler to run his hands across them. Columbine clustered amid lupine and whorled penstemon add color to the green mats of swamp onion and gooseberry near the ford. (In late season fill your canteen at McCabe Creek, for there is no more water until Glen Aulin.) Beyond this ford the trail begins long switchbacks across a slope moderately forested with fine specimens of silver pine, lodgepole and occasional red fir. These rocky switchbacks terminate at the McCabe Lake Trail junction, where our route turns right and descends gently over a duff surface. Birdlife abounds through the moderate-to-dense forest cover of red fir, lodgepole and silver pine, and the hiker is very likely to see chickadees, juncos, warblers, flycatchers, woodpeckers, bluebirds, robins and evening grosbeaks in these precincts.

A short ¾ mile beyond the last junction, close under Point 9186, you may find water even in late season. Then your route declines gently through cool, moist forest to a fairly large meadow east of Elbow Hill. After threading a course through a few stands of pines, you emerge in an even larger meadow—about 2 miles long, although the trail does not trace all 2 miles of it. At a stream fork shortly beyond a *very* large boulder to your west, you may find water even in late season. Then the trail climbs over a saddle in a low, forested ridge and gently descends for about ½ mile. Over the next mile, always near Cold Canyon creek, the level, rutted path passes many possible campsites in pleasant meadowy areas studded with small lodgepole pines.

From this camping region a series of easy switchbacks accomplish about half the descent to the Tuolumne River, and where the trail re-reaches the creek there is another good campsite. On the final rocky downhill mile to the river, you catch glimpses of Tuolumne Falls and White Cascade, and their roar carries all the way across the canyon.

Finally, you reach "civilization" at the Glen Aulin High Sierra Camp. Within sight of the camp you pass the Tuolumne River Trail westbound, and in 15 yards come to the little spur trail that crosses Conness Creek on a bridge to the camp. Very meager supplies are sometimes available here. The backpacker campsites just upstream from the "lodge" are very popular with bears, and you would be less likely to have ursine visitors at one of the campsites a mile or two before you reach Glen Aulin—though it would be no guarantee.

4th Hiking Day (**Glen Aulin** to **Tuolumne Meadows,** 5.7 miles— 9.2 km).

From Glen Aulin the trail crosses the Tuolumne River on a low steel bridge, from which one has excellent views of White Cascade and the deep green pool below it. In a few minutes we reach the May Lake Trail, ascending west, and continue our steep climb to gain the height of White Cascade and Tuolumne Falls. The trail passes a fine viewpoint below the falls, and if the light is right, you'll get a great photograph. Above the falls, the river flows down a series of sparkling rapids separated by large pools and wide sheets of clear water spread out over slightly inclined granite slopes.

Soon the trail crosses the river for the last time, on a boulders-and-steel bridge, and then climbs a little way above the gorge the river has cut here. Across the stream one can easily make out basaltic "Little Devils Postpile," the only volcanic formation anywhere around here. Then we descend to larger, polished slabs near the river, and follow a somewhat ducked route across them for about a mile beside the beckoning waters. When trail tread resumes, we soon cross the three branches of Dingley Creek, which may be dry in late season, and stroll along a "levee" built to raise the trailbed above the flood level here. About ½ mile of almost level walking in cool forest brings the long-distance trekker to the Young Lakes Trail junction, and then he touches the northwest edge of his destination, Tuolumne Meadows. Soon after, we cross three branches of Delaney Creek, the last being the only one of consequence. Just beyond this ford, a trail veers left, bound for the Tuolumne Meadows Stables. We instead veer right and ascend a long, dry, sandy ridge. From the tiny reeded lakes on top of this ridge, the trail drops gently down through meadowed pockets and stands of lodgepole pine to Soda Springs, once a drive-in and then a walk-in campground, but since 1976 closed to camping.

From the effervescent springs, in their dilapidated enclosure, the trail follows a closed-off dirt road east above the north edge of Tuolumne Meadows, the largest subalpine meadow in the Sierra Nevada. The spiring summits of the Cathedral Range across the meadow provide challenging vistas as we stroll the last, level ¾ mile to a parking lot beside State Highway 120, the Tioga Road.

47   Green Creek to Virginia Lakes

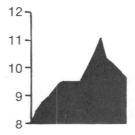

TRIP   From Green Creek Roadend to Virginia Lakes Campground (shuttle trip). Topo map *Matterhorn Peak*. Best mid or late season; 10 miles (16.1 km).

Grade	Trail/layover days	Total recommended days
Leisurely	2/1	3
Moderate	2/0	2
Strenuous	....	....

HILITES   This **U**-shaped trip circles around Kavanaugh Ridge and Dunderberg Peak, and in its passage touches 14 alpine and subalpine lakes. Scenery along this route is mostly of the open alpine variety, and the route is a fine sampling of the majestic Sierra crest. For the beginner or for the experienced back-country traveler, this trip is an excellent choice for a weekend excursion.

DESCRIPTION

1st Hiking Day: Follow Trip 45 to **East Lake**, 3.5 miles (5.6 km).

2nd Hiking Day (**East Lake** to **Virginia Lakes Campground**, 6.5 miles—10.5 km): Proceed to the Virginia Lakes Trail junction as described in the 2nd hiking day, Trip 46. At this junction our trail turns left (southeast) and climbs steeply up a series of switchbacks that overlook the Hoover Lakes in the valley of East Creek below. Beyond these zigzags we reach a sloping, willowed bowl surrounded by many snowbanks into late season. Then, under a small red cliff, the trail switchbacks up again, to cross the northern of the two streams in this two-headed canyon. Again the way steepens, and at frequent rest stops you can see the small white petals of Douglas phlox and the purple trumpetforms of Davidson's penstemon. There are even a few specimens of a yellow flower hardly ever found below 10,000 feet: alpine gold. Finally we cross the divide at 11,000 feet, where the red rocks of the crest on our right contrast with the somber dark grays of Black Mountain straight ahead.

The trail ahead has been altered slightly from that shown on the topo map, now being located farther south where it drops down the tundra steps of Frog Lakes. In Frog Lakes and in the willowed stream between them, anglers will find fair fishing for eastern brook and rainbow trout. Just north of Cooney Lake the new trail and that shown on the topo map once more coincide. This lake, with its willowed inlet and its precipitous outlet, contains thriving populations of eastern brook and rainbow.

Continuing the moderate descent over a rocky ledge system, the trail winds down through sparse clumps of whitebark pine past a mining claim, and then fords the willowed outlet stream of Moat Lake. In the wetter stretches here, wildflower fanciers will delight in the lush clumps of columbine, swamp onion and shooting star. Under the steep, avalanche-scarred south face of Dunderberg Peak, the second-highest peak in the North Boundary Country, the trail slopes down on a rocky traverse to the outlet of Blue Lake. The broken talus and scree to the north are a haven for marmots and conies, whose scats and hay harvests can be found on and between the rocks next to the trail. Like Cooney Lake, Blue Lake has a fishery of eastern brook and rainbow trout. Past Blue Lake the descending trail is within sight of one more tiny, unnamed lake. Soon the trail splits and ramifies, and even some roads appear, but route-finding is not a problem, because following any of them will in about ¼ mile bring you to Virginia Lakes Campground (9760').

48   Hetch Hetchy to Rancheria Creek

TRIP   From O'Shaughnessy Dam (Hetch Hetchy Reservoir) to Rancheria Creek (round trip). Topo maps *Hetch Hetchy Reservoir*. Best early season; 13 miles (21 km).

Grade	Trail/layover days	Total recommended days
Leisurely	2/0	2
Moderate	....	....
Strenuous	....	....

HILITES   Early season is the ideal time to view the falls along this route, and eager opening-day anglers will find the good fishing along Rancheria Creek a satisfying clumination to a fine trip.

DESCRIPTION

1st Hiking Day (**O'Shaughnessy Dam** to **Rancheria Creek**, 6.5 miles—10.5 km): From the trailhead at the south end of the dam, the thunder from the spillway accompanies the traveler as he crosses the 600-foot-long dam. Views across the reservoir waters are flanked by waterfalls on the left and spectacular Kolana Rock on the right. The first 0.7 mile of this route follows the service road to Lake Eleanor. Then the trail branches right and undulates through alternating timber (digger pine) and meadowed terrain on a long terrace above the reservoir. Grass-pocketed granite slabs where meadow foam blooms in spring at the foot of Tueeulala Falls are a fine place for a breather stop. The trail gets rockier as it approaches larger Wapama Falls, and beneath the rooster-tail spray from the falls it is slippery. This spectacular water drop, little-heralded in Yosemite Park publicity, plummets a total of 1200 feet in a stepladder succession of falls, the last step being 200 feet. In years of heavy snowmelt, the creek beneath these falls may be impassable until June, despite the bridges.

From the bridges across the multibranched creek below the falls, the trail climbs steeply on switchbacks through a bower of bay trees and golden oaks, with here and there some ponderosa pine, incense-cedar and digger pine. Leveling out, the trail threads a number of little pocket meadows strung along a high, narrow ledge. After topping a small summit, the trail rollercoasters down and then up, crossing several intermittent runoffs. High points of this segment offer excellent views of the bay into which Tiltill and Rancheria creeks empty. A moderate ascent of another ½ mile takes the hiker to the steel bridge across Tiltill Creek, beyond which the trail climbs steeply for several hundred rocky yards. As one nears Rancheria Creek, he has exciting views of a fine granite bedrock chute over which the creek makes a white ribbon.

Glaciated fields of granite mark the remaining ½ mile of easy climb to the fair campsites (4550′) along Rancheria Creek below the falls. These campsites are reached by taking a lateral trail ¼ mile before the junction of the Tiltill Valley Trail. Fishing is fair for rainbow (to 13″) on Rancheria Creek below Rancheria Falls. Bears are common and persistent around here.

2nd Hiking Day: Retrace your steps, 6.5 miles (10.5 km).

Hikers near O'Shaughnessy Dam

49   Hetch Hetchy to Tiltill Valley

TRIP   From O'Shaughnessy Dam (Hetch Hetchy Reservoir) to Tiltill Valley (round trip). Topo maps *Lake Eleanor*, ***Hetch Hetchy Reservoir***. Best early season; 18.6 miles (30 km)

Grade	Trail/layover days	Total recommended days
Leisurely	4/0	4
Moderate	3/0	3
Strenuous	2/0	2

HILITES   Like the previous trip, this route tours the northern edge of Hetch Hetchy Reservoir. Across the lake the views of Kolana Rock and the sheer granite walls of the Grand Canyon of the Tuolumne provide a majestic accompaniment. The contrasting intimate serenity of Tiltill Valley is a pleasant terminus to this early-season trek.

DESCRIPTION (Leisurely trip)

1st Hiking Day: Follow Trip 48 to **Rancheria Creek**, 6.5 miles (10.5 km).

2nd Hiking Day (**Rancheria Creek** to **Tiltill Valley**, 2.8 miles—4.5 km): From the junction of the Pate Valley/Tiltill Valley trails above the campsites, the trail to Tiltill Valley climbs steeply for a full 1200 feet up to a timber-bottomed saddle. As the trail descends on the north side of the saddle, it traverses a pine forest with a sprinkling of incense-cedar and black oak. When this duff trail emerges at the east end of Tiltill Valley, it meets a trail to Tilden Canyon and Benson Lake. The valley is a long meadow which in early spring is usually quite wet and boggy at the east end. Lodgepole pine fringes the meadow, and the valley is flanked by polished outcroppings of granite and by brush-covered slopes. The trail crosses to the north side of the meadow and winds west to the excellent campsites just south of the Tiltill Creek ford (5600'). These camping places, located in an isolated stand of lodgepole and sugar pine, afford excellent views in both directions down the meadows. Campers have an uninterrupted vantage point from which to watch the large variety of wildlife that make this meadow their home. Fishing on Tiltill Creek for rainbow (to 10″) is excellent in early season.

3rd and 4th Hiking Days: Retrace your steps, 9.3 miles (15 km).

Rancheria Falls

50   Saddlebag Lake to McCabe Lakes

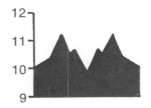

TRIP   From Saddlebag Lake to Lower McCabe Lake
            (round trip). Topo map *Tuolumne Meadows*. Best
            mid or late season; 11 miles (17.8 km).

Grade	Trail/layover days	Total recom- mended days
Leisurely	3/0	3
Moderate	2/1	3
Strenuous	....	....

HILITES   Alpine from beginning to end, this trip crosses the
            Sierra crest between the east end of Shepherd
            Crest and North Peak. High tundra meadows,
            sparkling clear-water lakes and weathered white-
            bark pines are hallmarks of this loftily routed
            excursion. Although the route is not marked as a
            trail on the topo map, there is sometimes a well-
            worn trace and sometimes adequate duck-on-
            the rock markings to delineate the route. This is
            a good trip selection for both intermediate and
            advanced backpackers.

DESCRIPTION (Moderate trip)

1st Hiking Day (**Saddlebag Lake** to **Lower McCabe Lake,** 5.5
miles—8.9 km): Saddlebag Lake (10,087'), caught in the
barren alpine basin between the Tioga Crest and the main
Sierra divide, is one of the largest lakes of the North Boundary
Country. About 340 acres in area, it is a long lake to walk
around, and hikers may elect to use the boat-taxi that runs the
length of the lake from Saddlebag Lake Resort. Rates are
reasonable, and the service convenient. Those who wish to
walk should take the mining road that leaves from the east
end of the resort area, rounds the south end of the lake, and
then skirts the rocky, open northeast side. At various times
dating back to the 1880s, it provided access for the numerous

mining ventures that occupied the basin above Saddlebag Lake and nearby Lundy Canyon. One claim is still registered as active.

To the east, the gently rounded summits of the Tioga Crest dip to Dore Pass, and hikers with a little imagination can see and hear the struggling men and animals of the winter of 1882 as they "snaked" and hauled 16,000 pounds of mining machinery across this pass on balky skid sleds. Bound for Bennettville, the sleds were lowered to the edge of Saddlebag Lake and run across on the thick midwinter ice.

Near the northwest end of the lake, the mining road meets a short trail leading up from the boat-taxi dock, and through a sparse forest cover of stunted lodgepole pine it continues west to the north shore of Greenstone Lake. This rocky lake is backgrounded by the glacier-footed crest of Mt. Conness, and its cold waters hold cutthroat and eastern brook trout. The road then winds gently up through swales in the buckling fields of glacially smoothed granite and past several small tarns to Wasco Lake. The wonderful variety of alpine flora along this gentle ascent sees the appearance of the whitebark pine in the sparse forest cover. Among the profuse wildflowers are primrose, heather, paintbrush (several varieties), wallflower, monkey flower, penstemon, corn lily, Douglas phlox, alpine columbine and aster.

The road then descends along the gullied stream flowing into Steelhead Lake, and at the south end of Steelhead Lake the cross-country route we will follow branches left around the west side of Steelhead Lake. Crossing granite ledges, the route fords Mill Creek, and then veers west around the small, unnamed lake to the northwest. At this point, anglers may wish to sample the golden trout fishing at Cascade Lake before going on. The steep rock-and-grass-ledge ascent of the crest begins as our route turns northwest beside a flower-lined inlet stream. The course of this tiny rill bends northward, and our route follows it faithfully to the small, unnamed lake it drains, locally called Secret Lake.

Pausing at Secret Lake to survey your route up the headwall, you have three choices. Adept mountaineers can attack the wall directly, preferably keeping just to the right of the black, lichen-stained vertical streak on the headwall. Hikers who want to put out some extra effort to achieve certainty and lack of steep exposure can arduously pick their way up the scree north of Secret Lake to the lip of what looks like—but isn't—a lake basin. From there, they will traverse slightly upward to their left, under the solid face of the east end of

Shepherd Crest, to the low point on the headwall divide. Probably most people choose the third way: From the south side of Secret Lake walk directly up the increasingly steep headwall until, about halfway up, you come to a long ledge that slopes slightly up to the south. Many ducks mark this route, but they are not always easy to see. About 200 yards south up this ledge, you leave it and follow ducks almost directly up to the ridgecrest. Once on it, follow it north to the low point of the divide to find the ducked route descending on the west side of the ridgecrest.

Excellent views northwest from the ridgecrest include Tower Peak and Saurian Crest. Descending from this ridge, a steep, eroded trail follows the gully northeast of upper McCabe Lake. This section levels out near some small tarns, and our route continues to the north shore of upper McCabe Lake. (One could camp here in a small stand of whitebark pines.) Turning west along the shore, we ford the outlet and then strike out for the low, rock-cairned saddle due west of the outlet. Beyond this saddle, the best route drops past snowmelt tarns not shown on the topo map and then winds down through a dense forest cover of lodgepole, whitebark pine and hemlock to the east shore of beautiful lower McCabe Lake (9850'). The best campsites on the lake are near the outlet. Fishing for eastern brook (to 12") is excellent.

2nd Hiking Day: Retrace your steps, 5.5 miles (8.9 km).

Peak 11282 over Nelson Lake

Saddlebag Lake to Tuolumne Meadows **51**

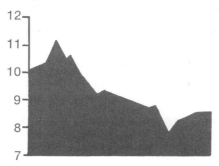

TRIP   From Saddlebag Lake to Tuolumne Meadows via
Lower McCabe Lake, Cold Canyon and Glen Aulin
(shuttle trip). Topo map *Tuolumne Meadows.* Best
mid or late season; 20.4 miles (32.9 km).

Grade	Trail/layover days	Total recom- mended days
Leisurely	4/1	5
Moderate	3/1	4
Strenuous	3/0	3

HILITES   Some hikers may choose this trip for its easy
shuttle, but the country that this route tours
should be adequate reason in itself. The variety of
a trip that is part cross country, part on trail and
part over water should appeal to the most jaded
mountaineer's appetite. This route does that and
more. Crossing the Sierra crest above upper
McCabe Lake, the trip traverses the long meadows
of Cold Canyon, and finishes by touring the
splashing cascades and roaring falls of the
Tuolumne River.

DESCRIPTION (Moderate trip)

1st Hiking Day: Follow Trip 50 to **Lower McCabe Lake**, 5.5 miles
(8.9 km).

2nd Hiking Day (**Lower McCabe Lake** to **Glen Aulin**, 9.2 miles—
14.8 km): From the campsites at the outlet of lower McCabe
Lake the trail descends along the west side of the stream
through a moderate-to-dense forest cover of hemlock,
lodgepole, whitebark and silver pine and occasional red fir.

The trail between lower McCabe Lake and the place where it veers west is usually very wet and swampy, a soggy condition hospitable to the fields of corn lily that line the way. As the trail veers west it becomes drier, and most of the timber near the trail is lodgepole pine. Flowers indigenous to better-drained soils are found along this section of trail, including wallflower, Douglas phlox, lupine, buckwheat, aster and pussy paws. The descent becomes gentle as the trail passes through a "ghost forest" caused by the needleminer moth and crosses an unnamed tributary of McCabe Creek before reaching the junction with the Virginia Canyon Trail. At this junction our route turns left (west) and continues to Glen Aulin as described in the third hiking day, Trip 46.

3rd Hiking Day: Follow the 4th hiking day, Trip 46, 5.7 miles (9.2 km).

White Cascade near Glen Aulin

National Park Service

Saddlebag Lake to Twin Lakes 52

TRIP　From Saddlebag Lake to Twin Lakes via Lower
McCabe Lake, Matterhorn Canyon, Burro Pass,
Upper Piute Creek and Crown Lake (shuttle trip).
Topo maps *Tuolumne Meadows, Matterhorn Peak.*
Best mid or late season; 34.5 miles (55.6 km).

Grade	Trail/layover days	Total recommended days
Leisurely	8/2	10
Moderate	5/2	7
Strenuous	4/2	6

HILITES　Of the many crestal routes throughout the Sierra,
this is one of the most exciting. The scenery is wild
and rugged, the six watersheds visited provide
excellent fishing, and the route touches some of
the most remote country of Yosemite National
Park. Most of the campsites mentioned below are
situated in central locations that invite side trips,
and the visitor is advised to allow enough layover
days for such trips.

DESCRIPTION (Moderate trip)

1st Hiking Day: Follow trip 50 to **Lower McCabe Lake**, 5.5 miles
(8.9 km).

2nd Hiking Day (**Lower McCabe Lake** to **Matterhorn Canyon**, 9
miles—14.5 km): This is the longest hiking day of the trip, and
the prudent hiker will get an early start. From the outlet of
Lower McCabe Lake the trail descends to the Virginia Canyon
Trail junction as described in the 2nd hiking day, Trip 51. At
this junction our route turns right and descends down the

steep switchbacks into Virginia Canyon. The trail along these switchbacks is **T**-blazed, and the deep layers of bark that have built up around these blazes give the passerby an indication of this trail's age. Blazed by the U.S. Cavalry under the acting superintendency of Captain Abram Epperson Wood in the 1890s, this trail was once used for access to the more remote portions of the North Boundary Country. As the intimidated sheepmen who had been encroaching on Park lands moved their herds northward, it became necessary for the Army caretakers to widen the area of their patrols. The traveler of today, like the mounted cavalryman of yesterday, may pause in wonder at the magnificent specimens of red fir and silver pine along this descent.

The trail descends nearly to Return Creek before turning northeast to ford McCabe Creek. Near the ford are magnificent examples of water-sculpting on the granite bedrock of Return Creek, and this bedrock is bordered with colorful patches of columbine, tiger lily and shooting star.

A short way beyond the ford of McCabe Creek the trail passes a packer campsite and there fords to the north side of Return Creek, where it meets the Summit Pass Trail. Our route turns left (southwest) and ascends moderately across the easy juniper-crowned divide to Spiller Canyon. One's first views of Spiller Creek are those of open granite bedrock, over which Spiller Creek splashes in a series of lovely chutes and miniature falls. The trail ascends along the creek for about ¼ mile and then fords it.

Through a moderate forest cover that now includes hemlock, the trail then climbs by steady switchbacks. At the hairpin turns one has fine views up Spiller Canyon all the way to the sky-parlor meadows at its headwall, and south across Return Creek to North Peak and Mt. Conness. The trail descends briefly through a long, dry, sandy meadow, and then ascends again over a grassy saddle. From the saddle, the trail dips gently to beautiful Miller Lake. Foregrounded by a large green meadow, the sparkling waters of this small lake tempt the traveler to stop and rest, but drama lies right around the bend.

From Miller Lake the rutted trail bends north, up a grassy swale to a timbered saddle. The views from this saddle burst upon the traveler as he is suddenly confronted with the chasm of Matterhorn Canyon and the distant teeth of the Sawtooth Ridge. This viewpoint marks the beginning of a long, switchbacking descent into Matterhorn Canyon, until finally the rocky trail levels off in the sand of the meadowed junction with the Matterhorn Canyon Trail (8480'). There are good campsites in the meadow and more just upstream. Fishing for eastern brook (to 12″) is good in Matterhorn Canyon creek, and the granite potholes upstream from the junction provide fine swimming in late season.

3rd, 4th and *5th Hiking Days*: Follow the 6th, 7th and 8th hiking days of Trip 44, 20 miles (32.2 km).

Ragged Peak over Young Lake

53   Tuolumne Meadows to Young Lakes

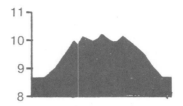

TRIP   From Tuolumne Meadows to Young Lakes (semi-
            loop trip). Topo map *Tuolumne Meadows*. Best mid
            or late season, 15.1 miles (24.3 km).

Grade	Trail/layover days	Total recom- mended days
Leisurely	....	....
Moderate	2/1	3
Strenuous	2/0	2

HILITES   The three Young Lakes, cupped under soaring
            Ragged Peak, offer a large selection of campsites,
            some in heavy woods and some at timberline.
            These camps provide a base for exciting excursions
            into the headwaters of Conness Creek and for
            climbing Mt. Conness itself.

DESCRIPTION

1st Hiking Day (**Glen Aulin TH** to **Young Lakes**, 8.2 mi.—13.2
km): The first part of this trip follows the Glen Aulin
"highway," a heavily traveled path from Tuolumne Meadows
to the High Sierra Camp down the Tuolumne River. From the
parking area west of State Highway 120 we stroll down a dirt
road, pass a locked gate that bars autos, and continue west
along the lodgepole-dotted flank of Tuolumne Meadows, with
fine views south across the meadows of Unicorn Peak,
Cathedral Peak and some of the Echo Peaks. Approaching a
boulder-rimmed old parking loop, we veer right and climb
slightly to the now-closed Soda Springs Campground. Once this
campground was the private holding of John Lembert,
namesake of Lembert Dome. His brothers, who survived him,
sold it to the Sierra Club in 1912, and for 60 years Club
members enjoyed a private campground in this marvelous
subalpine meadow. But in 1972 the Club deeded the property
to the National Park Service so that everyone could use it.

From the Soda Springs the sandy trail undulates through a forest of sparse, small lodgepole pines, and then descends to a boulder ford of Delaney Creek. Immediately beyond the ford we hop a branch of Delaney Creek, then hop another in 300 yards. Soon our trail almost touches the southwest arm of Tuolumne Meadows before ascending to the signed Young Lakes Trail. From the junction we ascend slightly and cross a broad expanse of boulder-strewn, grass-pocketed sheet granite. An open spot affords a look south across broad Tuolumne Meadows to the line of peaks from Fairview Dome to the steeplelike spires of the Cathedral Range. After crossing the open granite, our trail climbs a tree-clothed slope to a ridge and turns up the ridge for several hundred yards before veering down into the meadowy, bouldery, shallow valley of Dingley Creek, an easy ford except in early season. In the first mile beyond this small creek, we jump across its north fork and wind gently upward in shady pine forest carpeted with a fine flower display even into late season. Groundsel, daisies, lupine, squawroot and gooseberries all are colorful, but one's admiration for floral beauty concentrates on the delicate cream flower cups of Mariposa lily, with one rich brown spot in the throat of each petal. Near the ridgetop, breaks in the lodgepole forest allow us glimpses the whole Cathedral Range.

On the other side of the ridge a new panoply of peaks appears in the north—majestic Tower Peak, Doghead and Quarry peaks, the Finger Peaks, Matterhorn Peak, Sheep Peak, Mt. Conness, and the Shepherd Crest. From this viewpoint a moderate descent leads to a ford of a tributary of Conness Creek, where more varieties of flowers decorate the green banks of this icy, dashing stream. Soon our downwinding trail reaches the Dog Lake Trail junction, where we veer left and descend into thickening hemlock forest. On a level stretch of trail we cross another branch of Conness Creek, and then switchback ¼ mile up to a plateau from where the view is fine of the steep north face of Ragged Peak.

After passing a meadow which was the fourth Young Lake before it filled in with stream sediments, we descend to the west shore of lower Young Lake (9850'). There are both primitive and well-developed campsites along the north shore of this lake. More secluded campsites may be found on middle Young Lake by following the trail east from the ford of the lower lake, and forking right at a junction 400 yards beyond. From the middle lake you can go up the inlet to the upper lake (10,200'), which is the most attractive but also the most exposed. Fishing on the Young Lakes is fair-to-good for brook trout (to 12″).

2nd Hiking Day (**Young Lakes** to **Glen Aulin TH**, 6.9 mi.—11.1 km): After retracing our steps to the Dog Lake Trail junction, we turn left onto the southwest spur of Ragged Peak and ascend a sandy, boulder-scattered slope under a moderate lodgepole-and-hemlock forest cover. As the trail ascends, the trees diminish in density and change in species, to a predominance of whitebark pine, the highest-dwelling of subalpine trees. From the shoulder of Ragged Peak the trail descends through a very large, gently sloping meadow. This broad, well-watered expanse is a wildflower garden in season, laced with meandering brooks. Paintbrush, lupine and monkey flower in the foreground set off the great views of the entire Cathedral Range, strung out on the southern horizon.

Near the lower edge of the meadow we cross the headwaters of Dingley Creek, and then descend, steeply at times, some 300 feet through a moderately dense forest of lodgepoles and a few hemlocks. Then the trail levels off and veers east on a gently rolling course through more lodgepole forest where the sandy soil sprouts thousands of prostrate little lupine plants. Beyond is a very large level meadow where the reddish peaks of Mts. Dana and Gibbs loom in the east, Delaney Creek meanders lazily through the grass, and Belding ground squirrels pipe away. The Delaney Creek ford is difficult in early season; shallower fords may be found upstream. Beyond the creek, you will find the trail about 20 yards upstream from the main ford. After crossing a little ridge, our route drops once more toward Tuolumne Meadows. Lembert Dome, the "first ascent" of so many visitors to Tuolumne Meadows, can be glimpsed through the trees along this stretch of trail. The trail levels slightly before it meets the 0.1 mile lateral to Dog Lake. Then it passes a junction with a trail that leads east along the north side of Lembert Dome, and fords Dog Lake's outlet. The 560-foot descent from here is terribly dusty as it switchbacks down close under the steep west face of Lembert Dome. At the bottom of the deep dust, the trail splits into three paths. The right one leads to the stables, the left one to the parking area where we started.

Southern Yosemite/Devils Postpile

This region's topography is varied and complex, ranging from the yawning chasm of Yosemite Valley to the snowy heights of the Sierra crest's peaks, some over 13,000 feet. In profile this section ascends in a long, gentle slope, increasing in height and power until it climaxes at the white-peaked crest. It then drops away suddenly, in an escarpment, to Mono and Long valleys. The more gradual western slope is wrinkled into a complex of lesser crests and valleys that roughly parallel the north-south main crest, and this corrugated surface is broken by the networks of the three major rivers of the area: the Tuolumne, the Merced, and the San Joaquin.

Southern Yosemite National Park provides the grandest scenery in this region. But if Yosemite is first in grandeur, the Devils Postpile area, including the spectacular Ritter Range, is a close second. Combined, these two regions afford some of the best backpacking country in the world.

In all, Yosemite offers the traveler over 700 miles of trail, a figure that does not include the outside-the-Park portions of trails originating in the Park. Because of the number of people traveling the Yosemite backcountry, the Park Service has now instituted a policy of allowing camping with fires only at designated camping spots (and no fires above 9600 feet) and wilderness permits are required. Forest Service fire permits are required for trips outside the Park. (See the chapter on wilderness permits.) The credit for the well-maintained trails of this area belongs to trail crews of the U.S. Forest Service and of the National Park Service. Backpackers in Yosemite soon become familiar with the i tree blaze of the Forest Service and with Yosemite's distinctive T. The T blaze was first used when the U.S. Calvary administered the Park.

The general landforms of the southern Yosemite and Devils Postpile regions are similar because both were created by mountain-building forces followed by erosion by glaciers and rivers. However, anyone who hikes the backcountry of southern Yosemite and of the Ritter Range will see the marked differences between the two areas. In Yosemite, one is struck with the gargantuan scale of the landscape. Vast expanses of solid white granite give a sense of colossal immobility. By contrast, the dark heights of the Minarets of the Ritter Range appear almost like chocolate icing—decorative and ephemeral. The difference between the two areas is in the type of rock, the Yosemite high country being primarily massive, resistant granites, and the Ritter Range being mostly metamorphosed volcanic rocks, alternating with some metasedimentary layers. The softer rock of metamorphosed volcanic origin was more easily quarried by the ice and water, allowing the more delicate and fragile sculpting.

This dramatic landscaping is the product of many inundations by glaciers, and evidences of these ancient ice fields are readily seen along trails in both Yosemite and the Devils Postpile/Ritter Range country. The size of some of these glaciers is hard to imagine, for, combined, they covered hundreds of square miles. The most impressive was the great Tuolumne glacier, emanating from the region of Mt. Lyell and Mt. Dana, which carved and polished the present Tuolumne and Tenaya basins. Incredible as it may seem, the Tenaya basin was scoured by an incidental overflow from the primary Tuolumne basin glacier, which was a *mer de glace* that once filled the Grand Canyon of the Tuolumne to its brim! The top of the Devils Postpile, a fascinating columnar basaltic formation, offers mute testimony to the awesome power of the shearing action of these glaciers. Feeder glaciers, like the ones that carved Echo Creek canyon, Triple Peak Fork canyon, Chain Lakes basin and Shadow Creek canyon, are responsible for much of the scenery described in the following trips. Huge deposits of rocky glacial debris called moraines compose significant parts of the landscape (e.g., the lateral moraines along the descent from Clouds Rest to Little Yosemite Valley). Other glacial manifestations that backpackers will see include domes, U-shaped valleys, glacial polish, erratics (boulders left by receding ice fields), striae (grooves) and hanging valleys (the valleys out of which leap the falls of Yosemite Valley are classic examples).

Man on this scene seems almost an afterthought. The first men were the Indians of the Mono and Ahwahneechee tribes. Primarily peaceful, seminomadic peoples, they hunted and fished the idyllic Yosemite and Mono regions long before white men came. Virtually all that remains to mark their occupancy of the land are place names. They carried on some trade and social intercourse with each other—the primary trade route was via Tuolumne Meadows and the present

Sunrise Trail—but for the most part they remained isolated.

The Mariposa Battalion of 1851 was the first white party to penetrate the Yosemite Valley, but the trapper Joseph Walker first crossed the Park and saw the Valley as early as 1833. From 1848 until the 1860s gold fever brought white men into the Sierra in swarms. By 1853 Lee Vining had made prospecting forays into the Mt. Dana country, and by 1859 a temporary boomtown grew up around Dogtown on what is now U.S. 395 near Conway Summit. After the discovery of the fabulous Comstock Lode east of Lake Tahoe, gold fever subsided in the Yosemite/Devils Postpile region, except for a brief flurry caused by the abortive excitement of the Tioga Mine near Tioga Pass, and it had all but died by the turn of the century. This speculative mine, although it never opened or mined a ton of ore, was responsible for the building of the Tioga Road.

In Yosemite Valley a burgeoning tourist trade arose, centering about the natural wonders of the Valley. In 1864 President Lincoln signed an Act of Congress giving Yosemite over to the care of the State of California in the form of a public-land grant. Galen Clark, who established Clark's Station, the current site of Wawona, was appointed Yosemite's first guardian, and he served in this capacity until 1879. In 1890 Yosemite was made a National Park, the grant to be administered by the U. S. Cavalry. This Army administration lasted until 1916, when the National Park Service was established. Short as it was, this interim period of U. S. Army administration based at Wawona saw many "firsts" in the Park. Its boundaries were patrolled to keep out infringing cattle- and sheepmen; fish were introduced to high-country lakes and streams (the new strains included golden, brook, brown, cutthroat, Dolly Varden and grayling); and an exploration and trail-blazing program was carried out that created trails still used today. This was an exciting pioneer period, and today's backpacker can glean a taste of its fascination by visiting the Pioneer Yosemite History Center at Wawona.

Anglers will find that this region abounds in "hot fishing spots." Some of them are the Merced River east of Little Yosemite Valley, the Royal Arch Lake-Chilnualna Lakes area and the Chain Lakes basin. Today four species of trout—rainbow, brook, brown and golden—make up the primary fishery of this area, although an occasional catch will be made of a hybrid or a cutthroat. Nearly all the lakes and streams of the high country have been planted in the past, but a new policy in Yosemite National Park calls for no more planting there. The effects of this policy remain to be seen.

Fishing on the lakes is best during the first three weeks after the ice has cleared (from late June to the end of July, depending on the altitude) and during the last few weeks of the season before the first snows (late September to mid October). After the streams clear up, fishing is generally good all summer long. Usually they clear up by early July; however, this date can be affected by late rains and by the ground cover on the particular stream's watershed.

Flies are preferred to bait by most backpackers for reasons of sport, esthetics and weight, and the clear waters of the high-country lakes and streams behoove the angler to use fine leader material and a wary approach. Experienced backpacking fishermen use a light-action fly rod (3-5 sections) strung with tapered line and leader. Novice anglers find that a spinning rod with a bubble-fly combination or a metal wobbler is easily mastered, and is effective against blustery afternoon winds on lakes.

Anglers should keep only the fish they will eat. A fishing trip's success is never measured solely by the number of pounds in the creel.

NOTE: Bears are now a problem in the Devils Postpile area as well as in Yosemite.

The Trailheads

Gibbs Lake Trailhead. Go 1.3 miles south from the junction of U.S. 395 and State Highway 120 just south of Lee Vining, turn right on the road signed *Horse Meadow*, and go 2.1 miles up it.

Tuolumne Meadows Campground. Turn south off State Highway 120 in Tuolumne Meadows east of the store and drive up the road nearest the river.

Tuolumne Meadows Lodge. Following State Highway 120 in Tuolumne Meadows, drive ½ mile east from the bridge over the Tuolumne River, turn right on a paved road, and go ¾ mile to the roadend parking lot to let your passengers out. You must park at one of the two backpackers' parking lots along this road.

Tioga Road Trailhead. Go 0.5 mile west of the Visitors Center in Tuolumne Meadows, or 0.5 mile east of the west end of the meadows.

Tenaya Lake. Park in the lot at the west end of Tenaya Lake on State Highway 120 in Yosemite, where signs indicate the Walk-in Campground.

Agnew Meadows. Go 9 miles west from U.S. 395 through Mammoth Lakes and over Minaret Summit. Turn right 2.7 miles from Minaret Summit and go ¼ mile to a parking area. There is an overflow parking area just beyond it. You may have to park just before Minaret Summit and take a shuttle-bus.

Devils Postpile. Go 9 miles west from U.S. 395 through Mammoth Lakes and over Minaret Summit. Turn right 6.7 miles from Minaret Summit to go 0.35 mile to a parking area at the spur road's end. You may have to park just before Minaret Summit and take a shuttlebus.

Glacier Point. Drive 9.3 miles up State Highway 41 from Yosemite Valley, turn left, and drive 15.5 more miles to a parking lot at road's end.

Happy Isles. Take the Yosemite Valley shuttle bus to Happy Isles, or park at Camp Curry and hike along a trail 1 mile southeast to Happy Isles.

Bridalveil Creek. Drive 9.3 miles up State Highway 41 from Yosemite Valley, turn left, drive 7.6 more miles to the Bridalveil Campground road, branching right, and follow this road through the campground to the southeast end of it.

Chiquito Pass Trailhead. From the north shore of Bass Lake, drive northeast 20 miles up Beasore Road 434 (which becomes Road 5S07) to Globe Rock. There, turn left and drive 2.4 miles up Road 5S04 to a signed trailhead atop a small, flat ridge area.

Granite Creek Campground. From the north shore of Bass Lake, drive northeast 20 miles up Beasore Road 434 (which becomes Road 5S07) to Globe Rock, then continue 9.8 miles along your road to the Minarets road, which goes south 52 paved miles to the town of North Fork. Still on Road 5S07, you reach the Clover Meadow Ranger Station in 1.7 miles, then continue past it for 0.5 mile to Road 4S57. Branch right on this road and follow it 1.0 mile to a hikers' parking area in Granite Creek Campground. Road 4S57 may be undrivable as late as early July.

Old Strawberry Mine Road. From the north shore of Bass Lake, drive northest 20 miles up Beasore Road 434 (which becomes 5S07) to Globe Rock, then continue on you road to Road 5S05, just 100 yards past Ethelfreda Creek. Veer left on Road 5S05 and follow it 2.3 miles to a trailhead at road's end.

54   Horse Meadow to Gibbs Lake

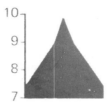

TRIP

From Horse Meadow to Gibbs Lake; round trip. Topo map *Mono Craters*. Best mid or late season; *8 miles* (12.8 km).

Grade	Trail/Layover days	Total recommended days
Leisurely	2/0	2
Moderate	....	....
Strenuous	....	....

HILITES

The destination of this trip is a little-known lake in the Minarets Wilderness on the dramatic east slope of the Sierra east of Yosemite Park. It's a great place to find peace and quiet, and for serious anglers there is a chance to catch some beautiful golden trout.

DESCRIPTION

1st Hiking Day (**Horse Meadow** to **Gibbs Lake**, 4 miles—6.4 km): Ordinary cars will have to park 2.1 miles up the dirt road from U.S. 395 in a little meadow that has a grove of aspen trees and a stream that runs until August. More mountain-worthy cars can ascend another mile to upper Horse Meadow.

We leave the lower meadow on a well-used dirt road that climbs through sagebrush and pinon pine, where Clark nutcrackers glide between scattered Jeffrey pines. After a short, moderate ascent the road arrives at long upper Horse Meadow, rimmed by aspens, white firs and Jeffrey pines, and threaded by an all-year stream. At the meadow's upper end we enter national forest, but remain in the lumber cutter's land, still looking forward to the true wilderness ahead.

Past the upper meadow the road forks, and 0.1 mile up the left fork is the trailhead that mountain-worthy cars can reach. We climb up a north-trending ridge, to an overlook of Lee Vining Canyon, 1000 feet below. Continuing the steep climb, we walk through more timber eligible for cutting and pass a road leading left (east). Just beyond a deer hunter's camp we come to a water ditch and then a sign heralding the wilderness ahead. From the ditch, the road ascends gently for ¼ mile and then mercifully ends. From the roadend, a trail takes off up a dry ravine that lies over a little ridge east from Gibbs Canyon creek. Then it crosses the ridge and dips down near the stream, where recent blazes mark the trail. We ascend through a cool forest of lodgepole, whitebark and silver pine, with an occasional mountain hemlock and with much Labrador tea along the creek, to the signed border of Minarets Wilderness. Here, perhaps, one will feel a distinct relief that autos and the rest of civilization are locked out beyond the invisible gate Congress erected here in 1963.

The remaining gentle climb to Gibbs Lake proceeds through moderate-to-dense forest near Gibbs Canyon creek, as we catch glimpses through the trees of the great Sierra crest dead ahead. There are fair-to-good campsites south of the outlet and west of the inlet of emerald-green Gibbs Lake (9500'). For the adventurous camper, an easy if steep route to Kidney Lake goes up the forested south side of the stream, and the expansive views of Mono Lake and the mountains around it are worth the climb. Most of the shore of this lake is barren, but some whitebark pines at the east end provide shelter for a primitive camp.

2nd Hiking Day: Retrace your steps, 4 miles (6.4 km).

Gibbs Lake

55   Tenaya Lake to Sunrise Camp

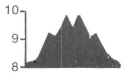

TRIP   From Tenaya Lake Walk-In Campground to Sunrise High Sierra Camp (round trip). Topo map *Tuolumne Meadows*. Best mid or late season; 11.4 miles (18.4 km).

Grade	Trail/layover days	Total recommended days
Leisurely	2/1	3
Moderate	2/0	2
Strenuous	....	....

HILITES   Although this route is very popular, being within the Yosemite High Sierra Camp network, the superb, unusual scenery of the high country makes this trip a must. The spectacular topography of the Tenaya canyon and of the serrated northwestern end of the Cathedral Range combine to overcome the most strident objections of the solitude-seeker.

DESCRIPTION

1st Hiking Day (**Tenaya Lake Walk-in Campground** to **Sunrise Camp**, 5.7 miles—9.2 km): From the campground parking lot (8149') the trail crosses the outlet of Tenaya Lake and skirts the meadowy edge of the walk-in campground. For a mile the trail winds south through moderate forest cover interrupted by small meadows where the quiet early-morning hiker will probably see browsing mule deer. The first part of this trail is lush with wildflowers as late as July, and one can expect to see blooming lupine, aster, larkspur, brodiaea and buttercup. Just past the stream from Lower Sunrise Lake the ascent begins to steepen, and soon it becomes a long series of rocky switchbacks up a slope clothed with pine and hemlock. From these switchbacks one can see the highway and can hear passing autos, but these are infinitesimal compared to the polished granite expanses of Tenaya Canyon. The Indian name for Tenaya Creek, Py-wi-ack ("Stream of the Shining Rocks"), was quite apt, for this canyon exhibits the largest exposed granite area in Yosemite, and its shining surfaces are barren except for sporadic clumps of hardy conifers that have found root in broken talus pockets.

Where the trail begins to rise, the long, gradual slope falling from the promontory called Clouds Rest comes into view in the south. This slope is a 4500-foot drop, one of the largest continuous rock slopes in the world. The traveler who feels sated by the panorama will find a different world to wonder at, right at his own boot-clad feet, for these slopes grow dozens of wildflower species, among them pussy paws, penstemon, paintbrush, lupine, streptanthus, aster, larkspur, brodiaea and buttercup. Finally the switchbacks end and the trail levels as it arrives at a junction with the lateral trail to Sunrise camp. Turning left (east), we stroll on a nearly level path under a sparse forest cover of pine and fir until the trail dips for about ¼ mile to the first Sunrise Lake. After passing the west side of the lake on a trail fringed with red mountain heather, we cross the outlet and ascend gradually northeast. Then the trail levels off and wanders roughly north through a sparse lodgepole forest. The second Sunrise Lake comes into view on the left, but we veer east and climb away from it, paralleling its inlet some distance from the cascading water. The few trees here are not enough to block our views of granite domes all around. Then our trail skirts the south side of the highest Sunrise Lake and begins a gradual ascent by crossing the lake's inlet stream.

Continuing southeast, we cross a little saddle and descend gradually almost straight south from the upper lake. After passing most of the hogback lying east of us, we swing northeast and switchback down to the floor of Long Meadow, intersecting the John Muir Trail at the south end of the meadow. There are fair campsites or, if advance reservations have been made, one may enjoy the luxury of a hot shower, a hot meal and a made-up bed at the High Sierra Camp (9320′). *2nd Hiking Day:* Retrace your steps. 5.7 miles (9.2 km).

56   Tioga Road to Cathedral Lake

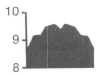

TRIP   From Trailhead on the Tioga Road (Tuolumne
          Meadows) to Cathedral Lake (round trip). Topo
          map *Tuolumne Meadows*. Best mid or late season;
          7.8 miles (12.6 km).

Grade	Trail/layover days	Total recom- mended days
Leisurely	2/0	2
Moderate	....	....
Strenuous	....	....

HILITES   Used since the time of the Indians, this trail offers
          some of the finest views of the Tuolumne Meadows
          region. Two large granite domes, Fairview and
          Medlicott, and the foremost landmark of the area,
          Cathedral Peak, line this route. Because of the
          relatively short mileage and the high-country
          scenery, this round trip is an excellent beginner's
          selection.

DESCRIPTION

1st Hiking Day (**Trailhead on Tioga Road** to **Cathedral Lake**, 3.9
miles—6.3 km): From the parking area (8560') on the Tioga
Road, we follow a gently ascending trail that is quite
objectionably dusty except after rainy sprinkles. (After this
initial section the trail itself is not bad at all, and the
panoramic views more than make up for the early unpleas-
antness.) A few steps from the trailhead our route crosses the
Tenaya Lake/Tuolumne Meadows Trail and then begins to
climb more steeply. After ½ mile of ascent under a welcome
forest cover, the trail levels off and descends to a small
meadow that is boggy in early season. From here we can see
the dramatically shaped tops of Unicorn Peak and The
Cockscomb, and the apparent granite dome in the south is in
reality the north ridge of Cathedral Peak, whose steeples are
out of sight over the "dome's" horizon.

The trail cruises gently up and down through more little meadows set in hemlock forest and then dips near a tinkling stream whose source, we discover after further walking, is a robust spring on a shady set of switchbacks. Beyond this climb our tread levels off on the west slope of Cathedral Peak and makes a long, gentle, sparsely forested descent on sandy underfooting to a junction with the spur trail to lower Cathedral Lake, where our route turns right. Periodically the traveler has westward views of another granite sentry left by the glacial ice, Medlicott Dome, and one can easily discern the difference between the rounded, polished tops of the domes and the jagged crest of Cathedral Peak. The domes were completely covered by the ice, whereas the top few hundred feet of Cathedral Peak stood above the grinding glacier, and hence was not rounded and smoothed by the ice.

From the junction, a ⅓-mile stroll across stream-braided meadows leads to the shores of lower Cathedral Lake (9320′). Fishing is poor for rainbow and brook (to 9″) but swimming is good. The views more than make up for the shortcomings, however, for from here Polly Dome, Cathedral Peak, Echo Peaks, Medlicott Dome and Unicorn Peak provide a rugged glacial setting.

2nd Hiking Day: Retrace your steps, 3.9 miles (6.3 km).

Tuolumne Meadows *National Park Service*

7   Tioga Road to Sunrise Camp

TRIP   From Trailhead on the Tioga Road (Tuolumne Meadows) to Sunrise High Sierra Camp (round trip). Topo map *Tuolumne Meadows*. Best mid or late season; 18.4 miles (29.6 km).

Grade	Trail/layover days	Total recommended days
Leisurely	4/1	5
Moderate	3/1	4
Strenuous	2/1	3

HILITES   The Sunrise Trail, of which this is the first leg, is a justly famous and popular route. Superlative views confront the traveler at every summit and oftentimes in between—views of whole ranges in the distance as well as spectacular peaks nearby.

DESCRIPTION (Leisurely trip)

1st Hiking Day: Follow Trip 56 to **Cathedral Lake**, 3.9 miles (6.3 km).

2nd Hiking Day (**Cathedral Lake** to **Sunrise High Sierra Camp**, 5.3 miles—8.5 km): First retrace the steps of the 1st hiking day to the Sunrise Trail at the foot of Cathedral Peak. Here our route turns right (south) and ascends gently to upper Cathedral Lake, a few yards to the right of the trail. Though camping is prohibited here, one may enjoy a stop for a snack and a swim. Our trail then skirts the east side of the lake and ascends to Cathedral Pass, where the excellent views include Cathedral Peak, Tresidder Peak, Echo Peaks, Matthes Crest, the Clark Range farther south and Matterhorn Peak far to the north. Beyond the pass is a long, beautiful swale, the headwaters of Echo Creek, where the midseason flower show is alone worth the trip. Our path traverses up the east flank of Tresidder Peak on a gentle climb to the actual high point of this trail, at a marvelous viewpoint overlooking most of southern Yosemite Park. The inspiring panorama includes the peaks around Vogelsang High Sierra Camp in the southeast, the whole Clark Range in the south, and the peaks on the Park border in both directions farther away. Then our high trail switchbacks quickly down to the head of the upper lobe of Long Meadow, levels off, and leads down a gradually sloping valley dotted with little lodgepole pines to the head of the second, lower lobe of l-o-n-g Long Meadow. Passing a junction with the trail down Echo Creek, this route continues its meadowy descent to the fair campsites along the stream at the south end of the meadow, past Sunrise High Sierra Camp, which is near the south end of the meadow, almost out of sight off to the west of the trail.

3rd and 4th Hiking Days: Retrace you steps, 9.2 miles (14.8 km).

Upper Cathedral Lake, Cathedral Peak

58   Tioga Road to Merced Lake

TRIP   Trailhead on the Tioga Road to Merced Lake via
             Echo Creek (shuttle trip). Topo maps *Tuolumne
             Meadows, Merced Peak*. Best mid or late season;
             34.2 miles (55.1 km).

Grade	Trail/layover days	Total recommended days
Leisurely	5/1	6
Moderate	4/1	5
Strenuous	3/0	3

HILITES   This looping excursion out of Tuolumne Meadows
              samples everything the Cathedral Range has to
              offer, from sweeping vistas at 10,000-foot passes to
              the deeply glaciated Merced River canyon to
              forested side streams with secluded campsites. For
              anglers there are lakes large and small, mead-
              owed creeks, and huge river pools.

DESCRIPTION (Leisurely trip)

1st Hiking Day: Follow Trip 56 to **Cathedral Lake**, 3.9 miles (6.3 km).

2nd Hiking Day (**Cathedral Lake** to **Echo Creek Crossing**, 9.0 miles—14.5 km): First, follow Trip 57 to the trail junction in Long Meadow. Here we turn left (east) on the signed Echo Creek Trail and ford the Long Meadow stream on boulders. The trail quickly switchbacks up to the top of the ridge that separates this stream from Echo Creek and then descends through dense hemlock-and-lodgepole forest toward the Cathedral Fork of Echo Creek. Where our route approaches this stream, we have fine views of the creek's water gliding down a series of granite slabs, and then the trail veers away from the creek and descends gently above it for more than a mile. Even in late season this shady hillside is watered by numerous rills that are bordered by still-blooming flowers. On this downgrade the trail crosses the Long Meadow stream, which has found an escape from that meadow through a gap between two large domes high above our trail.

Then our route levels out in a mile-long flat section of this valley where the wet ground yields a plus of wildflowers all summer but a minus of many mosquitos in early season. Beyond this flat "park," the trail descends a more open hillside, and where it passes the confluence of the two forks of Echo Creek, we can see across the valley the steep course of the east fork plunging down to its rendezvous with the west fork. Finally the trail levels off and reaches the good campsites just before a metal bridge over Echo Creek (8100'). Fishing in the creek is good for rainbow and golden trout to 10".

3rd Hiking Day (**Echo Creek Crossing** to **Merced Lake**, 4.9 miles—7.9 km): After crossing the bridge over Echo Creek, our trail leads down the forested valley and easily fords a tributary stream, staying well above the main creek. This pleasant, shaded descent encounters fibrous-barked juniper trees and then tall, brittle red firs as it drops to another metal bridge 1 mile from the last one. Beyond this sturdy span, the trail rises slightly and the creek drops precipitously, so that we are soon far above it. Then our sandy tread swings west away from Echo Creek and traverses down a hillside where views are excellent of Echo Valley, a wide place in the great Merced River canyon below. Our trail passes a junction with the High Trail, which leads west to the Sunrise Trail, and then descends south to a green-floored forest of mixed conifers threaded by a tinkling all-year stream and decorated with a brilliant array of mountain wildflowers.

Then a last series of switchbacks span the descent to the floor of Echo Valley, where we meet and turn left (east) on the Merced River Trail. After crossing several forks of Echo Creek on wooden bridges, we pass a burn area where a 1966 fire killed most of the mature trees. But already new, small lodgepoles grow by the hundreds, and the grassy valley floor is extensively decorated with the blue flowers of lupine and the white blossoms of yarrow and yampah. Leaving Echo Valley, the trail leads up immense granite slabs. In places, the path is an elevated dirt strip on the slabs held in place between two parallel rock walls; in other places the route is simply indicated by two rock borders on the slabs.

At the hairpin angle of a set of switchbacks, the trail comes
very close to the cascading Merced River, and a breather stop
here will allow the traveler to drink in the sights and sounds of
this dramatic part of the river—a long series of chutes,
cascades, falls, cataracts and pools that are all due to the
glacier which roughened up the formerly smooth bed of the
Merced River. Above this turbulent stretch, the trail levels off
beside the now-quiet river and arrives at the outlet of Merced
Lake (7216'). This large lake has a High Sierra Camp at its
east end, where the only presently legal campsites are. You
can buy a few provisions at the small store, or even rent a
rowboat to try your luck for rainbow and brown trout to 9". Be
sure to bearproof your food.

4th Hiking Day (**Merced Lake** to **Emeric Lake**, 5.6 miles—9.0
km): The first short mile of this day's hike follows an almost
level, wide, sandy path under a green forest canopy of fir and
pine, juniper and aspen. Immediately beyond a bridge over
roaring Lewis Creek we arrive at the Merced Lake Ranger
Station (emergency services available in summer) and beside
it find the Lewis Creek Trail, leading north. Quickly the
ascent up this cobbled trail becomes steep, and it remains so
for a panting half-mile-plus. Fortunately, Sierra junipers and
Jeffrey pines cast plenty of morning shade. The trail levels
momentarily as we pass a fine viewpoint for taking pictures of
Merced Lake, far below, and Half Dome, due west. One more
cobbled, steep climb leads to a junction with the Fletcher
Creek Trail, and we turn left onto this path. Several
switchbacks then descend to a wooden bridge over Lewis
Creek. From here the trail enters more open hillside as it
climbs moderately on a cobbled path bordered by proliferating
bushes of mountain whitethorn and huckleberry oak. Just
past a tributary ½ mile from Lewis Creek, we have fine views
of cataracts and waterfalls on Fletcher Creek where it rushes
down open granite slopes dotted with lodgepole pines. The
trail then passes very close to the creek before veering south
and climbing, steeply at times, on the now-familiar cobbling
placed by trail crews. Here one has more good views of
Fletcher Creek chuting and cascading down from the notch at
the base of a granite dome before it leaps off a ledge in free fall.
The few solitary pine trees on this otherwise blank dome
testify to nature's extraordinary persistence.

At the notch, our trail levels off near some nice but illegal
campsites, and then soon passes a side trail to Babcock Lake.
From this junction the sandy trail ascends steadily through a
moderate forest cover just east of Fletcher Creek. After a mile

this route breaks out into the open and begins to rise more steeply via rocky switchbacks. From these zigzags one can see nearby in the north the outlet stream of Emeric Lake—though not the lake itself, which is behind a dome just to the right of the outlet's notch. Leaving the trail, we cross Fletcher Creek, follow up this outlet and stroll along the northwest shore of Emeric Lake (9370′) to the excellent campsites midway along this shore. Fishing is often good for rainbow trout to 12″. Sometimes windy, this lake was nevertheless so still one night that one could see the Milky Way clearly reflected in it.

5th Hiking Day (**Emeric Lake** to **Tuolumne Meadows**, 10.8 miles—17.4 km): This is the longest hiking day on this trip, but the ascent is not too severe and it comes at the beginning. From Tuolumne Pass at the crest of the Cathedral Range, the rest is downhill.

After circling the head of Emeric Lake and crossing the inlet stream without benefit of trail, we find a trail at the northeast corner of the lake, at the base of a granite knoll. This trail leads east-northeast for 0.6 mile to an **X** junction in the valley of Fletcher Creek. Taking the left branch up the valley, we follow a rocky-dusty trail through the forest fringe of the long meadow that straddles Fletcher Creek. This trail climbs farther from the meadow and passes northwest of a bald prominence that sits in the center of the upper valley of Fletcher and Emeric creeks, separating the two. Topping a minor summit, the trail descends slightly and then winds levelly past a long series of lovely ponds that are interconnected in early season. Then, immediately beyond an abandoned section of old trail, there is a lakelet 100 yards in diameter that would offer good swimming around late August. Just beyond it, the old trail veers sharply right, and our rutted meadow trail, going left, ascends to the top of a little swale with another good swimming pond and reaches an overlook above Boothe Lake. Our trail contours along this meadowy hillside about 50 vertical feet above the lake, passing a junction with a rutted use trail down to the lake. About ¼ mile farther we reach west Tuolumne Pass and a junction with the trail to Vogelsang High Sierra Camp, from where we retrace most of the steps of Trip 64.

59   Tioga Road to Tenaya Lake

TRIP   Trailhead on the Tioga Road to Tenaya Lake via
              Cathedral Pass, Echo Creek and Sunrise Creek
              (shuttle trip). Topo maps *Tuolumne Meadows,
              Merced Peak*. Best mid or late season; 25.6 miles
              (41.2 km).

Grade	Trail/layover days	Total recom- mended days
Leisurely	4/1	5
Moderate	4/0	4
Strenuous	3/0	3

HILITES The first and last parts of this trip are along
             favorite and well-used trails, but in the middle we
             follow a little-used stretch of trail in the heart of
             Yosemite's spectacular glaciated highlands.
             Views of the immense domes and deep-cut canyons
             will impress the traveler's eye forever.

DESCRIPTION (Leisurely trip)

1st and 2nd Hiking Days: Follow Trip 58 to the **Echo Creek
crossing**, 12.9 miles (20.8 km).

3rd Hiking Day (**Echo Creek Crossing** to **Sunrise Creek**, 5.1
miles—8.2 km): First follow the third hiking day, Trip 58, to
the junction of the Echo Creek and High trails above the
Merced River. Here our route turns right (west) and climbs
rockily several hundred feet before leveling off above the
immense Merced River canyon. This trail segment was part of
the route from Yosemite Valley to Merced Lake until a path up
the canyon was constructed in 1931. Before that, the steep
canyon walls coming right down to the river near Bunnell
Point, the great dome to our southwest, had made passage
impossible. Finally a trail was built that bypasses the

narrowest part of the canyon by climbing high on the south wall, and the trail we are now on fell into relative disuse.

With fine views of obelisk-like Mt. Clark in the south, we descend gradually for ½ mile over open granite in a setting that is sure to give you a feeling of being above almost everything. Then the trail passes a stagnant lakelet and ascends to even better viewpoints for appreciating the grandeur of the glaciated granitic wonder of nature spread out before you. It takes time to grasp the immensity of Mt. Clark, Clouds Rest, Half Dome, Mt. Starr King, Bunnell Point, and the great unnamed dome across the canyon west of it. Our continuing ascent then rounds a ridge and veers north into a forest of handsome Jeffrey pines. Here the trail levels off, and it remains level for a mile of exhilarating walking through Jeffreys, lodgepoles and red firs which shade patch after patch of vivid green ferns and a complement of multihued floral displays. Still in forest, we descend slightly to meet the John Muir Trail, go right on it for 150 yards to the Forsyth Trail, and then go left up it 150 yards to the fair campsites on Sunrise Creek (8080'). Fishing in this enticing stream is only fair for small rainbow and brook trout.

4th Hiking Day: Reverse the steps of the 1st hiking day, Trip 61, 7.6 miles (12.2 km).

Looking up the Merced River Canyon

60   Tioga Road to Yosemite Valley

TRIP   From Trailhead on the Tioga Road (Tuolumne
                  Meadows) to Yosemite Valley via the Sunrise
                  Trail (shuttle trip). Topo maps *Tuolumne Meadows,
                  Merced Peak, Yosemite*. Best mid or late season;
                  21.8 miles (35.0 km).

Grade	Trail/layover days	Total recom- mended days
Leisurely	4/0	4
Moderate	3/0	3
Strenuous	2/0	2

HILITES   The Sunrise Trail route from the Meadows to the
                  Valley (a segment of the John Muir Trail) is one of
                  the Park's most famous and most used knapsack
                  routes. Its reputation is an honest one, for these
                  miles contain a magnificent range of flora and
                  fauna, and the trail surveys some of the Park's
                  best-known landmarks. This is a fine trip for the
                  beginning knapsacker who has a couple of shorter
                  trips under his (or her) belt, and has a taste for
                  more.

DESCRIPTION (Leisurely trip)

1st and 2nd Hiking Days: Follow Trip 57 to **Sunrise High Sierra
Camp**, 9.2 miles (14.8 km).
3rd Hiking Day (**Sunrise High Sierra Camp** to **Sunrise Creek**, 5.1

miles—8.2 km): The trail from Sunrise High Sierra Camp continues south through Long Meadow, undulating gently below the eastern crest of Sunrise Mountain. After climbing to a forested saddle over a mile past the meadows, the trail parallels the headwaters of Sunrise Creek, descending steeply by switchbacks down a rocky moraine. This moraine is the largest of a series of ridgelike glacial deposits in this area, and the gigantic granite boulders along their sides testify to the power of the *mer-de-glace* that once filled Little Yosemite Valley and its tributaries. One such "erratic," about the size of a compact car, was found poised on the side of Moraine Dome to the southwest, and geologists have determined that it came from the slopes of the peaks at the northwest end of the Cathedral Range. The current belief is that there were at least three and possibly four ice ages that covered the country with glaciers. Because of the glacial moraines, the forest cover—mainly lodgepole pine—occurs in splotchy, broken stands. On the descent of the moraine, where Sunrise Creek is in a gully on the left, a remarkable flower display will tempt one to stop and try to identify a species or two. At the foot of the morainal descent, the trail crosses Sunrise Creek, and then descends on a westward course to the fair campsites on Sunrise Creek (8080') 150 yards up the Forsyth Trail from our trail's junction with it. Fishing on Sunrise Creek is poor-to-fair for rainbow and brook (fry).

4th Hiking Day (**Sunrise Creek** to **Yosemite Valley**, 7.5 miles—12.0 km): First retrace your steps 150 yards south to the first junction. Back on the John Muir Trail, our route continues southwest on a gradual descent, passing the High Trail to Merced Lake. Our trail is bounded on the north by the Pinnacles, on the south ridge by the Clouds Rest eminence, and on the south by Moraine Dome. Francois Matthes, in an interesting "detective story" written in the form of a geological essay (Professional Paper 160), discusses Moraine Dome extensively. He deduced, using three examples (one was the "erratic" cited above), that the moraines around the dome were the product of at least *two* glacial ages—a notion contrary to the thinking of the time. The morainal till of the last glacial age characterizes the underfooting of our descent into Little Yosemite Valley. A mile from the last junction is a ford of Sunrise Creek in a red-fir forest whose stillness is broken by the creek's gurgling and by the occasional screams of Steller jays. In another mile we pass the trail to Clouds Rest, and about ½ mile from there, the lateral to Half Dome (about 4 miles round trip). From this junction our shady path switchbacks down through a changing forest cover that comes to include some stately incense-cedars with their burnt orange, fibrous bark.

There are improved campsites on Sunrise Creek at the foot of the descent, and more numerous ones along the Merced River south of the river trail. A summer ranger is on duty near the trail junction. This is prime bear territory, so be sure to secure your food.

From here, reverse the steps of the 1st hiking day, Trip 81, to Yosemite Valley.

Half Dome from Glacier Point

Tenaya Lake to Yosemite Valley **61**

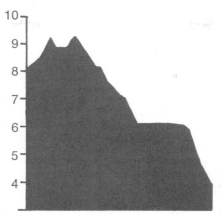

TRIP From Tenaya Lake Walk-in Campground to Yosemite Valley (shuttle trip). Topo maps *Tuolumne
Meadows, Merced Peak, Yosemite*. Best mid or late
season; 15.1 miles (24.2 km).

Grade	Trail/layover days	Total recom-mended days
Leisurely	2/1	3
Moderate	2/0	2
Strenuous	....	....

HILITES Through an elevation change of over 5000 feet
(mostly down hill) this route covers most of
Yosemite's spectrum of life zones. Views from
various points above Tenaya Canyon are breathtaking in their panoramic scope. By contrast, a
different kind of appreciation is evoked when
walking alongside the serene waters of the Merced
River as it serpentines across the floor of Little
Yosemite Valley. The ever-changing nature of a
river is a high point of this trip—slides, cascades,
and earth-shaking waterfalls add exclamation
points. This route is a fine selection for the
intermediate backpacker who has never had a
taste of Yosemite's varied backcountry.

DESCRIPTION

1st Hiking Day (**Tenaya Lake Walk-In Campground** to **Sunrise Creek**, 7.6 miles—12.2 km): First, follow Trip 55 to the junction of the trail going east to Sunrise Camp. From the junction, our trail makes a 320-foot descent on switchbacks, rises over a talus-swollen little ridge, and drops beside a pleasant-looking lakelet. The lightly forested hillside ahead leads up to three unnamed streams that we cross in quick succession. This watery slope is boggy till midseason, and the plentiful groundwater nourishes rank gardens of wildflowers throughout the summer. Leveling off beyond the streams, our trail meets the 2-mile trail to the summit of Clouds Rest. Hikers with plenty of energy may take this short lateral to this lofty prominence. Views from Clouds Rest are among the most spectacular in the Sierra, including a 4500-foot continuous granite slope stretching all the way down to Tenaya Creek and rising on the other side—the largest exposed granite area in the Park.

From the Clouds Rest junction, the trail meanders over sandy, level terrain for ½ mile, detouring around many fallen trees, before it starts its plunge down toward Sunrise Creek. This switchbacking descent is a little tough on the knees but in repayment the green fir-and-pine forest is a classic of its kind, and occasional views down into the Merced River Canyon are sweeping in their range. Finally our trail approaches a stream, parallels it for almost ½ mile, fords it and then fords Sunrise Creek to the fair campsites on the creek (8080'). Fishing for rainbow and brook (fry) is poor-to-fair.

2nd Hiking Day: Follow the 4th hiking day, Trip 60, 7.5 miles (12.0 km).

Tuolumne Meadows to Nelson Lake 62

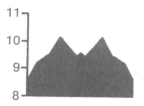

TRIP   From Tuolumne Meadows Campground to Nelson Lake (round trip). Topo map *Tuolumne Meadows*. Best mid or late season; 11.8 miles (19.0 km).

Grade	Trail/layover days	Total recom- mended days
Leisurely	....	....
Moderate	2/1	3
Strenuous	....	....

HILITES   This interesting and varied route visits the scenic Elizabeth Lake basin and then crosses the serrated Cathedral Range to Nelson Lake. No trail route offers finer views of those geologic wonders called Unicorn Peak and the Cockscomb. Open, meadow-fringed Nelson Lake makes a pleasantly fitting end to this exciting trip, and anglers can look forward to good brook-trout fishing on the placid waters of this alpine gem.

DESCRIPTION

1st Hiking Day (**Tuolumne Meadows Campground** to **Nelson Lake,** 5.9 miles—9.5 km): To reach the trailhead, walk to the Group Camping Section of the Tuolumne Meadows campground, where the signed trail begins across from a masonry building. In a few hundred feet we cross the Tenaya Lake/Lyell Canyon Trail and then continue a steady southward ascent. The shade-giving forest cover is almost entirely lodgepole pine as the trail crosses several runoff streams that dry up by late summer. More than a mile from the start, our route veers close to Unicorn Creek, and the music of this dashing, gurgling, cold-water stream makes the climb easier. When the ascent finally ends, the hiker emerges at the foot of a long meadow containing Elizabeth Lake, at the foot of striking Unicorn Peak.

Past Elizabeth Lake, the meadow gives way to a moderately dense forest cover of lodgepole interspersed with mountain hemlock, and the trail climbs, steeply, then moderately, and steeply again. A few hundred feet before you reach the ridge crest, you come to a late-lingering snowbank where the trail splits. If you go left, you will pass through a narrow gully between granite walls. If you go right, you will walk up a bare granite-sand slope. I recommend that if you have a full pack, you take the right trail going to Nelson Lake and the left one returning, because of some steep places on the left trail just beyond the crest.

Because of the close proximity of the Cockscomb, about 1 mile due west, the hiker has excellent views of that knifelike spire from just beyond the left pass. Well-named by Francois Matthes, this slender crest bears clear marks of the highest level reached by the ice of the last glacial episode. Its lower shoulders reveal the rounded, well-polished surfaces that betray glacial action, while its jagged, sharply etched crest shows no such markings. Further evidence of glacial action may be clearly seen on the steep descent into the head of long, typically **U**-shaped Echo Creek valley. The shearing and polishing action of the ice mass that shaped this rounded valley is evident on the cliffs on the west side.

About ⅓ mile from where the trail split, and several hundred yards beyond the crest, the forks come together again on a steep, tree-dotted, ravined hillside. As our route descends along winding, clear, meadowed Echo Creek for about 2 miles, the valley floor is lush with wildflower growth. During midseason the passerby can expect to see Davidson's penstemon, Douglas phlox, groundsel, red heather, lupine and swamp whiteheads. At the end of the second large meadow in this canyon, our trail leaves Echo Creek and veers east up a low, rocky ridge, undulating through sparse forest. One is almost at Nelson Lake (9636') before he can see his destination, meadow-fringed at the foot of imposing granite Peak 11282. Good campsites may be found on the southeast and southwest sides. Anglers will find the lake's waters good fishing for brook trout (7-11").

2nd Hiking Day: Reverse your steps, 5.9 miles (9.5 km).

Tuolumne Meadows to Lyell Canyon 63

TRIP
From Tuolumne Meadows Lodge to Lyell Base Camp (round trip). Topo map *Tuolumne Meadows*. Best early, mid or late season; 17.4 miles (28.0 km).

Grade	Trail/layover days	Total recommended days
Leisurely	2/0	2
Moderate	....	....
Strenuous	....	....

HILITES
Alpine meadows have a fascination that claims the trail traveler, whether he be novice or hoariest veteran. Campers' descriptions of favorite camping places invariably favor the forested western fringe of a remote meadow (your camp gets the first warming sunlight there). The meadows of Lyell Canyon are the stuff of which such memories are built. Idyllic from beginning to end, this long, gentle grassland with its serpentining river is a delight to travel.

DESCRIPTION

1st Hiking Day (**Tuolumne Meadows Lodge** to **Lyell Base Camp**, 8.7 miles—14.0 km): The trailhead is in the Tuolumne Meadows Lodge grounds, southwest of the office-dining room. The route goes about 100 yards to the Dana Fork of the river, and crosses it on a bridge. Then this segment of the John Muir Trail leads over a slight rise and descends to the Lyell Fork, where there is a substantial double bridge. The meadows above this bridge are among the most delightful in all the Sierra, and anytime you happen to be staying all night at the lodge or nearby, they are a wonderful place to spend the last hour before dinner. Mts. Dana and Gibbs fill the eastern horizon, catching the late sun, and the river has good fishing for brown trout.

About 50 yards past the bridge we meet the trail that comes up the river from the campground, turn left (east) onto it, and skirt a long, lovely section of the meadow. This re-routed trail is relatively new, established because of extensive trail wear and subsequent erosion of the old route. Re-routing is one of several far-sighted Park Service policies that have been adopted to allow areas in the wilderness a "breather"—a chance to recover from overuse. Going through a dense forest cover of lodgepole pine, our route passes the trail that ascends south to Tuolumne Pass and Vogelsang High Sierra Camp, and then fords Rafferty Creek. This ford may be difficult in early season, but you may find a log 200 yards down stream.

From this point on, the trail traverses alternating meadowed and forested sections as it veers southward, and the silent walker may come upon grazing deer in the meadows and an occasional marmot that has ventured from the rocky hillside on the right. Fields of wildflowers color the grasslands from early to late season, but the best time of the year for seeing this color is generally early-to-mid season. From the more open portions of the trail, one has excellent views of the Kuna Crest as it slopes up to the southeast and the river itself has delighted generations of mountain photographers. Our route then passes a trail branching southwest to Evelyn Lake and Tuolumne Pass. There are fair campsites around this junction. Beyond this junction the trail fords Ireland Creek (difficult in early season), passes below Potter Point, and ascends gently for 2 miles to the fair campsites at Lyell Base Camp (9040'). Fishing is fair for brook trout. This base camp, surrounded on three sides by steep canyon walls, marks the end of the meadowed sections of Lyell Canyon, and is the traditional first-night stopping place for those touring the John Muir Trail beginning at Tuolumne Meadows.

2nd Hiking Day: Retrace your steps, 8.7 miles (14.0 km).

Mt. Lyell above Lyell Canyon

Tuolumne Meadows to Vogelsang **64**

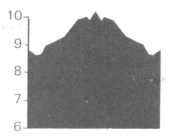

TRIP   **Tuolumne Meadows Lodge** to **Vogelsang High Sierra Camp** (round trip). Topo map *Tuolumne Meadows*. Best mid or late season, 15.4 miles (24.8 km).

Grade	Trail/layover days	Total recom- mended days
Leisurely	2/1	3
Moderate	2/0	2
Strenuous	....	....

HILITES   Vogelsang Camp has the most dramatic setting of all the famous High Sierra Camps. Located right under the somber north face of Fletcher Peak, it has an authentic alpine atmosphere. Many nearby lakes offer exciting side-trip possibilities for anglers, swimmers and picnickers.

DESCRIPTION

1st Hiking Day (**Tuolumne Meadows Lodge** to **Vogelsang High Sierra Camp**, 7.7 miles—12.4 km): First, follow Trip 63 to the John Muir Trail-Rafferty Creek Trail junction. Here our route turns right and immediately begins the toughest climb of this entire trip. Even so, the grade is moderate as often as it is steep, the trail is fairly well shaded by lodgepole pines, and the length of the climb is well under a mile. Then, as the ascent decreases to a gentle grade, we pass through high, boulder-strewn meadows that offer good views eastward of reddish-brown Mts. Dana and Gibbs, and gray-white Mammoth Peak. Soon the trail dips close to Rafferty Creek, and since this stream flows all year you can count on refreshment here. Then the nearly level trail passes above an orange snowcourse marker in a large meadow below and continues its long, gentle ascent through a sparse forest of lodgepole pines unmixed with

a single tree of any other species. About ⅓ mile beyond a
stream that dries up in late summer, we ford another that also
does in some years and immediately veer right at a junction
where the abandoned old trail up the long meadow veers left.
Our relocated trail up a cobbly hillside was built to allow the
damaged meadow below to recover from the pounding of too
many feet—people's and, especially, horses'.

Finally the exclusive lodgepole pines allow a few whitebark
pines to join their company, and these trees diminish the force
of the winds that often sweep through Tuolumne Pass.
Through breaks in this forest one has intermittent views of
cliff-bound, dark-banded Fletcher Peak and Peak 11799 in the
south. Then our path leaves the green-floored forest and leads
out into an area of bouldery granite outcroppings dotted with a
few trees. Around this granite and past these trees we wind
down to the west side of saucer-shaped Tuolumne Pass, a
major gap in the Cathedral Range. Taking the signed trail to
Vogelsang here, we follow a rocky-dusty path up a moderately
steep hillside below which Boothe Lake and its surrounding
meadows lie serene in the west. Finally, our trail reaches the
top of this climb, and suddenly we see the tents of Vogelsang
High Sierra Camp (10,180′) spread out before us. A few snacks
may be bought here, or dinner or breakfast if you make a
reservation. There are good campsites by Fletcher Creek just
beyond the camp, but remember the bears that live here are
always interested in your food.

2nd Hiking Day: Retrace you steps, 7.7 miles (12.4 km).

Looking north from Tuolumne Pass

Tuolumne Meadows to Emeric Lake **65**

TRIP   From Tuolumne Meadows Lodge to Emeric Lake via Vogelsang, Lewis Creek and Fletcher Creek; semiloop trip. Topo maps *Tuolumne Meadows, Merced Peak.* Best mid or late season; 28.8 miles (46.3 km).

Grade	Trail/layover days	Total recom- mended days
Leisurely	4/1	5
Moderate	3/0	3
Strenuous	2/0	2

HILITES   With Tuolumne Pass as the neck of the noose, this trip "lassos" Vogelsang Peak by dashing down the valley of Lewis Creek and then cruising back up the valley of Fletcher Creek. In addition to the spectrum of views of this fine peak, the traveler will constantly have good vistas of many parts of the Cathedral Range, and for anglers there is good fishing in both creeks and at Emeric Lake.

DESCRIPTION (Leisurely trip)

1st Hiking Day: Follow Trip 64 to **Vogelsang High Sierra Camp,** 7.7 miles (12.4 km).

2nd Hiking Day (**Vogelsang High Sierra Camp** to **Florence Creek,** 4.3 miles—6.9 km): Taking the Vogelsang Pass Trail from the camp, we descend slightly to ford Fletcher Creek on boulders and then begin a 550 foot ascent to the pass. The panting hiker is rewarded, as always in the Sierra, with increasingly good views. Fletcher Peak rises grandly on the left, far north is Mt.

Conness, and Clouds Rest and then Half Dome come into view in the west-southwest. The trail skirts above the west shore of Vogelsang Lake as we look down on the turfy shores and the large rock island of this timberline lake. Nearer the pass, views to the north are occluded somewhat, but expansive new views appear in the south: from left to right are Parsons Peak, Simmons Peak, Mt. Maclure, the tip of Mt. Lyell behind Maclure, Mt. Florence and, in the south, the entire Clark Range, from Triple Divide Peak on the left to Mt. Clark on the right.

From the windswept pass the trail rises briefly northeast before it follows steep switchbacks down into sparse lodgepole forest where many small streams provide moisture for thousands of lupine plants, with their light blue, pea-family flowers. The singing of the unnamed outlet stream from Gallison Lake becomes clear as the trail begins to level off, and then we reach a flat meadow through which the stream slowly meanders. There is a fine campsite beside this meadow, though wood fires are illegal here. Proceeding down a rutted, grassy trail for several hundred yards, we come to a brief, steep descent on a rocky path that swoops down to the meadowed valley of multi-braided Lewis Creek. In this little valley in quick succession we boulderhop the Gallison Lake outlet and then cross Lewis Creek on a log. In a few minutes we pass the steep ½ mile lateral to Bernice Lake. The shady trail winds gently down east of the creek under a moderate overhead canopy of lodgepole pine mixed with some hemlock, crossing a little stream about ½ mile from the last ford. Then, after almost touching the creek opposite a steep, rusty west canyon wall, the trail veers away and crosses another small tributary stream as it winds through dense hemlock forest to the good campsites beside Florence Creek (9200'). This year-round creek cascades down to the camping area over steep granite sheets, and the water sounds are a fine sleeping potion at bedtime. Fishing in Florence and Lewis creeks is good for brook trout to 12".

3rd Hiking Day (**Florence Creek** to **Emeric Lake**, 6.0 miles—9.6 km): Leaving the densely shaded hemlock forest floor, our trail descends a series of lodgepole-dotted granite slabs, and Lewis Creek makes pleasant noises in a string of chutes not far away on the right. Then, where the creek's channel narrows, the traveler will find on his left a lesson in exfoliation: granite layers peeling like an onion. One is more used to seeing this kind of peeling on Yosemite's domes, but this fine example is located on a canyon slope. As the bed of Lewis Creek steepens to deliver the stream's water to the Merced River far below, so does the trail steepen, and our descent to middle altitudes reaches the zone of red firs and silver pines. After dipping beside the creek, the trail climbs away from it to a junction with the High Trail, which leads south along the rim of the Merced River canyon.

From this junction the Lewis Creek Trail, now out of earshot of the creek, switchbacks down moderately, sometimes steeply, under a sparse cover of red fir, juniper, and lodgepole and silver pine for 1 mile to a junction with the Fletcher Creek Trail. We turn right onto this trail and follow the latter part of the 4th hiking day, Trip 58, to Emeric Lake.

4th Hiking Day: Follow the 5th hiking day, Trip 58, to **Tuolumne Meadows**, 10.8 miles (17.4 km).

Mt. Clark above Emeric Lake

66   Tuolumne Meadows to Lyell Fork

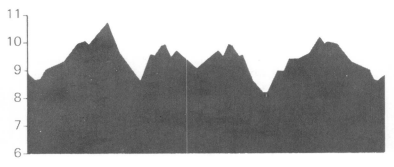

TRIP   From Tuolumne Meadows Lodge to Lyell Fork,
             Merced River, via Vogelsang, Lewis Creek, return
             via Fletcher Creek, Babcock Lake, Boothe Lake;
             semiloop trip. Topo maps *Tuolumne Meadows*,
             Merced Peak. Best mid or late season, 40.3 miles
             (64.9 km).

Grade	Trail/layover days	Total recom-mended days
Leisurely	7/1	8
Moderate	6/1	7
Strenuous	4/0	4

HILITES Every beginning backpacker sooner or later wants
             to try his newfound skills on a challenging trip of
             some length. This excursion in Yosemite Park is
             made to order for him: long mileage but not too
             long; tough climbs, but manageable ones; lonely
             stretches, but two popular campsites in between.
             And it's all wrapped up in some of the best scenery
             in Yosemite National Park.

DESCRIPTION (Moderate trip)

1st and 2nd Hiking Days: Follow Trip 65 to **Florence Creek**,
12.0 miles (19.3 km).

3rd Hiking Day (**Florence Creek** to **Lyell Fork**, 7.4 miles—11.9
km): First, follow the 3rd hiking day, Trip 65, to the junction of
the High Trail and the Lewis Creek Trail, and turn left. The
ascent from here is a tough, unrelieved 1000 vertical feet, but
fortunately most of it is in shady forest of red fir and silver

and lodgepole pine. Near the top, where the grade is a little less steep, the panting hiker is also shaded by altitude-preferring whitebark pines. At about 9000 feet, views to the west and north grow expansive, and one can make out Half Dome, Clouds Rest, the Cockscomb and Unicorn Peak. After crossing a ridge, our sandy path descends into a meadow long since invaded by lodgepole trees and reaches an all-year stream where you can refill your body's cooling system depleted by the long climb. Beyond this easy ford the High Trail lives up to its name as it traverses a broad bench about 10,000 feet above sea level. A second all-year stream, larger than the last, can present slight fording problems in early season. Then the trail climbs again, away from the lip of the main canyon, until it veers south back to the lip at a spectacular viewpoint for studying the headwaters of the Lyell Fork (in the east) and the Merced Peak Fork (in the south) of the Merced River. One could spend many days in these vast, trailless headwaters without seeing another human being.

From this overlook the trail descends a bit steeply in places to a third all-year stream, an easy boulderhop, and then continues down to the cascading, chuting Lyell Fork (9080'). The last segment of trail before the stream, over granite slabs, is a little hard to follow, but the route leads where you would expect it to. The campsites at the ford are poor, but good ones lie 150 yards downstream, where the chutes and rapids flowing over the sculpted granite bedrock are fine visual attractions and provide good music to sleep by. There are also good campsites ½ mile upstream, a better base if you are going to explore the remote lake basins at the headwaters of the Lyell Fork. Fishing in the Lyell Fork is good for brook trout to 11".

4th Hiking Day (**Lyell Fork** to **Babcock Lake**, 9.1 miles—14.7 km): First, retrace your steps to the Lewis Creek Trail and turn left (south). From this junction the Lewis Creek Trail, now out of earshot of the creek, switchbacks down moderately, sometimes steeply, under a sparse cover of red fir, juniper, and lodgepole and silver pine for 1 mile to a junction with a trail that comes steeply up from the main canyon floor. We turn right on this trail and follow several switchbacks down to a bridge over tree-shaded Lewis Creek. From here the rocky trail enters more open hillside as it climbs moderately on a cobbled path bordered by clumps of mountain whitethorn and huckleberry oak. Just past a tributary ½ mile from Lewis Creek we have fine views of cataracts and waterfalls on Fletcher Creek where it rushes down open granite slopes dotted with lodgepole pines. The trail then passes very close to the splashing creek before veering northeast and climbing, steeply at times, on the now-familiar cobbling placed by trail crews. Here one has more good views of Fletcher Creek chuting and cascading down from the notch at the base of a granite dome before it leaps off a ledge in free fall. The few solitary pine trees on this otherwise blank dome are mute testimony to nature's extraordinary persistence.

At the notch our trail levels off near some nice but illegal campsites and soon arrives at the trail to Babcock Lake. Turning left (north) we ford Fletcher Creek (difficult in early season) and follow a winding trail ⅓ mile west to narrow, granite-bound Babcock Lake (8983'). There are fine campsites all around this forested lake, and fishing is good for brook trout to 10".

5th Hiking Day (**Babcock Lake** to **Boothe Lake**, 4.4 miles—7.1 km): After retracing our steps to the Fletcher Creek Trail, we turn left (north). From this junction the sandy trail ascends steadily through a moderate forest cover just east of the verdant banks of rollicking Fletcher Creek. After a mile, the trail breaks out into the open and begins to rise more steeply via rocky but shaded switchbacks. These zigzags lead to another notch between two granite domes, and upon reaching this notch the slogging traveler suddenly achieves a wonderful panorama. A long, barely sloping, lush meadow stretches several miles ahead, and it is flanked on both sides by soaring, snow-streaked peaks. Down this meadow flows Fletcher Creek, meandering from pool to trout-holding pool. Here one has the feeling of being in truly high country, and the distance passes easily as we stroll to an **X** junction with trails to Emeric Lake and Vogelsang. From this junction follow part of the 5th hiking day, Trip 58, to the overlook of Boothe Lake (9900') and then leave the trail to find the good campsites on the south side of the lake.

6th Hiking Day (**Boothe Lake** to **Tuolumne Meadows Lodge**, 7.4 miles—11.9 km): First, hike briefly cross country back to the trail you left at the end of the previous hiking day. From that point, near broad Tuolumne Pass, hike up to the junction in the pass, and then retrace most of the steps of Trip 64.

Tuolumne Meadows to Triple Peak Fork 67

TRIP From Tuolumne Meadows Lodge to the Triple Peak Fork of the Merced River via Vogelsang, Lewis Creek, return via Washburn Lake, Fletcher Creek, Emeric Lake. Topo maps *Tuolumne Meadows, Merced Peak*. Best mid or late season; 51.0 miles (82.1 km).

Grade	Trail/layover days	Total recommended days
Leisurely	8/1	9
Moderate	7/0	7
Strenuous	4/0	4

HILITES The headwaters of the Triple Peak Fork of the Merced River are about as far as one can get from civilization, so this is a trip for those who feel they encounter too many people on most of their hikes. Their opportunity to view most of the High Sierra from the southern border of Yosemite is won by a long walk through grand high country.

DESCRIPTION (Moderate trip)

1st, 2nd and 3rd Hiking Days: Follow Trip 66 to the **Lyell Fork of the Merced River**, 19.1 miles (30.7 km).

4th Hiking Day (**Lyell Fork** to **Triple Peak Fork**, 6.9 miles—11.1 km): This day's hike starts off strenuously up switchbacks on the south wall of the Lyell Fork canyon. As we progress slowly up the rocky path, views open up to reward us for our struggle. In the northeast, on the Sierra crest, are Mt. Maclure and Mt. Lyell, highest point in Yosemite Park. After Lyell passes from view, Rodger Peak, second highest in the Park, appears as the dark triangle beyond the right flank of Peak 12132. Other towering peaks in view this side of the crest don't even have

names, but in the company of lesser summits they surely would
have. Where our trail extends close to the lip of the Merced
River canyon, we can step off the path to an overlook for
viewing most of the Clark Range in the southwest, and Clouds
Rest in the northwest.

Beyond the top of the ascent, the route winds among large
boulders on "gruss"—granite sand—which is the result of the
breakup of just such boulders by the fierce erosional forces at
work in these alpine climates. After crossing a seasonal
stream, the trail ascends to a second broad ridge from which
views through the whitebark-pine trees continue to be
excellent. About ½ mile beyond this ridge a trail to Foerster
Lake veers off to the left. This unsigned trail is indicated by
parallel rock borders and occasional flame-shaped blazes on
trees. Secluded Foerster Lake has no fish, but swimming and
camping there are excellent.

From this spur trail our route makes a long descent,
paralleling Foerster Lake's outlet part of the way, to a boulder
ford of Foerster Creek. The well-shaded trail then undulates
past a number of pocket meadows to another small stream,
and yet another not shown on the map. A gentle traverse
downward extends almost a mile to a small creek that winds
through a flat area densely forested with hemlock and
lodgepole pine. From this flat the High Trail begins a climb
that doesn't end until it reaches the Yosemite border at Isberg
Pass. Very soon the trail fords the outlet of the unnamed lake
north of Isberg Peak, and in another 200 yards it reaches a
large cairn which marks the junction with a trail down to the
Triple Peak Fork. All hikers who arrive here with any surplus
energy will greatly enjoy a 4-mile round trip to Isberg Pass
before heading down to camp on the Triple Peak Fork.

The trail to the pass first climbs moderately for ¼ mile up a
beautiful hillside covered with whitish broken granite in
whose cracks a dozen species of alpine wildflowers grow.
Looking west and north from this slope, one can see all the
peaks of the Clark Range and most of the peaks of the
Cathedral Range. Using your *Tuolumne Meadows* map, you
can probably make out Tenaya Peak, Tressider Peak,
Cathedral Peak, Echo Peaks, Matthes Crest and the
Cockscomb. At the top of this little climb a truly marvelous
sight comes into view, for here we enter a large, high bowl
nearly encircled by great peaks which has in it an enormous
meadow and two sparkling lakes. Here and there, clumps of
whitebark and lodgepole pines help give scale to the vast
amphitheater, and the delicateness of the meadow flowers is a

perfect counterpoint to the massiveness of the encircling summits. The setting is absolutely euphoric.

On the far side of the bowl, the trail begins to rise toward the crest and soon comes to a junction where the right fork leads to Post Peak Pass and the left to Isberg Pass, ¾ mile away. The left fork ascends moderately a short way to reach the height of the pass, and then contours over to it. The best views—other than those we have already been enjoying for the last several miles—are to be had from a point on the ridgeline a few hundred yards beyond the sign-marked pass. You can see most of the High Sierra, from the Ritter Range close in the east, to peaks around Mt. Goddard southwest of Bishop.

Back at the cairned junction, our route turns west and starts straight downhill, then veers southwest and switchbacks down into deep hemlock forest, turning north for the last ¾ mile down to the river. There are good campsites around the junction of our trail and the trail to Red Peak Pass, which begins just across the placid Triple Peak Fork (9100'). Fishing is good for brook and rainbow trout to 9".

5th Hiking Day (**Triple Peak Fork** to **Washburn Lake**, 6.9 miles—11.1 km): Reverse the 4th and part of the 3rd hiking day, Trip 87, to the good campsites at the head of Washburn Lake.

6th Hiking Day (**Washburn Lake** to **Emeric Lake**, 7.3 miles—11.8 km): The sandy trail along the east side of Washburn Lake leads over slopes dotted with white fir, aspen, juniper, lodgepole pine and Jeffrey pine, and from these slopes on a typical morning, the still water makes a fine mirror for the soaring granite cliffs across the lake. Beyond this lake, our descending trail stays near the singing river in open forest, fording a small stream every quarter mile or so as it descends on a moderate grade. Then the canyon floor begins to widen, and the trail proceeds levelly under a canopy of imposing Jeffrey pines and other tall conifers to a junction with the Lewis Creek Trail beside the Merced Lake Ranger Station. Here we turn right and follow the latter part of the 4th hiking day, Trip 58, to Emeric Lake.

7th Hiking Day (**Emeric Lake** to **Tuolumne Meadows Lodge**, 10.8 miles—17.4 km): Follow the 5th hiking day, Trip 58.

68 Tuolumne Meadows to Agnew Meadows

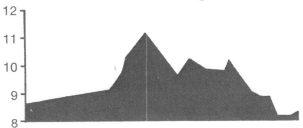

TRIP   From Tuolumne Meadows Lodge to Agnew
                 Meadows via Donohue Pass, Island Pass,
                 Thousand Island Lake, Shadow Lake (shuttle
                 trip). Topo maps *Tuolumne Meadows*, *Devils Post-
                 pile*. Best mid or late season; 28.2 miles (45.5 km).

Grade	Trail/layover days	Total recom- mended days
Leisurely	5/1	6
Moderate	4/1	5
Strenuous	4/0	4

HILITES   "Sky parlor" meadows, alpine lakes, clear, icy
                 streams, magnificent peaks—this trip has them
                 all. Except for the last 4 miles, this route follows
                 the well-known John Muir Trail as it tours Lyell
                 Canyon and the view-filled eastern slopes of the
                 Ritter Range. Because of its fame, this trail sees a
                 lot of use, but the incomparable scenery enroute
                 more than compensates for the lack of solitude.

DESCRIPTION (Moderate trip)

1st Hiking Day: Follow Trip 63 to **Lyell Base Camp**, 9 miles
(14.5 km).
2nd Hiking Day (**Lyell Base Camp** to **Rush Creek**, 7 miles—11.3
km): From Lyell Base Camp the trail ascends the steep,
southern terminal wall of Lyell Canyon above the west side of
the Lyell Fork. There is no water here in late season. Just
before the confluence of the Maclure Creek tributary of the
Lyell Fork, our route crosses a bridge to the east side and
switchbacks up to some very used campsites just before
another bridge. The rocky underfooting above here is
pleasantly relieved by superb alpine meadows. Along the first

3 miles of this day's ascent, views of the glaciers on the north faces of Mt. Maclure and Mt. Lyell are superlative.

From this ford our trail climbs steeply up rocky going to Donohue Pass (11,056') at the crest of the Sierra. This pass, lying between Donohue Peak (northeast) and Mt. Lyell (southwest), affords majestic views of the Sierra crest, the Cathedral Range and the Ritter Range—not right at the pass, but just before and just after. From Donohue Pass the trail descends by rocky switchbacks to sparse timber cover at the headwaters of Rush Creek, passing a lateral to Marie Lakes. As the trail levels out somewhat, it meets and then parallels a small, unnamed tributary of Rush Creek descending to join the main stream. In the Rush Creek watershed the forest cover of lodgepole and hemlock becomes denser, and the trail fords two tributaries to the "Improved" campsites on Rush Creek (9600"), where our route meets the Rush Creek Trail. Fishing is good for brook and rainbow (to 10").

3rd Hiking Day (**Rush Creek** to **Shadow Creek**, 8.0 miles—12.9 km): Through a continuing forest cover of lodgepole and mountain hemlock, our route ascends steadily beyond the junction with a trail to Davis Lakes, climbing southeast to the low saddle known as Island Pass (10,200'). Just south of this pass the trail passes two small lakes and then veers eastward across slopes. Along this trail the hiker will discover a verdant growth of wildflowers, including lupine, elephant heads, sulfur flower, Mariposa lily, goldenrod, fleabane, mountain aster, pussy paws, and streptanthus.

The trail emerges from the lodgepole-and-hemlock ground cover to a metamorphic slope above the outlet at the east end of Thousand Island Lake. Views from this rocky slope are sweeping, and the hiker immediately notices the difference between the predominantly darker rock of the Ritter Range and the lighter granite of the Sierra crest's alpine peaks. Geologically, the Ritter Range is made up of somewhat older rocks originally volcanic in nature, and the spectacularly jagged skyline from Banner Peak southward attests to the strength of this rock, which resisted the massive glaciers that gnawed at the range. As the trail switchbacks down to the outlet of Thousand Island Lake, there are classic views across the island-studded waters to the imposing east facades of Banner Peak and Mt. Ritter.

From Thousand Island Lake, proceed to Shadow Creek by reversing the 2nd hiking day of Trip 74.

4th Hiking Day (**Shadow Creek** to **Agnew Meadows**, 4.2 miles— 6.8 km); Reverse the 1st hiking day of Trip 69.

Several fair campsites may be found at the outlet and on the north side of Thousand Island Lake (9834'), the better ones being a mile or two west of the Muir Trail and back from the water. All these sites are somewhat exposed to the wind, but offer unexcelled views. Fishing for brook and rainbow (to 13") is poor-to-fair.

4th and 5th Hiking Days: Reverse the 2nd and 1st hiking days, Trip 74, 9.5 miles (15.3 km).

John Muir Trail, Mt. Lyell

Agnew Meadows to Shadow Creek　69

TRIP　From Agnew Meadows to Shadow Creek (round trip). Topo map *Devils Postpile*. Best mid or late season; 8.4 miles (13.6 km).

Grade	Trail/layover days	Total recommended days
Leisurely	2/0	2
Moderate	....	....
Strenuous	....	....

HILITES　Shadow Lake is subject to very heavy use, and in consequence this edition of *Sierra North* no longer recommends camping there but rather, up the inlet stream. If one needs an example to substantiate the necessity of the government's setting aside more wilderness areas, this high-country jewel is a case in point. This is a fine trip for beginning backpackers.

DESCRIPTION

1st Hiking Day (**Agnew Meadows** to **Shadow Creek**, 4.2 miles—6.8 km): From the trailhead west of the pack station (8335') our route skirts a flowery meadow before crossing a small ridge covered with red fir and lodgepole pine. Just under a mile from the start, and just beyond a long gully, we meet a trail from Agnew Meadows Campground, coming in on the right. In 80 yards the Pacific Crest Trail, which we've started west on, branches left to switchback down to the San Joaquin River while our route ahead descends steadily west toward the river. The first part of this downslope is interesting in that it incorporates many of the ground-cover changes typical of the Mammoth Lakes region. One moment you are in dense pine-and-fir forest, and the next you are walking on an exposed slope of pumice, growing manzanita and abundant wildflowers. In midsummer, watch for varieties of paintbrush, larkspur and streptanthus.

This trail re-enters forest cover near the bottom of the canyon, and skirts the northeast side of shallow, lily-padded Olaine Lake. Just past the lake we leave the River Trail,

which heads northwest up-canyon while our trail strikes west
to the river amid stands of quaking aspen and juniper. Beyond
the river ford our trail ascends the west wall of the canyon via
a rocky but well-maintained path. This path rises moderately
for 700 feet along juniper-dotted switchbacks, and has excellent views of tumbling Shadow Creek as it falls from the
eastern lip of Shadow Lake. Southeast from these switchbacks
one has picturesque views of the Mammoth Crest, **V**'d by the
steep San Joaquin River canyon walls. Arrival at lovely Shadow Lake (8760') is achieved via a bedrock notch that gives
the hiker a "fish's-eye view" of the lake and the background-
ing Ritter Range. Good campsites may be found along cascading Shadow Creek above the lake, about 100-200 yards up the
John Muir Trail.

2nd Hiking Day: Retrace your steps, 4.2 miles (6.8 km).

Shadow Lake

Ron Felzer

Agnew Meadows to Lake Ediza **70**

TRIP From Agnew Meadows to Lake Ediza (round trip).
Topo maps *Devils Postpile*. Best mid or late season;
14.0 miles (22.4 km).

Grade	Trail/layover days	Total recommended days
Leisurely	2/1	3
Moderate	2/0	2
Strenuous	....	....

HILITES This is one of the finest routes in the Mammoth
Lakes region for viewing the spectacular Ritter
Range, including Banner Peak, Mt. Ritter and the
Minarets. The pristine, alpine beauty of Sierra
lakes is nowhere better exemplified than at Lake
Ediza, where amid towering evidences of glacial
and volcanic action, the visitor can readily
appreciate the colossal natural forces that shaped,
thrust, and kneaded these natural landforms.

DESCRIPTION

1st Hiking Day (**Agnew Meadows** to **Lake Ediza**, 7 miles—11.2
km): First follow Trip 69 to **Shadow Creek**. From here our rising
trail parallels cascading Shadow Creek all the way to Lake
Ediza (9300'). Our route follows the John Muir Trail for about
⅔ mile to a junction where it branches off to Garnet and
Thousand Island lakes. From the junction our trail, though
heavily used, invites the traveler to stop and rest at one of the
several small waterfalls. Each has its own deep fishing or
swimming hole (late season, when the water has lost some of
its chill), and the granite slabs on the water's edge invite
sunbathing. Camping at Ediza Lake is legal only on the west
and southwest shores. Fishing is fair for brook (to 10″) in Lake
Ediza.

2nd Hiking Day: Retrace your steps, 7.0 miles (11.2 km).

71   Agnew Meadows to Devils Postpile

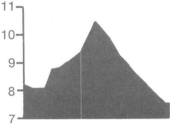

TRIP   From Agnew Meadows to Devils Postpile Campground (shuttle trip). Topo map *Devils Postpile*.
Best mid or late season; 16.2 miles (1 mile cross
country) (26.0 km).

Grade	Trail/layover days	Total recom- mended days
Leisurely	....	....
Moderate	3/0	3
Strenuous	....	....

HILITES   For those travelers who like their country high,
alpine and remote, this trip is ideal. However, this
route is recommended for highly experienced
backpackers only, because of the steep climb,
which is often made more hazardous by the late
snow melt between lower and upper Iceberg lakes.
There is no route that offers a finer view of the
spectacular and unusual Minarets.

DESCRIPTION (Moderate trip)

1st Hiking Day: Follow Trip 70 to **Lake Ediza**, 7.0 miles—11.2
km).

2nd Hiking Day (**Lake Ediza** to **Minaret Lake**, 3 miles—4.8 km):
The trail climbs south from the southeast end of Lake Ediza
over a steep, willow-covered slope. Often the path is almost
obliterated by the heavy growth, and some care should be
taken when it crosses and recrosses the outlet stream from
lower Iceberg Lake. A memorable view presents itself from the
top of the first rise. Below, the glacial cirque that cradles Lake
Ediza becomes very clear, and through a notch in the granite
to the northwest, Banner and Ritter thrust upward in a
side-on view. Immediately to the east, the massive 11,501-foot
heights of black Volcanic Ridge dominate the horizon. The
trail continues to ascend, winding through tiny alpine
meadows covered with the typical lupine, heather, and pussy

paws until it emerges at lower Iceberg Lake (9800'). Both
   Leaving the outlet of lower Iceberg Lake, the footpath
becomes somewhat indistinct as it rounds the eastern side and
then ascends 500 feet along the outlet stream from upper
Iceberg Lake. This particular ascent frequently has treacherous, late-melting snow on it, making it a route for experienced
knapsackers only. Upper Iceberg Lake (10,280') undoubtedly
has the choicest views of the Minarets. The trail, undiscerni-
ble at this point, rounds the eastern edge of the lake on the
broken black rock of Volcanic Ridge. From the southeastern
edge of the lake, there are awe-inspiring views of Clyde
Minaret, adjoining Minaret Lake, and Minaret Creek canyon.
The 500-foot descent to Minaret Lake is best made over the
rock-and-talus slope below this viewpoint, and it may entail
some rudimentary rock-climbing. A foot path going east along
the northern side of Minaret Lake joins the Forest Service
trail at the outlet, and good campsites dot this shore (9800').
Fishing in the lake is fair for brook (to 10").

3rd Hiking Day (**Minaret Lake** to **Devils Postpile Campground,**
6.2 miles—10 km): This day is a relatively steady descent of
2200 feet over a well-maintained but dusty trail. In its upper
reaches its dustiness is due to people and stock eroding the
decomposing granite; in its lower reaches the dustiness is due
to a deep layer of pumice (volcanic ash). From Minaret Lake
the trail descends over rocky switchbacks and enters red fir,
silver pine, lodgepole pine and mountain hemlock as it nears
the highest meadow on Minaret Creek. Just west of this trail
junction is a moderately warm lake with good swimming in
late season. After switchbacking down a granite slope beside
the cascades of Minaret Creek, the trail re-enters timber cover
and winds down a pumice slope to Johnston Meadow. This
meadow has a magnificent display of wildflowers that usually
lasts well into mid season. Part way through the meadow, the
trail rejoins the John Muir Trail, and soon fords Minaret
Creek. About ¼ mile southeast the route passes the trail to
Beck and Holcomb lakes, and from here the now very dusty
pumice trail drops steeply to a scissors junction with the
Pacific Crest Trail, which leads south from this junction, doing
double duty as the John Muir Trail too. We continue to descend on an old Muir Trail segment to the west edge of a long
meadow beside the San Joaquin River, where many Belding
ground squirrels are likely to be seen. Beyond the Summit
Meadow Trail, our route crosses the river via a large bridge at
the south end of the meadow, and then turns north to Devils
Postpile Campground.

72   Agnew Meadows to Devils Postpile

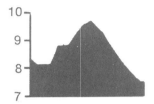

TRIP
From Agnew Meadows to Devils Postpile Camp-
ground (shuttle trip). Topo map *Devils Postpile*.
Best mid or late season; 12.2 miles (19.6 km).

Grade	Trail/layover days	Total recom- mended days
Leisurely	....	....
Moderate	2/0	2
Strenuous	....	....

HILITES
After crossing the Middle Fork San Joaquin, this
interesting route ascends to picturesque Shadow
Lake. Then, doubling back, it traverses the long,
narrow, lake-dotted bench that breaks the slope
from Volcanic Ridge to the river. Dense fir forests,
intimate lakes, and good fishing make this an
excellent beginner's weekend trip.

DESCRIPTION

1st Hiking Day (**Agnew Meadows** to **Rosalie Lake**, 5.4 miles—8.7
km): Follow the 1st hiking day, Trip 69, to Shadow Lake. At
the inlet to beautiful Shadow Lake, this route joins the John
Muir Trail and crosses Shadow Creek on a large log bridge.
The trail rounds the south side of the lake, and begins a series
of 22 switchbacks up a densely forested slope. Breather stops
along this 650-foot climb afford colorful views of the deep blues
and greens of Shadow Lake, and the crest of the ridge is soon
topped at a rocky saddle with a meadowy bottom. This saddle
leads to a good campsite by the outlet of charming Rosalie
Lake (9350'). Fishing is good for rainbow and brook (to 9″).
2nd Hiking Day (**Rosalie Lake** to **Devils Postpile Campground**,
6.8 miles—10.9 km): The trail soon climbs over the southeast
ridge that flanks Rosalie Lake. From the outlet of Gladys Lake
(known locally as Vivian Lake) one has views out over the San
Joaquin River canyon. To the west, the black, recrystallized

volcanic rocks of Volcanic ridge are on the skyline, and to the east the rock drops away into the San Joaquin and rises on the far side to red-topped San Joaquin Mountain and the distinctive Two Teats. From here the route drops down into the Trinity Lakes basin. Access to Castle and Emily lakes is via a short, steep foot trail that takes off from the western side of the trail, and fishing at these lakes is fair-to-good for rainbow and brook (to 8″). From the lowest of the Trinity Lakes, the trail descends steeply via dusty trail to Johnston Meadow, where it joins the trail from Minaret Lake. Follow this trail as described in the 3rd hiking day, Trip 71.

Mule ears

Jeff Schaffer

73 Agnew Meadows to Garnet Lake

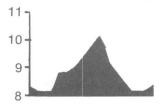

TRIP

From Agnew Meadows to Garnet Lake (loop trip). Topo map *Devils Postpile*. Best mid or late season; 14.1 miles (22.7 km).

Grade	Trail/layover days	Total recommended days
Leisurely	3/1	4
Moderate	3/0	3
Strenuous	2/0	2

HILITES

Employing about a 4-mile stretch of the well-known John Muir Trail, this trip surveys some of the northern Sierra's most dramatic country. In the region east of the jagged Ritter Range are some of the area's most vivid alpine lakes and spectacular landforms. This route traverses a section of this country in visiting Shadow and Garnet lakes.

DESCRIPTION (Leisurely trip)

1st Hiking Day: Follow Trip 69 to **Shadow Creek**, 4.2 miles (6.8 km).

2nd Hiking Day (**Shadow Creek** to **Garnet Lake**, 4.3 miles—6.9 km): On the John Muir Trail this route ascends west for ⅔ mile through Shadow Creek canyon before turning north. The trail suffers heavy use, and is likely to be dusty, particularly in late season. The dust, however, settles as the trail emerges from pine forest and tops the 1100-foot climb from the Shadow Creek Trail junction to the rocky ridge above Garnet Lake. This is an excellent place from which to appreciate the view of the lake itself, Ritter and Banner, and Mt. Davis to the west. The traveler will also note the striking change in the countryside. From the heavily timbered slopes of Shadow Creek canyon, the landscape, except for scattered stands of stunted hemlock, lodgepole and whitebark is now predominantly glacialy polished rock. From this viewpoint the trail descends 500 feet to the outlet of Garnet Lake (9680'). Fair campsites may be found on the north side of the lake west of the "no camping" zone, and several hundred feet below the outlet. Fishing for brook and rainbow (to 10″) is only fair.

3rd Hiking Day (**Garnet Lake** to **Agnew Meadows via the River Trail,** 5.6 miles—9.0 km): The lateral leading to the River Trail branches from the main trail on the south side of the outlet of Garnet Lake. It is a narrow footpath that descends steeply over a very rocky section, and backpackers should proceed with great caution. Three-fourths mile northeast it strikes the river, crosses on a log, and meets the River Trail, where our route turns right (southeast). The River Trail from this junction is a heavily timbered stretch of trail that passes the Agnew Pass Trail lateral and winds down the canyon. The sound of cascading San Joaquin River is a pleasant part-time accompaniment to this dusty descent when the river is nearby. Fishing on the San Joaquin for rainbow and brook (to 9″) is only fair, and swimming, even in late season, is likely to be somewhat chilly. This route meets the Shadow Lake Trail 2 miles from Agnew Meadows, whence it retraces part of the 1st hiking day.

Mt. Davis from near Rush Creek Trail

74 Agnew Meadows to 1000 Island Lake

TRIP   From Agnew Meadows to Thousand Island Lake
                via the River Trail (loop trip). Topo map *Devils
                Postpile*. Best mid or late season; 17.6 miles (28.3
                km).

Grade	Trail/layover days	Total recommended days
Leisurely	3/1	4
Moderate	3/0	3
Strenuous	2/0	2

HILITES   The climax of this trip is Garnet and Thousand
                Island lakes. Settings of alpine grandeur make
                these large lakes favorites of lensmen and
                naturalists alike. Although this trip can be made
                in a weekend, the superlative scenery warrants a
                slower pace. Almost half of this route follows the
                scenic John Muir Trail.

DESCRIPTION (Leisurely trip)

1st Hiking Day: Follow Trip 69 to **Shadow Creek**, 4.2 miles (6.8
km).
2nd Hiking Day (**Shadow Creek** to **Thousand Island Lake**, 6.3
miles—10.1 km): Follow the 2nd hiking day, Trip 73 to Garnet
Lake. Beyond the outlet of Garnet Lake, care should be
exercised when crossing the 500-foot talus-covered ridge that
separates Garnet and Thousand Island lakes. En route, the
trail circles the east shore of dramatic Ruby Lake, and then
drops down past colorful Emerald Lake to the outlet of
Thousand Island Lake (9834'). The island-dotted lake's
wind-swept surface reflects the imposing facade of Banner
Peak and the more sharply etched Mt. Ritter. Several exposed
campsites (subject to a great deal of wind) may be found on the
north side of the lake, the better ones being a mile or more
west of the Muir Trail and back from the water. Fishing for

rainbow and brook (7-13″) is particularly good in early and late season. Camping is also possible at the lakelet about ¼ mile east down the River Trail.

3rd Hiking Day (**Thousand Island Lake** to **Agnew Meadow** via the River Trail, 7.1 miles—11.4 km): This route leaves the John Muir Trail at the meadowy outlet of Thousand Island Lake, and proceeds northeast past several small snow tarns. The alpine setting is soon left behind as the trail re-enters forest cover. Our route then veers southeast to a junction with the High Trail, branches right at this junction, and slants down through dense lodgepole and fir to the Garnet Lake lateral, whence it proceeds as described in 3rd hiking day, Trip 73.

Ritter Range over upper Lost Lake

75 Agnew Meadows to 1000 Island Lake

TRIP   From Agnew Meadows to Thousand Island Lake
             via the High Trail (loop trip). Topo map *Devils
             Postpile*. Best mid or late season; 17.6 miles (28.3
             km).

Grade	Trail/layover days	Total recom- mended days
Leisurely	3/1	4
Moderate	3/0	3
Strenuous	2/0	2

HILITES   The San Joaquin River drainage provides this trip
             with a fascinating contrast. The imposing scenery
             viewed from the west side of the canyon below the
             Ritter Range has already been described, but few
             travelers have taken in the altogether different
             beauty of the slopes of the Sierra Crest. Here on
             the east side of the canyon the trail traveler passes
             through an entirely different kind of ground cover
             and he has unbroken views of the Ritter Range. A
             first assessment would indicate that this hillside
             was a scrubby, arid stretch, but it is not. Many
             streams interrupt the trail, even in late season,
             and wildflowers line the route.

DESCRIPTION (Leisurely trip)

1st and 2nd Hiking Days: Follow Trip 74 to **Thousand Island
Lake**, 10.5 miles (16.9 km).
3rd Hiking Day (**Thousand Island Lake** to **Agnew Meadows,** via
the High Trail, 7.1 miles—11.4 km): Follow the 3rd hiking
day, Trip 74, to the High Trail junction. From this trail
junction, the route ascends past meadowy Badger Lakes and
past a secondary lateral to Agnew Pass. On this first slope the
trail emerges from the dense forest cover, and then it winds up

and down through a ground cover that, except for a few
scattered stands of pine, is sagebrush, bitterbrush, willow, and
some mountain alder. When the trail descends to one of the
many tributaries of the San Joaquin River, the traveler should
observe the lush growth of wildflowers, including larkspur,
lupine, shooting star, columbine, penstemon, monkey flower,
scarlet gilia and tiger lily. For a while views are excellent of
the Ritter Range to the west; particularly impressive is the **V**'d
view of Shadow Lake directly across the San Joaquin River
canyon about 2¾ miles from the trailhead. But views soon
disappear, and you make a gradual descent, ending it with a
series of well-graded switchbacks to the parking lot north of
the pack station.

76   Chiquito Creek to Chain Lakes

TRIP   From Chiquito Creek Trailhead to Upper Chain
             Lake (round trip). Topo map *Merced Peak*. Best
             mid or late season; 14.8 miles (23.8 km).

Grade	Trail/layover days	Total recom-mended days
Leisurely	2/1	3
Moderate	2/0	2
Strenuous	....	....

HILITES   This round trip has several interesting route
              alternatives that will appeal to the experienced
              backpacker who is looking for a moderate
              weekend trip. Granite-bound Chain Lakes are a
              superlative high-country setting for a base camp,
              whether the purpose be angling, photography,
              hiking, or just communing.

DESCRIPTION

1st Hiking Day (**Chiquito Creek Trailhead** to **Middle Chain Lake**,
7.4 miles—11.9 km): From the trailhead (7320') the trail
immediately begins its 630-foot ascent to Chiquito Lake
(7940'). In about ⅔ mile, the abandoned pre-1970s trail to
Chiquito Pass comes in on the left, and then we traverse over
to the banks of sparkling Chiquito Creek. The next mile is
steep and dusty, and then the trail drops to ford Chiquito
Creek. Just before arriving at the Yosemite Park boundary at
Chiquito Pass, the trail passes marshy Chiquito Lake. At the
lake's southwest corner, a trail departs west to an alternative
trailhead at the end of a spur of Sky Ranch Road (see the topo
map). A few yards past the north end of the lake, an unmaintained but passable footpath veers off to the northeast, leading
to Spotted Lakes.

After crossing Chiquito Pass and its Buck Camp Trail junction, our route traverses to a crossing of the Spotted Lakes
Creek and then climbs moderately northward. Occasional

eastward glimpses may be had of vermilion-capped Red Top and the gray and ruddy tops of Sing and Gale peaks. Many of the large red firs and lodgepole pines that line this section of trail looked down on the U.S. Cavalry patrols which worked this part of the Park around the turn of the century. Immediately after fording the outlet creek of Chain Lakes, our route branches east along the creek, and it is a steep but short climb to the lower of the Chain Lakes. Fishing is excellent for brook (9-14"), subject to a midsummer slowdown. Swimming, particularly in late season, is good and good camping sites may be found at all three lakes. The middle lake (9100') is the prettiest—and the most-used. Many hikers who prefer the intoxicating atmosphere of a high-country, granite-bound lake will overlook the scarcity of timber at the upper lake. If you plan layover days, these lakes make an excellent base camp for cross-country side excursions to Spotted or Breeze lakes, where fishing is good to excellent for brook (9-14") with a midsummer slowdown.

2nd Hiking Day: Retrace you steps, 7.4 miles (11.9 km).

Middle Chain Lake   *National Park Service*

77 Chiquito Creek to Rutherford Lake

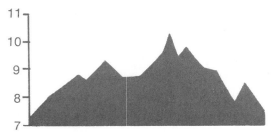

TRIP   From Chiquito Creek Trailhead to Trailhead on the old Strawberry Mine Road via Rutherford Lake (shuttle trip). Topo map *Merced Peak*. Best mid or late season; 25.5 miles (42.3 km).

Grade	Trail/layover days	Total recom- mended days
Leisurely	....	....
Moderate	3/1	4
Strenuous	3/0	3

HILITES Rarely does a backpack trip of 3 days' duration offer such a wide choice of recreational opportunities. Fishing on either side of Fernandez Pass is good-to-excellent, and alternative cross-country routes add a dash of spice for the more adventurous hiker. Scenery along the trail varies from dense red-fir forests to the wide-open vistas of high, alpine, glaciated lakes.

DESCRIPTION

1st Hiking Day: Follow Trip 76 to **Middle Chain Lake**, 7.4 miles (13.2 km).

2nd Hiking Day (**Middle Chain Lake** to **Rutherford Lake**, 9.4 miles—15.1 km): This route, via Moraine Meadow, descends along the Chain Lakes outlet stream to the junction (8500′), ½ miles below yesterday's junction, of the Buck Camp and Moraine Meadow trails. The trail north to Moraine Meadow ascends gradually on duff composed largely of lodgepole-pine needles. Shortly after fording the South Fork Merced River, the trail strikes the Fernandez Pass Trail, and at this point our route turns east for a mile, and then re-fords the river. Fishing is fair-to-good for rainbow and brook (to 9″). Then the trail turns south and ascends 400 feet to two unnamed lakes fed by the outlet stream from Breeze Lake, crossing this stream midway to the two lakes. Fishing at these lakes is fair-to-good for brook and rainbow (to 8″) but anglers will probably wish to bypass these lakes and after ½ mile take the short (0.7 mile) side trail to Breeze Lake for a try at the larger brook trout (9-14″). Breeze Lake, scooped out of the north face of Gale Peak, is a large (35-acre) glacial lake that has an honest claim to its name. The large granite wall bordering the east side gives way to a long, glacially polished scoop on the southeast that acts as a flue to channel the wind across the blue surface of the lake.

From the Breeze Lake side trail, it is but another 600 feet by short, rocky, eroded switchbacks to Fernandez Pass (10,200′). This pass, and the lakes of the same name 1 miles east, were named for Sgt. Joseph Fernandez, U.S. Cavalry. Fernandez was among the members of the Benson exploration party seeking the headwaters of the Merced River in 1895-97, and he was later instrumental in planting the first fish in this section of the Park. Views from Fernandez Pass are splendid of both the San Joaquin and Merced River basins, and on a clear day one can see Banner, Ritter, and the Minarets to the east. Fernandez Pass marks the Park boundary. On the new trail on the northeast side of the pass we first ascend several switchbacks before starting down. The trail drops into a fine little basin, climbs out of it, and then descends over steep, rocky switchbacks to the Rutherford Lake Trail. From here it is but ¼ mile, with a 250-foot elevation gain, to the lake (9760′), a large lake in a rocky basin at timberline. Fishing at the lake is fair, with the notorious midsummer slack period, for golden and brook trout (to 16″).

3rd Hiking Day (**Rutherford Lake** to **Trailhead on the old Strawberry Mine Road**, 8.7 miles—14 km): After retracing the ¼ mile to the Fernandez Pass Trail, our route turns east along it. This trail switchbacks down a morainal slope where one has frequent views of the south part of the Clark Range, then turns east into cool lodgepole forest. Near an easy ford of Fernandez Creek are some good campsites and a junction with the Post Peak Trail. A short mile beyond, on the east shoulder of a low exfoliation dome, we veer away from the abandoned trail that goes past Twin Lakes and dive south down a dark gully to a swampy flat, where we encounter the Rainbow Lake Trail, going right. Some further gentle descent on a sandy slope dotted with glacial erratics and sparse pines leads to a junction with the trail to Lillian Lake. Here our route veers east to lead about ¾ mile to a junction from where the abandoned Twin Lakes segment heads northwest, and we take the maintained Fernandez Pass Trail southeast, dropping moderately and then more steeply, even switchbacking in places, to a junction ½ mile below the switchbacks. Just 70 yards north up the side trail here is a fork from which the left branch climbs to a campsite on West Fork Granite Creek and the right branch is the Timber Creek Trail. From the junction our trail descends briefly to Madera Creek, and on a north-bank flat at another trail junction we leave the Fernandez Trail to head left (east) for 250 yards to a ford of the creek (difficult in early season). Beyond this ford our trail switchbacks steeply up to a nearby gap from where the crest panorama extends from Madera Peak in the south past Sing, Gale, Triple Divide and Post peaks to Timber Knob. The last 2¾ miles of unsigned, narrow trail are mostly downhill or easy traversing, ending at the old, abandoned Strawberry Mine Road. The present trailhead on this old road is just ½ mile south.

Belding ground squirrel

National Park Service

Chiquito Creek to Bridalveil Creek 78

TRIP

Chiquito Creek Trailhead to Bridalveil Campground (shuttle trip). Topo maps *Merced Peak*,
Yosemite. Best mid or late season; 29.4 miles (48.6
km).

Grade	Trail/layover days	Total recom- mended days
Leisurely	4/1	5
Moderate	4/0	4
Strenuous	3/0	3

HILITES

This is a shuttle trip that crosses some of the more
scenic southern Yosemite National Park boundary country. Some of the finest fishing in the Park
is found along this route at Chain and Royal Arch
lakes, and bonus angling spots can be explored on
layover days at Breeze, Spotted, Johnson and
Crescent lakes. The gigantic, sweeping effects of
glacial action are seen throughout this trip. The
resulting cirques, **U**-shaped valleys, jagged
ranges, and polished granite are a constant source
of awe and delight to the traveler.

DESCRIPTION (Leisurely trip)

1st Hiking Day: Follow Trip 76 to **Middle Chain Lake**, 7.4 miles
(13.2 km).

2nd Hiking Day (**Upper Chain Lake** to **Royal Arch Lake**, 9 miles—
14.5 km): First, retrace your steps to yesterday's junction, and
then continue downstream. In ⅓ mile the trail veers north to a
junction, where we turn left (west) and parallel the outlet
creek from Chain Lakes as it falls to rendezvous with the
South Fork Merced. Just before the South Fork a signed lateral trail leads south ¼ mile to good camping at Soda Springs.

Our route fords the South Fork and swings southwest over a lodgepole-covered slope. The depth of the U-shaped, glacially formed slopes gives a good account of the forces that were at work when the ice flow originating in the Clark Range to the north was in its heyday.

After fording Givens Creek the trail passes a southbound trail to Chiquito Pass. Just 60 yards farther we choose a well-used left fork over a little-used right fork and then continue ½ mile to meet the Buck Camp/Merced Pass Trail on a ridgetop. Turning southwest, we descend through red-fir forest and then climb northwest to the meadowy precincts of Buck Camp. At Buck Camp Yosemite National Park has a summer ranger station, and emergency services may be obtained. From Buck Camp the trail ascends a tough 750 feet via switchbacks, then drops 350 feet to a junction with the Royal Arch Lake Trail. From this point it is but ¾ mile to Royal Arch Lake (8700'). Large, black, rainbow-arched striations across the eastern wall of polished granite gave this picturesque lake its name. These distinctive markings are the result of water discoloration due to centuries of seepage. They make a magnificent backdrop to the excellent fishing for brook and rainbow (8-14") and anglers may well regard this relatively small lake as the high point of the trip. Numerous good campsites are on the west shore, and this lake makes an excellent base camp for scenic and angling excursions to nearby Buena Vista, Johnson and Crescent lakes. Swimming is good in late season.

3rd and 4th Hiking Days: Reverse the steps of the 2nd and 1st hiking days, Trip 82, 13 miles (20.9 km).

Royal Arch Lake   *National Park Service*

Granite Creek Road to Rutherford Lake 79

TRIP
From Trailhead on the Old Strawberry Mine Road to Rutherford Lake (semiloop trip). Topo map *Merced Peak*. Best mid or late season; 20.2 miles (32.5 km).

Grade	Trail/layover days	Total recommended days
Leisurely	3/1	4
Moderate	3/0	3
Strenuous	2/0	2

HILITES
The lake-filled area east of Gale and Sing peaks provides a choice trip for the angler. Except for a midsummer slack period, these lakes are good producers of brook, rainbow, and even golden trout. Add to this benefit the dramatic peaks that lie to the west, and the 35-mile views to the south, and every hiker will find cause for visiting this country. This trip is the answer for the hiker with a short time for travel who wishes to get into the spectacular south boundary country.

DESCRIPTION (Leisurely trip)

1st Hiking Day (**Trailhead on the old Strawberry Mine Road** to **Vandeburg Lake**, 4 miles—6.4 km): From the old road, the trail bears northwest for a steady uphill climb 900 feet through a forest of fir and lodgepole, Jeffrey and sugar pine. Bird fanciers will find this stretch of trail of particular interest because of the large variety of birdlife. Early-season hikers should listen for the distinctive pulsating "whump-whump-whump" mating call of the ventriloquist grouse. The "chirr" of the white-headed woodpecker may be heard at any time of the season, and the monotonous cry of the junco will dog one's footsteps for the entire trip. Other birds one may encounter are the white-crowned sparrow, chickadee, and olive-sided flycatcher. In this initial section we pass two trails going left to Norris Creek, after ⅓ mile, and then a mile later.

As the trail crosses the ridge into the Madera Creek watershed, there are views through the thinning timber of Banner Peak, Mt. Ritter and the Minarets to the northeast. Southward one has views across the canyon of the Middle San Joaquin to Kaiser Ridge, up the canyon of the South San Joaquin, and down the main river to the sides of Mammoth Pool. On this ridgetop our route turns left from the Fernandez Trail and begins 2 easy, forested miles of trail where mosquitoes are thick in early season. Then the trail climbs through a bedrock notch in a granitic crest and enters the basin of Vandeburg Lake (8680′), which lies below the trail. Here beneath the brooding black granite of Madera Peak, Vandeburg and Lady lakes provide good fishing for brook (to 9″) except in midsummer.

2nd Hiking Day (**Vandeburg Lake** to **Rutherford Lake**, 7.5 miles—12.1 km): This day offers many possible stopping places to fish, eat, look, or just sit. The trail curves around the north side of Vandeburg Lake to a junction where we take the right fork to Stanford Lakes, a mile away over a low crest. Named after an old Fresno family, they lie on the Shirley Creek tributary of West Fork Granite Creek. Anglers will find brook (to 9″). From Stanford Lakes one has a choice. He may (1) choose the trail to Lillian Lake, or (2) take the unmarked trail up Shirley Creek to little (5-acre) Shirley Lake (9180′), which is situated in a shallow granite basin at timberline (good fishing for brook to 12″). Anglers may want to cross the granite shoulder south from Shirley Lake to Chittenden Lake, for the excellent fishing for brook (to 12″). The basin in which these lakes lie affords good views westward of Sing and Gale peaks, whose present shapes were created during a Pleistocene ice age. Then, great ice masses formed on the then-much-rounder slopes of the peaks, and the jagged tops that remain are the "islands" that escape the plucking and grinding of the glaciers.

If the hiker chooses to go via Shirley Lake, he can then reach Lillian by crossing a slight divide toward the east (cross country) and following the inlet stream. Lillian Lake is the largest lake (35 acres, 8840′) in the Granite Creek basin, and has fair fishing for brook and rainbow (to 11″), best in early and late season. It is a natural lake, but a flow-maintenance dam was added in 1953, and today it controls the level of the lake and the flow in the outlet stream. Cut timber along one side intrudes on the wilderness feeling of this lake.

From Lillian Lake a well-marked trail leads east to the junction with the Fernandez Trail. Turning left, our route makes a gentle ascent in open lodgepole forest to the Rainbow Lake Trail, where we turn left again, beside a small swamp. The trail to Rainbow Lake winds south to cross the tiny outlet stream of unseen Flat Lake, then ascends southwest on a broken exfoliation slope to a fine overlook of the Lillian Lake basin, backdropped by vermilion-stained Madera Peak. From this overlook our route descends north, crosses the outlet of Rainbow Lake and ascends through pine and hemlock to the campsites on the east shore of Rainbow Lake.

From this east shore, we head cross country for the saddle north of the lake, where we find a well-used and exorbitantly ducked route that leads past Fernandez Lake to the old Fernandez Trail at its junction with the old Rutherford Lake Trail Crossing the former, we ascend the latter to the new Fernandez Trail and continue ahead for the last ¼ mile to 28-acre Rutherford Lake (9800'). There are fair-to-good campsites on the west side of the lake south of the outlet, and fishing is fair for golden and brook (to 16').

3rd Hiking Day: Follow the 3rd hiking day, Trip 77, 8.7 miles (14 km).

80   Granite Creek Road to Isberg Lakes

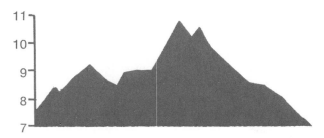

TRIP   From Trailhead on the Old Strawberry Mine Road
to Granite Creek Campground (shuttle trip). Topo
map *Merced Peak*. Best mid or late season; 28.2
miles (45.5 km).

Grade	Trail/layover days	Total recom- mended days
Leisurely	5/1	6
Moderate	4/1	5
Strenuous	3/1	4

HILITES   This is a challenging hike, with an altitude change
of over 3000 feet. Scenery varies from the cloisters
of dense forests and the intimacy of small
meadows to the overwhelming panoramas from
two high passes. Fishing is best in early or late
season, and ranges from fair to excellent.

DESCRIPTION (Leisurely trip)

1st Hiking Day: Follow Trip 79 to **Vandeburg Lake**, 4 miles (6.4
km).

2nd Hiking Day (**Vandeburg Lake** to **Fernandez Creek Meadow**,
5.7 miles—9.2 km): Follow the 2nd hiking day, Trip 79, to the
junction of the Fernandez Trail and the Rainbow Lake Trail.
Staying on the former trail, we hike north up a dark gully past
a low exfoliation dome on the west. Heading toward the divide
that is the border of Yosemite Park, our route passes the
abandoned trail leading southeast to Twin Lakes and a mile
farther comes to a meadow with good campsites at the junction
of the Fernandez Trail and the Post Peak Pass Trail. Small
brook trout are plentiful here on pleasant Fernandez Creek.

3rd Hiking Day (**Fernandez Creek Meadow** to **Isberg Lakes**, 7.8 miles—12.6 km): Two passes, both over 10,500 feet, are the reward for this day's efforts. From Fernandez Creek Meadow the Post Peak Pass Trail leads east along Fernandez Creek to cross it after 250 yards. Then it fords the Slab Lake creek and climbs gently for over a mile to Post Creek (9040'). Fishing on the creek is good for brook (to 8"). Then the trail switchbacks steadily up exposed granite to 1-acre Porphyry Lake (10,100'), where fishing is fair for brook and rainbow. This deep, rocky lake was named for the extraordinary looking porphyritic granite that surrounds the area. A breather here is well-earned, and the arresting scenery makes it a good choice for a break, though there's no decent camping.

From Porphyry Lake it is 1.5 steep, rocky miles to the highest point on this route, Post Peak Pass (10,750'). The pass marks the divide between the Merced and San Joaquin river drainages. After a 1½-mile, very scenic visit in Yosemite Park, our route recrosses this divide at Isberg Pass (10,500'). From this section of trail the hiker has grand views of the Clark Range to the west, the Cathedral Range to the north, the tops of Banner, Ritter and the Minarets to the east, and a large part of the entire High Sierra farther south. This route was discovered and named by a military expedition in 1895 under the command of Lt. N. F. McClure. From Isberg Pass the trail descends 1 mile on the southeast slope to upper Isberg Lake, and ½ mile beyond to lower Isberg Lake (9800'). Fishing on these lakes is fair-to-good for brook and rainbow (to 8") but swimming is poor. There are a few fair campsites at the lower lake.

4th Hiking Day (**Isberg Lakes** to **Cora Lakes**, 5.7 miles—9.2 km,—6.7 miles by cross country to East Fork Granite Creek): From lower Isberg Lake the trail soon re-enters timber, and about a mile beyond skirts the side of Sadler Lake (9345'). Named for another member of the McClure expedition of 1895, Sadler Lake today affords excellent fishing for brook (7-10") in early and late season. The lodgepole pines cluster on the south shore, leaving the north, west and east sides open to alpine meadows. These meadows are a splash of wildflower color in early season. From Sadler Lake the trail passes through scattered stands of hemlock and silver pine as it descends steadily southward, and then passes the Timber Creek lateral to Joe Crane Lake. This trail segment parallels the East Fork of Granite Creek, and fishing for brook (some rainbow and brown) is good (to 10") on the stretches just below Sadler Lake and above Detachment Meadow. However, many anglers will

pass up the stream fishing for the slightly larger trout of Cora
Lakes (8400'). The largest of the three Cora Lakes is middle
Cora (16 acres), where the best camping may be found.

The hiker who is seeking an alternative route and a
camping place away from the trail, and whose feet do not balk
at a 2-mile cross-country walk, may elect to turn right (west)
at the south end of middle Cora Lake. This unmarked route
crosses an easy rocky ridge, veers southwest, and descends to
the secluded streamside campsites along the East Fork
Granite Creek. The deep pools and one dashing water slide
make this a pleasant night's stop. To join the route described
for the 5th hiking day, this cross-country route continues
down the East Fork of Granite Creek and it meets the Granite
Creek Campground Trail at the foot of Green Mountain.

5th Hiking Day (**Cora Lakes** to **Granite Creek Campground**, 5
miles—8.1 km): Within a mile of Cora Lakes the trail rejoins
the East Fork of Granite Creek, and follows it closely as far as
the rocky west shoulder of Green Mountain, fording the creek
midway down. The trail then veers away from the creek and
descends rapidly for 2.2 miles before rejoining the stream just
north of Granite Creek Campground. This 1000-foot descent is
marked by the reverse order of the groundcover change noted
in the 1st and 3rd hiking days. The ford of the West Fork of
Granite Creek is a wet one unless you go 120 yards
downstream and cross it on a horse bridge.

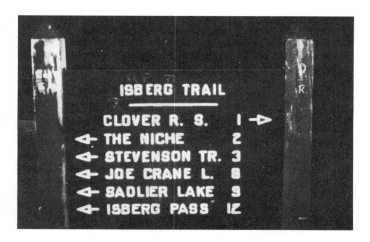

Yosemite Valley to Merced Lake 81

TRIP

From Yosemite Valley to Merced Lake (round trip). Topo maps *Yosemite, Merced Peak*. Best early season; 26.8 miles (43.2 km).

Grade	Trail/layover days	Total recommended days
Leisurely	4/0	4
Moderate	3/0	3
Streuous	2/0	2

HILITES

An early-season trip (low altitude, early snowmelt), this route offers all the scenic grandeur of the Valley attractions, plus the intimate knowledge of the back country that only the backpacker can have. Fishing is good during early season on the Merced River and at Merced Lake. Swimming is poor during the early season, owing to the chilly waters, but photographers and naturalists will find an exciting area of geologic spectacle and history.

DESCRIPTION (Leisurely trip)

1st Hiking Day (**Yosemite Valley** to **Little Yosemite Valley**, 4.7 miles—7.6 km): This trip is graded as leisurely, but any hiking day that includes an elevation change of 2200 feet must entail some strenuous exertion. The strenuous climb is hereby granted. However, this ascent is not too rough if undertaken during the cool of the morning. The trail begins at Happy Isles and climbs steadily under golden oak and Douglas-fir around Sierra Point to the Vernal Fall bridge. If one hits the trail early enough, he will see the rising sun's rays haloing in the mist of Vernal Fall. The sight is a memory to sustain one over the steady slog up numerous shaded switchbacks on the lower slopes of Panorama Cliff. Finally the switchbacks end and the trail arrives at Clark's Point, an overlook whence views are excellent of Half Dome, Grizzly Peak, Liberty Cap and Nevada Fall. From this point a short lateral trail leads down to the river above Vernal Fall.

Then more switchbacks continue to a junction with the Panorama Trail. From here it is but a short distance to the top of Nevada Fall. The Merced River here takes its mightiest plunge (594') and its roar signals what to expect long before the traveler arrives at its edge. The view from the brink of Nevada Fall is unforgettable—the cauldron of flying water stands in stark relief to the serenity of the trail, and the barren solidity of Liberty Cap is a reassuring reminder of the solid rock on which the viewer stands.

Beyond the bridge over the Merced River, the sandy trail winds among groves of Douglas-fir and lodgepole and Jeffrey pine and then executes a few little switchbacks under the shadow of Liberty Cap to reach the 3-mile-long flat floor of forest-covered Little Yosemite Valley. Enjoying frequent glimpses of the immensely appealing river, we stroll for one mile to a junction with the trail to Half Dome, Clouds Rest and Tuolumne Meadows, first passing an unsigned shortcut that veers northeast over to this trail. Abundant signs inform you about where you may camp, where toilets are, and how to keep your food safe from the numerous bears that live around here. Near the trail junction there is also a summer ranger station. Fishing in the river is fair for rainbow, brook and brown trout (to 10").

2nd Hiking Day (**Little Yosemite Valley** to **Merced Lake**, 8.7 miles—14 km): The pleasant jaunt up this valley is shaded by a moderate forest of large Jeffrey and sugar pines, and smaller lodgepole pines. As the trail winds along close beside the now-serene Merced River, the green depths invite a fishing line. Ahead, the granite valley walls begin to close in, and we pass another group of campsites. As the trail winds up the easy 200-foot ascent to Lost Valley, it passes by silent, swift-running chutes and roaring cascades. By contrast, once in Lost Valley, the Merced regains its placid appearance. As this route enters Lost Valley, a sign points out the extreme fire hazard of the valley. Heavy "fall" and channeled winds make this short stretch of trail a fire threat. At the end of Lost Valley the trail begins an 800-foot climb along the Bunnell Cascade. The early part of this climb brings the traveler above the timber, and it is time well spent to stop and look back at the granite domes that flank the trail. On the north side Moraine

Dome (8055') dominates the skyline, while on the south loom Mt. Starr King (9092') and Bunnell Point (8193'). Ahead the trail climbs above the channeled gorge of the now-writhing, twisting, tormented river. Once over the shoulder of Bunnell Point, the trail starts down, recrossing the river below the foot of Echo Valley. Our route passes the Echo Creek Trail and continues on a gradual ascent to Merced Lake (7216'). The High Sierra Camp and the hikers' campground are located at the eastern end of the lake. (Advance reservations are necessary for meals and lodging at the camp.) Fishing is good for rainbow and brook (to 9"). Again, bear-proof your food.

3rd and 4th Hiking Days: Retrace your steps, 13.4 miles (21.6 km).

Bearbagging at Merced Lake

82   Bridalveil Creek to Royal Arch Lake

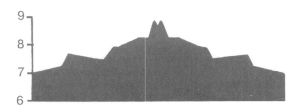

TRIP   From Bridalveil Campground to Royal Arch Lake
(round trip). Topo map *Yosemite*. Best early-to-mid
season; 26 miles (41.8 km).

Grade	Trail/layover days	Total recom- mended days
Leisurely	4/0	4
Moderate	3/0	3
Strenuous	2/0	2

HILITES In early season this trip route is lush with
wildflowers of every variety, and color film is a
must for the photographer. Anglers will find few
lakes within the Park to rival the fishing at Royal
Arch Lake. The easy grade of the topography
makes this an excellent early-season choice.

DESCRIPTION (Leisurely trip)

1st Hiking Day (**Bridalveil Campground** to **Turner Meadows**, 6.3
miles—10.1 km): From the trailhead at the southeast end of
the campground, the trail begins winding southeastward
along meandering Bridalveil Creek. The grade is gentle as the
trail winds through the dense lodgepole forest. Periodically,
the thick undergrowth gives way to intimate, mountain-
bluebell-filled meadows. Near Lost Bear Meadow the trail
veers south beside one of the larger tributaries of Bridalveil
Creek. It crosses this tributary twice, and each fording is
heralded by banks covered with shooting stars. The second
crossing marks the beginning of an easy 400-foot climb over
the ridge that separates the Bridalveil Creek and Alder
Creek watersheds. In early and mid season this ridge is colorfully decked out in lush pink and white fields of pussy paws
and Douglas phlox. From the top of this ridge, the trail drops to
the Deer Camp Trail junction, climbs over Turner Ridge and

then offers a short walk to Turner Meadows and the campsites at the southern end. The cabin site at the head of the meadows (indicated by the rock fireplace) is all that remains of Bill Turner's pioneer abode. He occupied these grasslands while running cattle around the turn of the century. There is good stream water except in late season.

2nd Hiking Day (**Turner Meadows** to **Royal Arch Lake**, 6.7 miles—10.8 km): Before leaving Turner Meadows, one should take the opportunity to study the wildlife that frequents the meadows, particularly in the early morning. Within ½ mile from Turner Meadows, the trail passes the Wawona Trail, which branches south, and ¾ mile farther it passes the Chilnualna Lakes Trail branching east. These trails were used by U.S. Cavalry patrols at the turn of the century. Their purpose was to facilitate administration of the Park, which at that time meant keeping the poachers, cattlemen and sheepmen out. Along this stretch the ground cover of red fir gives way to lodgepole pine.

Once past a second trail lateral to Wawona, the trail climbs to Johnson Lake (8300') via Grouse Lake (off the trail to the right) and Crescent Lake, where fishing is poor-to-fair for brook. Johnson Lake, however, affords good fishing for brook and rainbow (9-13"). Johnson Lake was one of the Park's last acquisitions of private property within its boundaries, and two crumbling cabins remain to remind us of our homesteading era. The area around the lake is now reverting to its primitive state. The ¾ mile to the junction of the Royal Arch Lake Trail is a 250-foot ascent over a lodgepole-covered slope. Here our route leaves the Buck Camp Trail and turns north for a small climb through a dense forest cover. Royal Arch Lake (8700') is small but it is deep and it supports an excellent, self-sustaining fishery of brook and rainbow (8-14"). Its dramatic name derives from the blackened granite streaks that rainbow across the steep eastern face of the lake basin. Numerous good-to-excellent campsites are on the north and west shores.

3rd and 4th Hiking Days: Retrace your steps, 13 miles (20.9 km).

83 Bridalveil Creek to Glacier Point

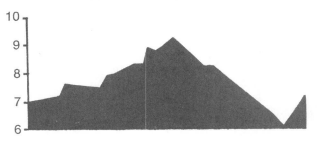

TRIP   From Bridalveil Campground to Glacier Point
                (shuttle trip). Topo maps *Yosemite, Merced Peak*.
                Best early-to-mid season; 28.8 miles (46.3 km).

Grade	Trail/layover days	Total recom- mended days
Leisurely	5/1	6
Moderate	4/1	5
Strenuous	3/0	3

HILITES   This long circle trip covers some of the more scenic
                portions of the southern part of the Park, and has
                the advantage of a very short shuttle between the
                beginning and ending points. Anglers have a wide
                choice of lake and stream fishing which is among
                the best in Yosemite. Despite the attractions, the
                route is not heavily traveled, and those seeking
                some solitude will find it on this trip.

DESCRIPTION (Leisurely trip)

1st and 2nd Hiking Days: Follow Trip 82 to **Royal Arch Lake**, 13
miles (20.9 km).

3rd Hiking Day (**Royal Arch Lake** to **Edson Lake**, 5.6 miles—9
km): The 2½-mile ascent from Royal Arch Lake to Buena
Vista Lake (9080′) is an easy one across granite dotted with
stands of lodgepole and hemlock. At Buena Vista Lake anglers
can unlimber their rods for good fishing for brook and rainbow
(9-13″). Those fishermen desiring a change of scenery (or luck)
will elect to continue ½ mile to the Buena Vista summit and
the junction with the trail to Chilnualna Lakes. At this
summit photographers may wish to capture the sweeping
view. Beginning with Half Dome just west of north, one can
make out Mt. Hoffman, Mt. Starr King, Clouds Rest,

Cathedral Peak, the Cockscomb, Matthes Crest, Mt. Clark, Gray Peak, Red Peak, Merced Peak, Triple Divide Peak, Gale Peak, Sing Peak and Madera Peak, It is only another 0.7 mile, but a 480-foot descent, down the side trail to Upper Chilnualna Lake (8500'). Fishing on this small (7-acre) lake is excellent for brook (8-14"). From Buena Vista summit our trail drops down to cross and recross Buena Vista Creek and then climb abruptly back onto the shoulder of Horse Ridge, crossing the seasonal outlet of Hart Lakes as it does so. Dropping north, we reach an unmarked junction with a ducked footpath to Edson Lake (8160'). Fair campsites may be found on the north shore. Fishing at the lake is only fair for rainbow.

4th Hiking Day (**Edson Lake** to **Illilouette Creek**, 6.7 miles—10.8 km): Back on the Buena Vista Trail, the first part of this day's walk is a long, steady descent of 1000 feet on dusty, rocky underfooting. From Buena Vista Creek the 700-foot descent to Illilouette Creek is sandy. The dense red-fir forest is often interrupted by clumps of dead lodgepole pines, and the contrast is much like stepping from a cathedral into the adjoining graveyard. Periodically, the fir cover opens to give peephole views of the granite domes to the north and northeast, of which Mt. Starr King stands out above all the rest. Our trail dips close to the confluence of Buena Vista and Illilouette creeks, and then veers away from the latter as we follow its canyon downstream, jumping across several small tributaries. As we approach Illilouette Creek again, we meet the trail from Mono Meadow, and near this junction find campsites on both sides of the creek. Fishing on the creek is fair for rainbow (to 8").

5th Hiking Day (**Illilouette Creek** to **Glacier Point**, 3.5 miles—5.6 km): The trail descends gently beside Illilouette Creek for about 1½ miles before beginning to climb. As it ascends past the junction with a trail down to Illilouette Fall, each foot of altitude gain improves the view, giving the trail here its meaningful name, the Panorama Trail. From this trail, on a clear day (and it is clearer in the morning), one can look across the vast chasm of the Merced River, and with the aid of binoculars see hikers on the summit of Half Dome. Nearer at hand, we can see the work of avalanches that have thundered down from the heights, carrying rocks, trees and soil across the trail. The fine views from just below Washburn Point include Nevada Fall, Vernal Fall, Half Dome, Mt. Starr King, and many high peaks of eastern Yosemite, marching off to the southeast horizon. The last half mile to Glacier Point (7214') is accomplished by switchbacks that rise through a fine stand of red fir to the parking circle near this famous overlook.

84   Bridalveil Creek to Yosemite Valley

TRIP   From Bridalveil Campground to Yosemite Valley
            (Happy Isles), (shuttle trip). Topo maps (15′) *Yose-*
            mite, Merced Peak. Best early-to-mid season; 32.7
            miles (52.6 km).

Grade	Trail/layover days	Total recom- mended days
Leisurely	5/1	6
Moderate	4/1	5
Strenuous	3/0	3

HILITES This route traverses some of the finer forest stands
            in Yosemite, crosses the Buena Vista Crest, and
            concludes via the famous Panorama and Nevada
            Fall trails into the Valley. A feeling of remoteness
            from the start, combined with excellent fishing on
            several lakes, makes this a fine early-to-mid
            season trip.

DESCRIPTION (Leisurely trip)

1st and 2nd Hiking Days: Follow Trip 82 to **Royal Arch Lake**, 13
miles (20.9 km).

3rd and 4th Hiking Days: Follow the 3rd and 4th hiking days
of Trip 83 to **Illilouette Creek**, 12.3 miles (19.8 km).

5th Hiking Day (**Illilouette Creek** to **Yosemite Valley**, 7.4
miles—11.9 km—via the John Muir Trail, or 6.7 miles—10.8
km—via the Mist Trail): A short way up the east bank of
Illilouette Creek from the campsites is a junction, where our
route turns north across a sandy meadow. After jumping a

small, unnamed stream, we climb moderately to meet a trail coming in on the right. Continuing northward, our trail crosses a low, forested saddle and descends to the blacktopped Panorama Trail, where we turn right (east). This route skirts the edge of the sheer Panorama Cliff and then switchbacks down 500 feet to the lip of Nevada Fall, joining the John Muir Trail shortly before reaching the top of the fall. One of the finest falls in Yosemite, Nevada Fall drops 594 feet in one vertical plunge. Other falls in the Valley drop greater distances, but none has the volume of water that the Merced River has. The result is a thunderous roar that can be heard for miles. As the viewer stands facing out over the fall, the granite dome on his right is Liberty Cap; directly ahead and slightly above him is Glacier Point. Unfortunately, a shelf of the slope on the left hides the 370-foot Illilouette Fall. Should the traveler determine to conclude this day's hike via the John Muir Trail he will have to retrace his steps to the last junction and then retrace part of the 1st hiking day, Trip 81.

The more spectacular route, however, is the Mist Trail. As this route is spectacular, it is also quite difficult, owing to its steepness. The Mist Trail begins 0.2 mile northeast of the top of Nevada Fall. Progress down the Mist Trail is easily measured in relation to Nevada Fall, since the trail at one point comes down to the very base of the fall. At this point the immense power of the fall makes itself known. This route imposes an unforgettable humility on all those who tread it, for no sooner is Nevada Fall left behind than one is at the man-made railing on the brink of Vernal Fall. This site is a point of contrasts. Emerald Pool, just above the fall, is a placid flow of water that elicits a feeling of calm. Ten seconds away, the same water is catapulted with a roar into the misty chasm below. It is into this same chasm that the trail winds. On this trail section the trail's name gains meaning, and one emerges from the cloud of mist 800' lower with clothing damp and ears ringing with the sound of crashing water. At the Vernal Fall bridge the Mist Trail rejoins the John Muir Trail, which descends rather steeply to Happy Isles.

85 Bridalveil Creek to Royal Arch Lake

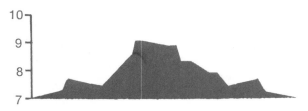

TRIP From Bridalveil Campground to Royal Arch Lake (semiloop trip). Topo map *Yosemite*. Best early-to-mid season; 27.2 miles (43.7 km).

Grade	Trail/layover days	Total recommended days
Leisurely	5/1	6
Moderate	4/1	5
Strenuous	3/0	3

HILITES For the first-timer, exploring Yosemite's south boundary country is a memorable experience, and this loop trip provides an exciting route. Angling on the many lakes around Buena Vista Peak is excellent, particularly in early season, and the easy access and return recommend this trip as an early-season "warm up."

DESCRIPTION (Leisurely trip)

1st Hiking Day: Follow Trip 82 to **Turner Meadows**, 6.3 miles (10.1 km).

2nd Hiking Day (**Turner Meadows** to **Upper Chilnualna Lake**, 4.9 miles—7.9 km): From Turner Meadows the trail continues southeast. One half mile from the campsites at the south end of the meadow our route passes the Wawona Trail, and ¾ mile later it turns east along Chilnualna Creek. This junction marks the beginning of a long, easy ascent that is pleasantly accompanied by the creek. Fishing along this cascading stream is fair (small brook and rainbow); most anglers will keep their lines dry until they reach Chilnualna Lakes (8480'). Here, all except the lowest lake provide excellent fishing for brook and rainbow (7-12"). Small (7-acre) upper Chilnualna Lake, alongside the trail, has several good campsites on its north side, but the best and most secluded Chilnualna Lake is the southernmost one.

3rd Hiking Day (**Upper Chilnualna Lake** to **Royal Arch Lake**, 3.0 miles—4.8 km): From the north side of the lake, the trail climbs steeply up the 480-foot, densely forested slope to a junction with the Buena Vista Trail. Our route turns right (southeast) and climbs the ridge to beautiful Buena Vista Lake (9080'). On this high lake fishing is good for rainbow and brook (9-13″) and anglers may wish to tarry. After a switchbacking 300-foot climb, the remaining 2 miles to Royal Arch Lake is a gentle descent across granite that exhibits a sprinkling of lodgepole pine and hemlock. Royal Arch Lake (8700') is a fine fishing lake (excellent angling for brook and rainbow to 14″), and there are numerous good-to-excellent campsites on the west shore. The lake's name is well-suited, deriving from the blackened granite streaks that rainbow across the sheer eastern facade of the lake basin.

4th and 5th Hiking Days: Reverse the steps of the 2nd and 1st hiking days, Trip 82, 13 miles (20.9 km).

Lyell Fork of the Tuolumne River

86   Glacier Point to Merced Lake

TRIP
From Glacier Point to Merced Lake (round trip). Topo maps *Yosemite, Merced Peak*. Best early season; 30.8 miles (49.6 km).

Grade	Trail/layover days	Total recommended days
Leisurely	4/1	5
Moderate	4/0	4
Strenuous	3/0	3

HILITES
This early-season excursion has all the scenic advantages of the Yosemite-Valley-to-Merced-Lake trip (Trip 81) without the 2000-foot climb from Happy Isles to Nevada Fall. Mild elevation change and solid mileage make this route a fine choice for the hiker who wants to shake winter's kinks out of early-season muscles.

DESCRIPTION (Leisurely trip)

1st Hiking Day (**Glacier Point** to **Little Yosemite Valley**, 6.7 miles—10.8 km): This trail begins at a large wooden sign above the parking lot at Glacier Point. Going east from the sign, we swing south and descend into Illilouette Gorge, where we can see the work of avalanches that have thundered down from the heights, carrying rocks, trees and soil across the trail. Across the gorge is a cliff from which a large rock face fell in a recent wet winter. This major act of erosion struck the area just below a viewpoint situated on the switchbacks that climb the east canyon wall from Illilouette Creek.

At the junction with the Buena Vista Trail, 1½ miles out, our route turns left (east) and begins a switchbacking descent of 560 feet to Illilouette Creek. About ⅓ mile before the creek bridge is a chasm viewpoint just off the trail behind a small fence. From here there is a striking view almost directly down to 370-foot Illilouette Fall. Beyond the bridge, the trail rises steeply for 400 feet and then skirts the edge of Panorama Cliff. As we climb higher, views expand greatly. The Valley floor is spread out below, and across the canyon the immense back of Half Dome dominates the scene.

After passing the Mono Meadow Trail our route switch-backs down 500 feet to join the John Muir Trail shortly below the top of Nevada Fall. From here we follow the latter part of the 1st hiking day, Trip 81, to Little Yosemite Valley.

2nd Hiking Day: Follow the 2nd hiking day, Trip 81, to **Merced Lake**, 8.7 miles (14 km).

3rd and 4th Hiking Days: Retrace your steps, 15.4 miles (24.8 km).

Merced Lake

87 Glacier Point to Rutherford Lake

TRIP   From Glacier Point to Rutherford Lake (loop trip).
             Topo maps *Yosemite, Merced Peak*. Best mid or late
             season; 69.0 miles (111.1 km).

Grade	Trail/layover days	Total recommended days
Leisurely	12/2	14
Moderate	11/2	13
Strenuous	7/2	9

HILITES Designed for the experienced backpacker, this trip
             offers a combination of excellent fishing and
             superlative vistas. Almost a dozen angling lakes,
             most of them in high-country settings, also
             provide swimming to alleviate the trail dust.
             Three major passes challenge the most ambitious
             hiker, and the wide variations in plants and
             wildlife will satisfy the most discriminating
             naturalist.

DESCRIPTION (Moderate trip)

1st Hiking Day: Follow Trip 86 to **Little Yosemite Valley**, 6.7
miles (10.8 km).

2nd Hiking Day: Follow the 2nd hiking day, Trip 81, to **Merced
Lake**, 8.7 miles (14 km).

3rd Hiking Day (**Merced Lake** to **Lyell Fork, Merced River**, 5.8
miles—9.3 km): Leaving "civilization" by the back door, we
follow a level, sandy, shady trail up the flat Merced River
valley for a short mile to the Merced Lake Ranger Station and
a junction with the trail up Lewis Creek, crossing this creek on
multiple bridges. Beyond the junction our route continues
almost level under imposing Jeffrey pines and other tall

conifers for more than a mile before beginning a perceptible ascent. This gentle climb crosses several tributaries, and each crossing is the center of a small sea of bracken ferns. On the right, the singing river is never far away, and the great height of the debris above summer water levels suggests what a massive torrent must rage here at the peak of the melt.

Arriving at Washburn Lake (7600′) one sees what looks like a dam at the outlet, but it is a natural dam—a bedrock granite ridge into which the river has cut a **V**. Fishing in this lake is good, especially in late season, for rainbow, brook and brown trout (to 9″). The shores are host to a great variety of trees and shrubs, including Jeffrey and lodgepole pine, white fir, Sierra juniper, aspen, manzanita, sagebrush, chinquapin and huckleberry oak, plus a field of grass just back of the swimmable sandy beach by the inlet. Above the lake our trail hops across a tributary stream and continues gently up on sandy underfooting for ½ mile to a twin waterfall about 10 feet high. Across the canyon is the notch through which the Red Peak Fork of the Merced River reaches the main canyon. Then our trail climbs less gently on an open slope up to another forested flat where a glorious understory of bracken ferns hundreds of yards long is shaded by tall red and white firs, Jeffrey and lodgepole pines, and quaking aspens. Under these stately trees, just before a bridge over the river and just below the confluence of the Lyell Fork, are several good campsites. Fishing in the river is fair for rainbow trout (to 10″).

4th Hiking Day (**Lyell Fork, Merced River**, to **Triple Peak Fork Meadow**, 4.2 miles—6.8 km): Beyond the sturdy wood bridge spanning the Merced River, our trail soon begins to climb south into the great granite **V** carved by the lower stretches of the Merced Peak Fork of the river. This ascent steepens as it enters the zone of red fir and juniper, and then the path levels momentarily where it crosses the Merced Peak Fork on another wooden bridge, which spans a short section of quiet water between roaring cascades above and below. Our trail leaves the riverside and climbs by long switchbacks up the north side of the bowl, leading to excellent viewpoints for visual enjoyment of the huge granite slabs, the aspen grove and the pockets of conifers below. Another overlook at a switchback turn is close beneath a cascade and a waterfall on the Triple Peak Fork, whose upper reaches our trail is searching out. It was in these upper reaches of the river that the Merced glacier began, and the polished granite on every hand is a constant reminder of its presence. Above the switchbacks our trail ascends gently to a verdant flat where the green Triple Peak Fork slowly winds among the tall trees. After one more steep—but short— climb, the trail ascends gradually near the river under a moderate forest cover of lodgepoles for 2 miles to the foot of long Triple Peak Fork Meadow. The river curves in lovely fashion through this mile-long grassland, past many campsites made illegal by the prohibition against camping within 100 feet of streams. Side pools out of the main current warm up enough to provide pleasant swimming in midsummer. The best campsites are at the south end of the meadow, near the junction with the Red Peak Pass Trail (9100'). Fishing is good for brook and rainbow trout (to 9").

5th Hiking Day (**Triple Peak Fork Meadow** to **Post Creek**, 7.2 miles—11.6 km): This hiking day begins with a gradually increasing climb for a long mile southward away from the Triple Peak Fork, out of lodgepole forest into dense hemlock. Then the duff trail turns northeast and climbs almost a mile on a traverse interrupted by two short switchbacks, to arrive at the rock monument at the junction with the high trail that goes along the top of the east wall of the Merced River canyon. Here our route turns right (south) and quickly ascends a beautiful hillside with broken, light-colored granite close on the left and the soaring Clark Range across the canyon on the right. The trail then levels off in a spectacular high bowl, encircled by Triple Divide Peak, Isberg Peak and some unnamed peaks between. The feeling of spaciousness here is worth the four days' hike to get to this Shangri-la, and in midseason the green grass and many-hued flowers add enough stimulation to surfeit the senses. After fording the unmapped, unnamed outlet of the unnamed but mapped lakes in this bowl, our trail dips into a bowl-within-the-bowl and there crosses another clear stream.

Finally we ascend out of the huge meadow and cross another stream before arriving at a hillside junction with the Isberg Pass Trail, where we turn right (south). Our Post Peak Pass Trail climbs to the ridgeline north of Post Peak, then follows this ridge south to the actual pass (10,700'). This ascent is not without compensation, for the views from the trail are among the most outstanding in the South Boundary Country. From this divide between the Merced and the San Joaquin River, the traveler has views of the Clark Range to the west, the Cathedral Range to the north and the tops of Banner Peak, Mt. Ritter and the Minarets to the east.

At this point our route leaves Yosemite, later to recross the boundary at Fernandez Pass—6 miles away. The trail descends 600 feet to little Porphyry Lake (10,100'), where fishing is fair for brook and rainbow. Below the lake, the trail improves slightly in the stretch to Isberg Meadow, then becomes fairly good. Conies and marmots may appear on the rocky portions of this trail, and deer, grouse and quail in the meadowy parts. After going almost level for ½ mile through several meadows, we enter lodgepole forest and descend moderately to the good campsites at Post Creek (9040'). Fishing along the creek is good for brook trout (to 8").

6th Hiking Day (**Post Creek** to **Rutherford Lake**, 3.9 miles—6.3 km): From Post Creek the trail crosses a small rise, passes two small, unnamed lakelets (no fish), and fords the West Fork Granite Creek. Shortly beyond, the trail fords Fernandez Creek and strikes the Fernandez Pass Trail. Here our route turns right (west) along a gently ascending, densely timbered stretch that offers fine views across Fernandez Creek. After a long ½ mile the trail switchbacks moderately up a morainal slope, trending northwest, to a junction with the Rutherford Lake lateral. Here our route turns right (north) and climbs steeply to the cirque nestling 28-acre Rutherford Lake (9800'). There are fair-to-good campsites on the west side of the lake south of the outlet. Views from these sites are excellent, and fishing is fair for brook and golden (to 16").

7th Hiking Day: Reverse the steps of the 2nd hiking day, Trip 77, to **Middle Chain Lake**, 7.7 miles (12.4 km).

8th Hiking Day: Follow the 2nd hiking day, Trip 78, to **Royal Arch Lake**, 9 miles (14.5 km).

9th, 10th and 11th Hiking Days: Follow the 3rd, 4th and 5th hiking days, Trip 83, 15.8 miles (25.4 km).

Clark Range from near Post Peak Pass

88 Glacier Point to Granite Creek

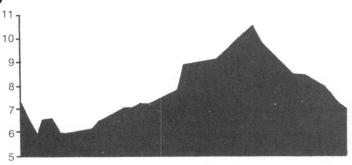

TRIP   From Glacier Point to Granite Creek Campground (shuttle trip). Topo maps *Yosemite, Merced Peak*. Best mid or late season; 41 miles (66 km).

Grade	Trail/layover days	Total recommended days
Leisurely	7/2	9
Moderate	6/1	7
Strenuous	4/1	5

HILITES   This route traverses the very heart of Yosemite's South Boundary Country, and crosses the divide of the Merced and San Joaquin River watersheds at Isberg Pass. Fishing on the lakes and streams is fair-to-excellent, and the life zones range from Canadian to Arctic-Alpine. Remoteness and panoramic vistas beckon the traveler to choose this trip.

DESCRIPTION (Leisurely trip)

1st Hiking Day: Follow Trip 86 to **Little Yosemite Valley**, 6.7 miles (10.8 km).

2nd Hiking Day: Follow the 2nd hiking day, Trip 81, to **Merced Lake**, 8.7 miles (14 km).

3rd and 4th Hiking Days: Follow the 3rd and 4th hiking days, Trip 87, to **Triple Peak Fork Meadow**, 10 miles (16.1 km).

5th Hiking Day (**Triple Peak Fork Meadow** to **Isberg Lakes**, 4.9 miles—7.9 km): First, follow the 5th hiking day, Trip 87, to the junction of the Post Peak Pass and Isberg Pass trails. From this junction at timberline, our route turns left (northeast) and climbs steadily among large blocks of talus. The views north and west, which already have been excellent, become even better as our route switchbacks farther up the ridge, as high as the pass we are approaching. Then the tread goes more or less level to signed Isberg Pass (10,500') and beyond it continues to weave sinuously along the crest. Finally it passes through a tiny defile between two stunted whitebark pines which frame a very dramatic view of the Ritter Range a few miles east. In the distance to the right of this dark range, most of the High Sierra is visible, and hikers who have rambled among its summits will spy some of their favorite monuments. From this pass between the Merced River and the San Joaquin River watersheds, the trail descends by switchbacks to rocky upper Isberg Lake, and then more gradually to lower Isberg Lake (9800'). Fishing in these lakes is fair-to-good for brook and some rainbow (to 8"). There are a few fair campsites at lower Isberg.

6th and 7th Hiking Days: Follow the steps of the 4th and 5th hiking days, Trip 80, 10.7 miles (17.2 km).

Unnamed lake, Triple Divide Peak

National Park Service

Fish Creek/Mono Creek

Surmounting Duck Pass from the north, one looks south across Cascade Valley to the Silver Divide. In the light of midday, the bleached granite of the divide imparts a glowing crown to the whole range and the impression is one of a royal diadem. Views such as this make the region a special place—a favorite to which one must return time and again lest a nuance of memory be lost. Since most of the region is now part of the John Muir Wilderness, its Sierran tranquility is assured.

The Silver Divide country, composed of the Fish and Mono Creek watersheds, lies southeast of Devils Postpile. It is bounded on the north by the Mammoth Crest, on the east by the Sierra crest, and on the south by the Mono Divide. Both Fish Creek and Mono Creek flow west from the Sierra crest, and their flow is augmented by feeder streams emanating from pocket lakes and cirque lakes of the Mono Divide, the Silver Divide and the Mammoth Crest. These feeder streams plunge and splash down from their alpine settings to densely forested canyon floors. The forest carpet in the canyons contrasts sharply with the barrenness of surrounding peaks, like Red Slate Mountain, Mt. Morgan, Mt. Mills, Mt. Gabb and Mt. Hilgard, all over 13,000 feet.

Glacially wrought, the Fish and Mono Creek canyons exhibit typical "hanging valleys," broad expanses of polished granite, amphitheater cirques, and arc-shaped moraines. An outstanding example of a terminal moraine may be seen when one looks back toward Long Valley from the eastern ascent to McGee Pass. The glacier that once filled this canyon was one of the Sierra's most ancient, and it is fitting that it was eroding the oldest rocks in the Sierra. Recent fossil identification has dated these rocks at four hundred million years. Nowhere in the Sierra is the birthplace of a glacier more vividly portrayed than in the Little Lakes Valley on the east side of Mono Pass. Backed by Mts. Mills, Abbot and Dade and Bear Creek Spire, this charming valley has the typical **U**-shaped profile. Lateral moraines pushed to the sides of the valley by the ebb and flow of ice are now topped by tiny lakelets.

The Indians were the first to appreciate the charm of high-country retreats like the Little Lakes Valley. On the east side, it was the Mono Indians who sought the high country in summertime. This country provided a plentiful natural larder, but the Indians, like us, also fled to the heights to escape the midsummer valley heat.

Prospectors, following the lure of "that one big strike," soon penetrated into the high country, but most of their efforts were confined to the area around Mono Lake. The first recorded visit to Mono Pass and the San Joaquin River was by the Brewer party in 1864. Led by an army cavalryman who claimed he had once pursued Indians over the pass, this tiny survey team topped the Sierra crest and followed the descent of the present Mono Creek Trail to Vermilion Valley (now covered by man-made Lake Thomas A. Edison). Using the valley as a base camp, they made an unsuccessful attempt to ascend Mt. Goddard before returning to Yosemite.

The Brewer party journals do not indicate the quality of fishing available in the area at the time. However, it is difficult to imagine much better angling than is offered there today. The appropriately named Fish Creek boasts a varied fish population of brook, rainbow and some golden trout—as does Mono Creek. On the Fish Creek side of the Silver Divide some of the better fishing spots are Cascade Valley, Tully Hole, Helen Lake and Warrior Lake. The Mono Creek watershed offers equally fine angling at Grinnell Lakes, Graveyard Lakes and Laurel Lake, and on the upper reaches of Mono Creek. State fishing licenses are required.

The Trailheads

Vermilion Campground. Go east from Clovis (near Fresno) 81 miles on State Highway 168 to the Florence Lake/Lake Edison junction, then 8 miles north on a mostly paved road to Vermilion Campground.

Coldwater Campground. Go west from U.S. 395 4 miles to Mammoth Lakes and veer left on the Lake Mary Road. Follow it 3.5 miles to the northeast shore of Lake Mary, where you turn onto a 1-mile road southeast to Coldwater Campground.

Mosquito Flat. Go 25 miles north from Bishop or 15 miles south from the Mammoth Lakes turnoff on U.S. 395 and then 11 miles on paved and dirt road to road's end in Mosquito Flat beside Rock Creek.

McGee Creek Roadend. Go 32 miles north of Bishop or 8 miles south of the Mammoth Lakes turnoff to a dirt road that leads west 4.0 miles to a roadend parking area.

89 Lake Edison to Graveyard Meadows

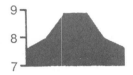

TRIP
From Vermilion Campground (Lake Thomas A. Edison) to Graveyard Meadows (round trip). Topo maps *Kaiser Peak, Mt. Abbot*. Best mid season; 10.4 miles (16.8 km).

Grade	Trail/layover days	Total recom- mended days
Leisurely	2/0	2
Moderate	....	....
Strenuous	....	....

HILITES
The grail at the end of this quest is a pretty, meadowed campsite within the boundaries of the John Muir Wilderness Area. This route travels densely forested country abounding in wildlife, and tops a crest offering superlative views.

DESCRIPTION

1st Hiking Day (**Vermilion Campground** to **Graveyard Meadows**, 5.2 miles—8.4 km): To reach the trailhead, proceed beyond the turnoff to the campground and follow the dirt road 0.15 mile to a parking area, turn right, up the hill, and go past the turnoff to the packstation (on the left) to a parking area at a Forest Service sign. Park here under the tall Jeffrey pines. After a stroll of 0.3 mile we reach a signed junction with the trail to Quail Meadows, and we veer right onto it and down, to the collapsed bridge across Cold Creek. Beyond the bridge, our route reaches a junction, where we take the Goodale Pass Trail, the left fork, and proceed under Jeffrey pines, white firs and junipers. We soon begin a long, dusty ascent under a dense cover of mostly Jeffrey pines. Our route passes a meadow on the lower part of this climb, but the ascent is fairly monotonous until very near the top, where we are rewarded with good views of Lake Edison and the peaks of the Mono Divide. From the crown of the climb it is but a short distance to Cold Creek, which we ford in order to join a jeep road for a short distance before we arrive at the signed boundary of the John Muir

Wilderness. Graveyard Meadows (8800') are on the right, and secluded camping can be found at the head of the meadows. Or, if one prefers, one can stay at the more well-used sites near the ford. Fishing in Cold Creek is poor-to-fair for brook (to 8").
2nd Hiking Day: Retrace your steps, 5.2 miles (8.4 km).

Cold Creek bridge before it collapsed

90 Lake Edison to Graveyard Lakes

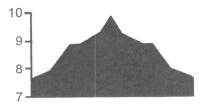

TRIP From Vermilion Campground (Lake Thomas A. Edison) to Lower Graveyard Lake (round trip). Topo maps *Kaiser Peak, Mt. Abbot.* Best mid or late season; 16.8 miles (27.2 km).

Grade	Trail/layover days	Total recommended days
Leisurely	4/1	5
Moderate	3/1	4
Strenuous	2/1	3

HILITES The California Department of Fish and Game has never been called overly creative, but it named the lakes in the Graveyard Lakes chain well. Beneath tombstone-granited Graveyard Peak lie lakes with DF&G names like Vengeance, Murder, Phantom, Headstone, Spook and Ghost. This country is worth investigating if for no other reason than to satisfy one's curiosity about these names. The truth is that this particular lake basin is one of the loveliest and most regal in the Silver Divide country.

DESCRIPTION (Leisurely trip)

1st Hiking Day: Follow Trip 89 to **Graveyard Meadows,** 5.2 miles (8.4 km).

2nd Hiking Day (**Graveyard Meadows** to **Lower Graveyard Lake,** 3.2 miles—5.2 km): From the south end of Graveyard Meadows, the trail enters the John Muir Wilderness and skirts the north edge of the meadows under a dense cover of lodgepoles and red firs. Birdlovers should keep an eye out for the Brewer blackbird, whitecrowned sparrow, Cassin finch, robin and sparrow hawk that inhabit this mountain field. At the north end of the meadow, the trail begins climbing moderately, and soon we cross Cold Creek on rocks (difficult in early season). This forested, duff trail ascends the narrowing Cold Creek valley, fording the creek in two places at the south end of Upper Graveyard Meadow. The trail continues its gentle-to-moderate ascent under lodgepoles to a junction with the trail to Graveyard Lakes. We turn left onto it and ford Cold Creek in Upper Graveyard Meadow. Beyond the ford, the trail enters a cover of lodgepole and hemlock and begins a steep, rocky climb to the basin above. The lodgepole pine and mountain hemlock at the top of this 600-foot ascent give way to lush meadows at the eastern fringes of beautiful lower Graveyard Lake (9900'). Good though heavily used campsites may be found in the lodgepole stands where the trail first meets the lake, or along the east side of the lake between this point and the inlet stream.

From any of these places, the camper has marvelous views of Graveyard Peak and the tumbled granite cirque wall that surrounds the entire Graveyard Lakes basin. It is easy to derive the logic behind the name, "Graveyard Peak." Tombstone-makers have for years shown a preference for this particular kind of salt-and-pepper granite. These campsites along the east side of lower Graveyard Lake make an excellent base camp from which to fish and explore the remaining five lakes in the basin. The three small lakes directly above offer pretty and cleaner camping, and they can be reached by following the trail around to the head of the lake and climbing the hill. Fishing is good on lower Graveyard Lake for brook trout (to 13") and fair-to-good on the upper lakes, due to poor spawning waters.

3rd and 4th Hiking Days: Retrace your steps, 8.4 miles (13.6 km).

Looking south over Lake Edison

91   Rock Creek to Chickenfoot Lake

TRIP   From Mosquito Flat (on Rock Creek) to Chickenfoot Lake (round trip). Topo maps *Mt. Tom, Mt.
Abbot*. Best mid or late season; 6 miles (9.6 km).

Grade	Trail/layover days	Total recommended days
Leisurely	2/0	2
Moderate	....	....
Strenuous	....	....

HILITES   Majestic scenery dominates this short, popular
trip. Because of its moderate terrain and high
country "feel" this route through the Little Lakes
Valley has been a long-time favorite of the
beginning hiker, and the varied and good fishing
for brook, rainbow and brown makes it also an
excellent angling choice.

DESCRIPTION

1st Hiking Day (**Mosquito Flat** to **Chickenfoot Lake,** 3 miles—4.8
km): The magnificent Sierra crest confronts the traveler at the
very outset of this trip. From the trailhead at Mosquito Flat
(10,300′), the wide, rocky-sandy trail starts southwest toward
the imposing skyline dominated by Bear Creek Spire. A short
distance from the trailhead, our route tops a low rocky ridge
just west of Mack Lake, and from this ridge one has good views
of green-clad Little Lakes Valley. Gazing out, one cannot help
but feel a sense of satisfaction that this beautiful valley enjoys
protection as part of the John Muir Wilderness. Aside from
some early, abortive mining ventures, this region remains
relatively unspoiled.

    Our trail, the Morgan Pass Trail, crosses the ridge and in a
short distance meets the Mono Pass Trail branching right.
Our route then skirts the west tip of Marsh Lake. Anglers will
wish to try their luck for the good fishing for brown and brook
in Marsh Lake and in the nearby lagoon areas of Rock Creek.
While fishing on the numerous lakes and streams of Little
Lakes Valley, one has views south into the long glacial
cirque—a long-time favorite of lensmen. Flanked by Mt. Starr

(12,870') and Mt. Morgan (13,748'), the valley terminates in the omnipotent heights of Mts. Mills, Abbot, Dade and Julius Caesar, and Bear Creek Spire, all over 13,000 feet. Still-active glaciers on the slopes of these prominences are reminders of the enormous forces that carved this valley eons ago, and the visitor cannot help feeling contrasting reactions of exhilaration and humility.

From the meadowed fringes of Marsh and Heart lakes the trail ascends gently past the western side of Box Lake to the east side of aptly named Long Lake. For the angler with a yearning to try different waters, the three unnamed lakes on the bench just to the east offer good fishing for brook and rainbow. Beyond Long Lake the trail ascends through a moderately dense forest cover to the fair campsites at the western edge of Chickenfoot Lake (10,761'). Overall, this lake does indeed look like a chicken's foot, but any further reference to domesticity in describing this high, glacial lake would be inappropriate. As in the streams and lakes in the north end of the valley, the fishing is good for brook, brown and rainbow (to 15"), and the views are magnificent. The close proximity of the Sierra Nevada crest makes Chickenfoot Lake a popular base camp for climbers.

2nd Hiking Day: Retrace your steps, 3 miles (4.8 km).

Bear Creek Spire, Mt. Dade

92   Rock Creek to Ruby Lake

TRIP   From Mosquito Flat to Ruby Lake (round trip).
                Topo maps *Mt. Tom, Mt. Abbot.* Best mid or late
                season; 5 miles (8 km).

Grade	Trail/layover days	Total recommended days
Leisurely	2/0	2
Moderate	....	....
Strenuous	....	....

HILITES   From the Little Lakes Valley upward to the
                heights of the Ruby Lake cirque, the traveler
                gains an appreciation of glacially formed country.
                One can almost see the main trunk of the glacier
                flowing northeast through the valley and being
                joined by the feeder glacier from the cirque that
                now holds Ruby Lake. The terminus of this trip,
                Ruby Lake, lies amidst the barren peaks of the
                awe-inspiring Sierra Nevada crest.

DESCRIPTION

1st Hiking Day (**Mosquito Flat** to **Ruby Lake,** 2.5 miles—4 km):
First, follow Trip 91 to the junction of the Morgan Pass and
Mono Pass trails. Here our route branches right (west) and
ascends steeply over rocky switchbacks. In the course of this
switchbacking ascent, the traveler will see the moderate-to-
dense forest cover of whitebark and lodgepole diminish in
density as we near timberline. Views during the climb include
the glacier-fronted peaks named above, and, midway up the
ascent, Mt. Morgan. Immediately below to the east, the deep
blue of Heart and Box lakes and some of the Hidden Lakes
reflects the sky above, and the viewer looking at the panorama
of the valley can readily trace the glacial history that left these
"puddles" behind.
    Near the meadowed edge of the outlet stream from Ruby
Lake is a junction, where we turn left. It becomes apparent
that a cirque basin is opening up, although one cannot see

Ruby Lake, which completely fills the cirque bottom, until one is actually at water's edge (11,000'). This first breathtaking view of the lake and its towering cirque walls makes the climb worth the effort. Sheer granite makes up the upper walls of the cirque, and the crown is topped by a series of spectacular pinnacles, particularly to the west. To the north, also on the crest, a notch indicates Mono Pass, and close scrutiny will reveal the switchbacking trail that ascends the south ridge of Mt. Starr. The lower walls of the cirque are mostly made up of talus and scree that curve outward to the lake's edge, and it is over this jumbled rock that ambitious anglers must scramble to sample the fair fishing for brook, rainbow and brown (to 12"). Good campsites can be found below the outlet of the lake. Lakeside campsites are exposed and usually windy.

2nd Hiking Day: Retrace your steps, 2.5 miles (4 km).

Outlet of Ruby Lake

93   McGee Creek to Steelhead Lake

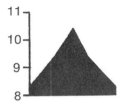

TRIP   From McGee Creek Roadend to Steelhead Lake
(round trip). Topo maps *Mt. Morrison, Mt. Abbot.*
Best mid or late season; 9 miles (14.4 km).

Grade	Trail/layover days	Total recommended days
Leisurely	2/1	3
Moderate	2/0	2
Strenuous	....	....

HILITES   Travelers new to east-escarpment entry to the
Sierra will find the ascent to Steelhead Lake fascinating because of the swirling patterns in the
highly fractured red metamorphic rocks of the
canyon wall. Though Steelhead Lake is relatively
easy to reach, the hiker may find seclusion there.

DESCRIPTION

1st Hiking Day (**McGee Creek Roadend** to **Steelhead Lake**, 4.5
miles—7.2 km): From the parking area (8100') the trail
ascends a short distance to a Forest Service sign proclaiming
the eastern boundary of the John Muir Wilderness. The route,
an old jeep road leading to the defunct Scheelore Mine,
traverses the north and then the west side of McGee Creek
canyon. The canyon is mostly sage- and rabbitbrush-covered
except for an anomalous grove of aspen in an apparently dry
area. Near the creek are more aspen, cottonwood, birch and
willow. Soon our trail fords the streams emanating from the
springs above Horsetail Falls, and the canyon narrows. As the
trail passes close to the creek, the grade eases, and our route
enters a lush area with a lovely floral display.

The gentle ascent continues to a ford of tree-lined McGee
Creek, where there is sometimes a log (difficult in early season). Then the unshaded trail climbs more steeply until it
passes a beaver dam. Above the dam, the creek wanders

through a meadow, above which the trail fords the creek via logs and boards to the west bank. As the trail loops west it becomes steeper and enters a moderately dense lodgepole forest. Then our route leaves the jeep road at a signed junction and continues its winding ascent to a junction with the Steelhead Lake lateral. (This junction is farther than indicated on the map; it is where the trail finally returns to creekside. Fording McGee Creek, this lateral climbs steeply by switchbacks along the north side of the outlet stream from Grass Lake. Fishing from the meadowed fringes of little Grass Lake is poor-to-fair for rainbow and brook. From Grass Lake the trail once more switchbacks up an abrupt, timbered slope, and ends at the good camping sites at the north end of fairly large (about 25 acres) Steelhead Lake (10,350'). Views from these campsites take in the granite grandeur of Mt. Stanford and Mt. Crocker to the south and west, and rust-and-buff-colored Mt. Baldwin to the north. Fishermen will find the angling for rainbow and brook excellent (best in early and late season). They will also find the name "Steelhead" Lake a misnomer, though an understandable error. Over the years, catches of rainbow trout from this lake have exhibited pale, faded-out markings, giving an appearance much like their silver cousins of coastal waters.

2nd Hiking Day: Retrace your steps, 4.5 miles (7.2 km).

94   McGee Creek to McGee Lake

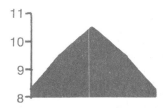

TRIP   From McGee Creek Roadend to Big McGee Lake
(round trip). Topo maps *Mt. Morrison, Mt. Abbot.*
Best mid or late season; 13 miles (21 km).

Grade	Trail/layover days	Total recommended days
Leisurely	2/1	3
Moderate	2/0	2
Strenuous	....	....

HILITES   In an alpine setting close under the Sierra crest,
Big McGee Lake shares a large granite basin with
three other fishable lakes. This beautiful spot
nestles under the sheer, colorful walls of Red and
White Peak, and close to impressive Mt. Crocker.

DESCRIPTION

1st Hiking Day (**McGee Creek Roadend** to **Big McGee Lake**, 6.5
miles—10.5 km): First, follow Trip 93 to the trail intersection
with the Steelhead Lake lateral, where the trail continues,
south over a forested, rocky slope. The ascent eases as the trail
passes a drift fence, and then we pass a tarn, climb above a
meadow where there is a campsite, and emerge from timber
into another meadow. The trail then undulates under a sparse
cover of whitebark pine to join the creek briefly and skirt a
smaller meadow from where an older section of trail heads
back down-canyon. Soon the trail reaches the rocky, open
slopes just north of Big McGee Lake (10480'). Fair-to-good
campsites may be found along the north shore. Fishermen will
enjoy the fair-to-good fishing for rainbow and brook (to 13") on
Big McGee Lake, and, if time and inclination allow, will want
to explore the equally good fishing at nearby Little McGee
Lake, Crocker Lake, or picture-book Golden Lake.
2nd Hiking Day: Retrace your steps, 6.5 miles (10.5 km).

McGee Creek to Lake Edison   95

TRIP   From McGee Creek Roadend to Vermilion Camp-
ground (Lake Thomas A. Edison) (shuttle trip).
Topo maps *Mt. Morrison, Mt. Abbot, Kaiser Peak.*
Best mid or late season; 33.6 miles (54.3 km).

Grade	Trail/layover days	Total recom- mended days
Leisurely	7/2	9
Moderate	5/2	7
Strenuous	4/2	6

HILITES   This trans-Sierra route is one of the finest in the
northern Sierra. Two scenic passes, both over
11,000 feet, cross the Sierra crest and the Silver
Divide. Between them the route visits alpine lakes
and streams offering excellent fishing for rainbow,
brook and golden trout. Pristine meadows, spectacular peaks, and dense forest mark this trip as a
must for any serious wilderness traveler.

DESCRIPTION (Leisurely trip)

1st Hiking Day: Follow Trip 94 to **Big McGee Lake,** 6.5 miles
(10.5 km).

2nd Hiking Day (**Big McGee Lake** to **Tully Lake**, 5.5 miles—8.9
km): With the colorful and majestic heights of Red and White
Mountain to the left (southwest) the route ascends steeply to
Little McGee Lake, passing a signed junction with the route to
Hopkins Pass. Fishing at this rockbound lake is fair for rainbow and brook. From Little McGee Lake our route swings
northward and ascends a narrow, rocky canyon toward McGee

Pass. The red rock walls of the canyon look very desolate, and the trail briefly disappears under snow until late season. The last few hundred feet of ascent are accomplished via rocky switchbacks up the west wall of a barren cirque. From McGee Pass (11,900′) views to the west are good of the peaks above Fish Creek.

An interesting turn-of-the-century legend has it that two Indian sheepherders running sheep around the headwaters of McGee Creek were returning from the high country. En route, a pack on one of their mules shifted, and they jury-rigged a large rock to balance the shifting action. Upon reaching their destination, they unloaded the jury-rigged balance and discovered that the rock felt abnormally heavy. As in all good gold legends, the rock assayed rich, and, ostensibly, neither the two Indians nor subsequent treasure-seekers have found the lode from which the rock was taken.

From the pass much of the descent to timberline is on new trail that has too many switchbacks for most people's taste. We reach timberline above a large meadow, and from here our trail follows a route north of that shown on the topo map. The trail descends through sparse timber and meets the creek at the foot of a meadow. Just below, the creek and the trail drop steeply and turn right. Ford the creek here and head south up a grassy swale to the good campsite in the trees above Tully Lake. Good campsites may also be found on the meadowed fringes along the northeast side of the lake. Tully Lake (10,400′) is a small (about 10 acres) high-country lake that sustains fair-to-good fishing for golden and brook (to 13″). Anglers will want to try the nearby waters of Red and White Lake, about 1 mile over the ridge to the east. Fishing here is also fair-to-good for rainbow that often run to 16″. Those wishing stream fishing can find smaller rainbow, brook and some golden along meandering Fish Creek.

3rd Hiking Day (**Tully Lake** to **Tully Hole**, 3 miles—4.8 km): This short trail day allows the traveler who admires wild back-country scenery to absorb the primitive beauty of this area. Anglers, particularly fly fisherman, will find the leisurely pace along Fish Creek satisfying. From Tully Lake retrace the route to the main Fish Creek Trail, where it turns left (west). The trail now follows the south bank of Fish Creek as it descends below treeline ¼ mile to a ford of Fish Creek, where it meets the trail that follows the outlet from Tully Lake. Our trail soon fords the creek again and enters timber. Here we pass a signed junction with the trail to Cecil and Lee Lakes. Then the descent steepens and the trail switchbacks down to lush Horse Heaven. Through the meadow, the trail is muddy into late season, and the ford at the west end of the meadow is difficult in early season. Beyond this ford the trail passes a drift fence and descends through lodgepole and hemlock on the south side of the creek to Tully Hole (9500'). Like the meadows at Horse Heaven, the grasslands of Tully Hole (9500') are also rife with wildflower color. The stream is sometimes bowered with willows, but the long, swirling, curved line of Fish Creek is for the most part an open, pleasant stretch of water with grassy, overhung banks and several deep holes. Good campsites at the northwest edge of the meadow near the John Muir Trail junction take advantage of the fine views up the meadow.

4th Hiking Day (**Tully Hole** to **Lake of the Lone Indian**, 5 miles— 8.1 km): The route at this point joins the John Muir Trail, and leaves Tully Hole by a gentle descent. From the trail, the traveler has splendid views and access to the numerous small falls and holes that characterize nearby Fish Creek. The trail then passes the junction with the Cascade Valley Trail and climbs steeply over a densely forested slope east of the outlet stream from Squaw Lake. Midway up this stretch the trail levels off, fords the stream twice in quick succession, and passes several campsites situated in picturesque meadows. Then it begins the final, long, steep climb to Squaw Lake. This section of trail is rocky, eroded and exposed.

Meadow-fringed Squaw Lake is a good place to stop and ponder the effects of glacial erosion—the clean granite cliffs the large erratics here and there, and the lake basin itself. Anglers will wish to fish Squaw Lake—and Warrior Lake above it—which offer good-to-excellent fishing for brook (to 9").

From Squaw Lake our route winds up the rocky slope to the southwest, and in ½ mile meets the Goodale Pass Trail at a small pool. Our route leaves the John Muir Trail here, turns right, tops a ridge, and descends through rocky meadows to the foot of turquoise Papoose Lake. This small lake (under 5 acres) affords good fishing for brook, as does Chief Lake, up the granite slope to the east. At the outlet of Papoose Lake our route branches north, and then descends over a long dusty traverse to the good campsites in the grassy pockets at the southwest end of Lake of the Lone Indian (10,200'). Angling is good for brook and rainbow (8-14").

5th Hiking Day (**Lake of the Lone Indian** to **Lower Graveyard Lake**, 5.2 miles—8.4 km): First retrace the steps of the previous day to the Goodale Pass Trail at the foot of Papoose Lake.

Our route then turns right (southwest), and 100 yards beyond the ford of Papoose Lake's outlet is a signed junction with the trail to Minnow Creek. Here our trail begins a steep, rocky ascent to a long, grass-bottomed swale below Goodale Pass. Where the trail levels off momentarily an unsigned trail goes right, down the hill to Lake of the Lone Indian. The exfoliating, rocky slopes of the Silver Divide show the usual signs of glaciation—polish, rounding and striation. The whistling of marmots that inhabit the jumbled slopes accompanies the traveler as he climbs the last leg to Goodale Pass (11,000'). From the pass views extend as far north as the Ritter Range and Yosemite, and south over the San Joaquin River watershed to the peaks beyond the Mono Divide. The first part of the descent down the south side of Goodale Pass is rocky and steep. As the switchbacking trail progresses, it offers fine views of the nearby cirque that feeds Cold Creek.

Soon the trail levels out somewhat and stepladders down through a series of charming green pocket meadows. As the trail descends in and out of lodgepole-pine stands, it crosses many small streams which pour out of the canyon's north wall. Unfortunately, some of these may be fouled by the summer cattle population. Soon after the ford of Cold Creek (difficult in early season) the trail arrives at the junction with the Graveyard Lakes Trail. Here our route branches right (west) onto it and follows the last part of the 2nd hiking day, Trip 90. *6th Hiking day:* Reverse the steps of the 2nd hiking day, Trip 90, 3.2 miles (5.2 km).

7th Hiking Day: Reverse the steps of the 1st hiking day, Trip 89, 5.2 miles (8.4 km).

Rock Creek to Lake Edison   **96**

TRIP
From Mosquito Flat (on Rock Creek) to Vermilion Campground (Lake Thomas A. Edison) via Mono Creek (shuttle trip). Topo maps *Mt. Tom, Mt. Abbot, Kaiser Peak*. Best late season; 21.4 miles (34.5 km).

Grade	Trail/layover days	Total recommended days
Leisurely	4/1	5
Moderate	3/1	4
Strenuous	2/1	3

HILITES
Taking this trans-Sierra crossing in late season gives the traveler three distinct plusses: First, the luxuriant aspen groves along Mono Creek take on their golden hue about this time. Second, the mid-season fishing slump usually ends as the weather cools off. Last, this popular route sees heavy foot and animal traffic during early and mid season, but this activity tapers off when the leaves begin to turn.

DESCRIPTION (Leisurely trip)
1st Hiking Day: Follow Trip 92 to **Ruby Lake**, 2.5 miles (4 km).
2nd Hiking Day (**Ruby Lake** to **Fish Camp**, 7.8 miles—12.6 km); First, retrace your steps back to the Mono Pass Trail. From the junction, the trail ascends steeply over the rocky switchbacks on the south slope of Mt. Starr to Mono Pass (12,000′), a notch in the cirque wall just west of Mt. Starr. Views from the pass are excellent, but those wishing a panoramic outlook on the

spectacular Sierra crest should ascend the granite shoulder of Mt. Starr, an easy climb to the east. From this vantage point one has a complete perspective of Pioneer Basin and Mts. Stanford, Huntington, Crocker and Hopkins, and Red and White Mountain to the north. To the south one has an "end-on" view of Mts. Abbot and Dade, Bear Creek Spire, and Mt. Humphreys.

From Mono Pass the trail descends over granite slopes past barren Summit Lake, and then drops more severely as it veers west above Trail Lakes (poor-to-fair fishing for brook). Our route then turns northward and fords Golden Creek. Following the north side of the stream in a moderately dense forest cover, the trail passes the lateral to Pioneer Basin (north) and the lateral to Fourth Recess Lake (south). Anglers may elect to try their luck at the good fishing for brook (8-14″) at Fourth Recess Lake, ½ mile south over a gentle climb.

Our route continues to descend, fording the outlet streams from Pioneer Basin and paralleling the westward course of Mono Creek. As the Mono Creek valley opens up beyond Mono Rock, the trail passes the steep lateral to Third Recess Lake (south), and, about a mile farther, descends past the turnoff to Lower Hopkins Lake and the Hopkins Lake basin. Anglers will find the many fine holes that interrupt dashing Mono Creek good fishing for the brook, rainbow and occasional golden (to 12″). In late season the groves of quaking aspen that line the stream's banks are an incomparably colorful backdrop to an otherwise steady conifer green. Owing to heavy traffic, this segment of trail becomes somewhat dusty where it passes the Grinnell Lake lateral and descends to Fish Camp (8500′). This traditional camping place marks the junction of the Mono Creek Trail with the Second Recess lateral. Due to heavy use here, the Forest Service encourages you to camp downstream.

3rd Hiking Day (**Fish Camp** to **Quail Meadows**, 5 miles—8.1 km): As this day's route descends along the north side of Mono Creek, the rich yellows of the aspen groves accompany the stream. Occasionally the traveler has views of the stern northern face of Volcanic Knob to the south, and from several spots along the trail one looks up the long, chutelike valley of the First Recess to the granite-topped heights of Recess Peak. Fishing for the brook, rainbow and occasional golden is much like that of the previous day, but the stream is somewhat less accessible from the trail. About 2½ miles below Fish Camp the trail turns right, away from the narrowing canyon, and climbs by rocky switchbacks to the crown of a ridge, where it joins the John Muir Trail. Thence it descends a short distance on the

east side of the North Fork of Mono Creek, and fords the
North Fork (difficult in early season) just above its confluence
with Mono Creek. From the ford to the edge of Quail Meadows
is a gentle downhill walk through dense forest cover. Fair-to-
good campsites can be found on the forested fringe of Quail
Meadows (7760'), downstream from the point where the John
Muir Trail branches left (south) and crosses Mono Creek.

4th Hiking Day (**Quail Meadows** to **Vermilion Campground**, 6.1
miles—9.8 km): Our route from Quail Meadows proceeds west
on a level stretch. Mono Creek now casades over a series of
granite-bedrocked holes (fine swimming in late season) before
flowing into the northeast tip of Lake Edison. This man-made,
granite-edged lake dominates the views to the south for the
remainder of this trip. A boat-taxi service operates the length
of the lake, based at a resort adjoining Vermilion Campground, but advance inquiry should be made about length of
operating season and ferry schedule. (Write to Vermilion
Valley Resort/Mono Hot Springs/California 93642.) The ferry
lands at the northeast tip of the lake, and the marked footpath
giving access to this point can be seen from the trail.

The trail along the upper reaches of the north side of Lake
Edison undulates severely over alternately rocky and dusty
stretches. At some points the trail crosses granite ridges 600
feet above the lake surface, and from these ridges the traveler
has fine views of heavily timbered Bear Ridge across the lake.
The forest cover reflects the lower altitude, as Jeffrey pine and
red fir mix with ever-present lodgepole. This forest becomes
quite dense as our route passes the trail going right (north) to
Graveyard Meadows and Goodale Pass. A faint trail to the left
(south)leads to another landing point, on a nearby bay. Our
route continues west, crosses the bridge over Cold Creek, and
passes the trail to Devils Bathtub. Beyond this junction the
hiker leaves the worst of the dust behind as the trail winds
through Jeffrey pine to a Forest Service road. This sandy road
descends gently to the east edge of Vermilion Campground
(7650').

97 McGee Creek to Rock Creek

TRIP   From McGee Creek Roadend to Mosquito Flat (on
Rock Creek) via McGee Pass, Red and White Lake,
Grinnell Lakes and Fish Camp (shuttle trip). Topo
maps *Mt. Morrison, Mt. Abbot, Mt. Tom.* Best late
season; 29.3 miles (47.1 km).

Grade	Trail/layover days	Total recom-mended days
Leisurely	6/2	8
Moderate	4/2	6
Strenuous	3/1	4

HILITES For *experienced knapsackers only*, this rugged
route (some cross-country) offers excitement and
challenge sufficient to satisfy the most jaded
appetite. High-country lakes surrounded by ram-
partlike peaks characterize this colorful route,
and the fishing is good-to-excellent.

DESCRIPTION (Leisurely trip)

1st and 2nd Hiking Days: Follow Trip 95 to **Tully Lake**, 11 miles
(17.7 km).

3rd Hiking Day (**Tully Lake** to **Grinnell Lake**, 3.5 miles—5.6
km—cross country): From the east shore of Tully Lake our
route ascends the grassy swale that lies due east of the lake. At
the outlet stream from Red and White Lake our route turns
right (south-east) and follows this stream to the lake itself.
Fishermen will wish to try these icy, clear, blue waters for
large rainbow (to 18″), although there's no good camping, Red
and White Lake offers an excellent vantage point from which
to take in the spectacular and aptly named heights of Red and
White Mountain. The saddle (11,600′) that this day's route
traverses is clearly discernible on the lowest point of the right

shoulder of Red and White Mountain, and the easiest route to the saddle takes the traveler around the rocky east shore of the lake. The steepest part of the ascent is over treacherous shale—or snow in early and mid season—and the climber is well-advised to take it slow and easy. Rope should be carried and used, especially if ascending the west side of the pass.

From the top one obtains a well-deserved and exciting view of the surrounding terrain. To the north the immediate, dazzling blue of Red and White Lake sets off the buff browns and ochre reds of the surrounding rock. Beyond this basin the meadowy cirque forming the headwaters of Fish Creek is a large greensward that contrasts sharply with the austere, red-stained eminence of Red Slate Mountain, and the distant skyline offers sawtooth profiles of the Ritter Range, with its readily identifiable Minarets, and the Mammoth Crest. To the south, the barren, rocky shores of the Grinnell chain of lakes occupy the foreground, and, just beyond, the green-sheathed slopes of the Mono Creek watershed drop away, rising in the distance to the Mono Divide. Like the ascent of this saddle, the descent should be taken with some care. The sudden, shaley drop terminates in a large "rock garden," a jumble of large boulders, just above Little Grinnell Lake. Our rock-hopping route takes us along the east shore of this tiny lake to the long, grassy descent leading to the west side of Grinnell Lake (10,800'). Midway along this side, where the most prominent peninsula infringes on the long lake, our route strikes the marked fisherman's trail that veers southwest down a long swale to tiny Laurel Lake. There are several fair campsites at this junction which offer excellent views due to their situation on a plateau above the lake. Fishermen will find Grinnell Lake fair-to-good fishing for brook and rainbow (8-14″). Alternative good campsites can be found along the meadowy fringes of Laurel Lake (10,300'), about 1 mile southwest. Fishing on this lake is excellent for brook (to 10″).

4th Hiking Day (**Grinnell Lake** to **Fish Camp**, 4.5 miles—7.2 km): The fisherman's trail from Grinnell Lake to Laurel Lake descends via a long, scooplike swale to the grassy meadows forming the headwaters of Laurel Creek. The trail, though very faint from Grinnell to Laurel Lake, becomes clearer as it descends gently along Laurel Creek. At this point the creek is still a "jump-across" stream, but a careful approach along the banks will reveal an abundance of brook trout (to 9″), and fly fishermen who favor stream angling will find this tiny watercourse a delight.

The gradual descent along the creek becomes somewhat

steeper just above the larger meadows. The pleasant, timber-fringed grassland is divided by the serpentine curves of Laurel Creek. The trail across the meadow is difficult to follow, and the traveler who loses it should cross to the west side of Laurel Creek and look for the trail in the vicinity of the campsites at the south end of the meadow. The dense lodgepole cover at the end of the meadow soon gives way to manzanita thickets and occasional clumps of quaking aspen as the trail reaches the steep, switchbacking descent above Mono Creek. These switchbacks are unmaintained, and are subject to heavy erosion. However, the difficult going is more than compensated for by the excellent views across the Mono Creek watershed into the Second Recess. Particularly impressive are the heights of Mt. Gabb and Mt. Hilgard, which guard the upper end of this side canyon. When our route strikes the Mono Creek Trail, it turns right (west) for a gently descending ½ mile to the campsites at Fish Camp (8500'). Due to heavy use here, the Forest Service encourages you to camp downstream. Fishing is good for brook and rainbow (to 12") on Mono Creek.

5th Hiking Day: Reverse the steps of the 2nd hiking day, Trip 95, 7.8 miles (12.6 km).

6th Hiking Day: Reverse the steps of the 1st hiking day, Trip 92, 2.5 miles (4 km).

Mammoth Lakes to Purple Lake   **98**

TRIP   From Coldwater Campground (Mammoth Lakes)
to Purple Lake (round trip). Topo map *Mt.
Morrison*. Best late season; 16 miles (25.8 km).

Grade	Trail/layover days	Total recom- mended days
Leisurely	3/1	4
Moderate	2/1	3
Strenuous	2/0	2

HILITES   The rewards for crossing a mountain pass amount
to more than the views that are presented. Most
experienced knapsackers know that passes have a
way of separating the day hikers from the over-
nighters. So it is with this trip across the
Mammoth Crest. Those seeking a modicum of
solitude, along with the satisfaction of seeing what
lies beyond the top of the hill, will find this hike a
worthwhile choice.

DESCRIPTION (Moderate trip)

1st Hiking Day (**Coldwater Campground** to **Purple Lake**, 8
miles—12.9 km): From Coldwater Campground (8960') the
Duck Pass Trail ascends on an alternately sandy and rocky
section along a moderately forested slope. The initial portion
of this trail, from the road end to Barney Lake, receives a good
deal of day hiker and fisherman use, so by midseason the trail
is fairly dusty. As the going levels off, after the first rise,
Arrowhead Lake is visible off to the left (east). Then the trail
ascends again to Skelton Lake. The lake was named for the
brothers Skelton, who, during this mining area's heyday,
established and maintained a stamp mill at the lower end of
the lake. Owing to heavy fishing pressure on these lakes, the
angling is only fair. As our route crosses the rolling terrain
south of Skelton Lake, the barren canyon walls along the
Mammoth Crest show the scouring action of the ancient
glaciers that once covered the land. From the rocky shores of

emerald-green Barney Lake the steep ascent to Duck Pass is easily seen. The switchbacks ascending this steep slope leave hemlock and lodgepole pine behind, and except for an occasional whitebark pine this climb is barren and exposed.

At Duck Pass (10,790′) there are views of the Mammoth Creek watershed and the Mammoth Crest to the northwest. Beyond, the skyline is dominated by the distinctive spires of the Ritter Range. To the south and southwest Pika and Duck lakes occupy the basin immediately below; and these blue, still waters are flanked by the green depths of Cascade Valley. Across the valley the Silver Divide's rocky peaks occupy the horizon. The short descent to the rocky shores of large Duck Lake passes a faint fisherman's trail to Pika Lake. The boulder-strewn west shore of Duck Lake is rugged going, and one has plenty of time during rest stops to admire the pure blue of the deep waters. Except for a few gnarled whitebark pines, the jumbled slopes and rocky crags surrounding the lake are barren and austere. From Duck Lake our route crosses the outlet and descends to join the scenic John Muir Trail. It then turns left (south), rounds a rocky, granite shoulder, and veers east to the several good campsites near the outlet at the south end of Purple Lake (9860′). Fishing is fair-to-good for rainbow and some golden and brook (8-13″). Purple Lake's partly timbered, rocky shoreline gives way to meadow at the northeast end of the lake. The rocks above the meadow give this lake its name; they have a rosy tint during the day, but around sunset they turn purple and violet.

2nd Hiking Day: Retrace your steps, 8 miles (12.9 km).

Mammoth Lakes to Lake Edison 99

TRIP From Coldwater Campground (Mammoth Lakes) to Vermilion Campground (Lake Thomas A. Edison) via Cascade Valley and Goodale Pass (shuttle trip). Topo maps *Mt. Morrison, Mt. Abbot, Kaiser Peak*. Best late season; 29.9 miles (48.1 km).

Grade	Trail/layover days	Total recom- mended days
Leisurely	6/1	7
Moderate	5/1	6
Strenuous	4/1	5

HILITES This trans-Sierra route explores two watersheds, ascends two passes, and offers a world of fine fishing along the way. About one fourth of the route follows the famous John Trail, and high, alpine scenery alternates with intimate, friendly meadows, fast-running streams, and lonely, placid lakes. Long mileage and stiff climbs make this a trip for the hiker who has prepared himself with a couple of early- or mid-season warm-ups, but the rewards, in views and fishing, repay him for the required effort.

DESCRIPTION (Moderate trip)

1st Hiking Day: Follow Trip 98 to **Purple Lake**, 8 miles (12.9 km).

2nd Hiking Day (**Purple Lake** to **Cascade Valley/Fish Creek ford**, 3.5 miles—5.6 km): From the outlet of Purple Lake our route branches right (southwest) from the John Muir Trail and descends gently at first, parallel to Purple Creek. The forest cover along this switchbacking descent is primarily lodgepole pine, giving way to Jeffrey pine and juniper near the valley floor. Manzanita is the main shrub on the steeper part of the descent. The hiker has fine views of the Silver Divide across the valley. The long switchbacks of this steep descent terminate in a large meadow on the floor of Cascade Valley. Here our route strikes the Cascade Valley Trail and turns left (east) along Fish Creek. The fairly level going along the valley floor gives the angler ample opportunity to test the good fishing for brook and rainbow (to 9″). California's DF&G *Anglers' Guide* says about Cascade Valley: "One of the finest trout streams left in the High Sierra; meandering and scenic with splendid campsites and forest cover." As the hiker works his way up the valley, Fish Creek rushes and then meanders on his right, and open meadow fringes beckon. Where this trail crosses Fish Creek via a wading ford, this hiking day ends at one of the many campsites (8560′). Fishing is good, as noted above.

3rd Hiking Day (**Cascade Valley/Fish Creek ford** to **Lake of the Lone Indian**, 4.8 miles—7.7 km): Beyond the ford of Fish Creek the trail ascends somewhat more steeply over rocky stretches. Fish Creek, now on the left, changes as the canyon narrows. The water flows faster and the creek becomes a riotous tumble of waterfalls and tiny holes. Just below the point where our route rejoins the John Muir Trail, the canyon wall on the north side of the valley becomes a sheer, dramatically polished granite surface. Our trail crosses the outlet stream from Helen Lake and meets the John Muir Trail, onto which we turn right (south). From this junction to Helen Lake the ascent is steep. The first part of the climb is densely forested as it works its way up the east side of the outlet stream from Helen Lake, and midway up, the trail passes several alternative meadowed campsites on the right. Beyond these campsites the trail becomes rocky, exposed and eroded as it makes the last steep climb to Helen Lake. One has excellent views back down the **U**-shaped valley with which to fill the breather stops, and as the trail crests at the granite lip of the Helen Lake cirque, one can see whence the glacier emanated that carved the valley below. Anglers will want to fish Helen Lake—and Bobs Lake about ½ mile southeast. Both offer good-to-excellent angling for brook (to 9″).

The trail then rock-hops the outlet of Helen Lake, passes two small alpine tarns, and branches right, leaving the John

Muir Trail, which continues south to Silver Pass. Our route
passes below rocky Papoose Lake, which offers good fishing for
brook trout, as does Warrior Lake, a short distance over the
granite to the east. At the outlet stream of Papoose Lake our
route branches north, away from the Goodale Pass Trail, and
descends over a dusty traverse to the good, grassy-pocketed
campsites at the southwest end of Lake of the Lone Indian
(10,200'). Fishing is good for brook and rainbow (8-14").

4th Hiking Day: Follow the 5th hiking day, Trip 95, 5.2 miles
(8.4 km).

5th Hiking Day: Follow the 2nd hiking day, Trip 90, and the
1st hiking day, Trip 89, 8.4 miles (13.5 km).

Polemonium

Jason Winnett

00 **Mammoth Lakes to Lake Edison**

TRIP   From Coldwater Campground (Mammoth Lakes)
                  to Vermilion Campground (Lake Thomas A. Edi-
                  son), via Cascade Valley, Tully Lake and Grinnell
                  Lakes (shuttle trip). Topo maps *Mt. Morrison, Mt.
                  Abbot, Kaiser Peak*. Best late season; 35.9 miles
                  (57.8 km).

| | Trail/layover | Total recom- |
Grade	days	mended days
Leisurely	8/2	10
Moderate	5/2	7
Strenuous	4/2	6

HILITES   This is a trip for *experienced backpackers only*.
                  Employing a short but strenuous cross-country
                  route over the Silver Divide, this unusual and
                  remote trip should appeal to fisherman, hiker and
                  naturalist—or any combination thereof. Travelers
                  looking for a trip of lonely alpine grandeur will
                  find it in the Silver Divide country.

DESCRIPTION (Leisurely trip)

1st and 2nd Hiking Days: Follow Trip 99 to **Cascade Valley/Fish
Creek ford**, 11.5 miles (18.5 km).

3rd Hiking Day (**Cascade Valley/Fish Creek ford** to **Tully Hole**, 2.8
miles—4.5 km): From the Fish Creek ford the trail ascends the
sometimes-rocky valley floor on the south side of Fish Creek.
This section offers splendid access to nice deep holes and
gurgling riffles, but as the canyon narrows, the trail becomes
steeper and the creek becomes faster, small waterfalls
alternating with noisy cascades. Looking up at the sheer

canyon walls, the hiker cannot help but be impressed with the glacial forces that polished their granite faces. Just below the junction with the John Muir Trail, the trail fords the outlet stream from Helen Lake. Here our route turns left (north) onto the John Muir Trail and crosses to the north side of plunging Fish Creek via a steel bridge. The trail then climbs steeply by switchbacks, offering fine views back to the falls above the bridge. The climb is short, and the trail levels out somewhat as it rejoins Fish Creek. The reunion with the creek is startling, for its waters are now almost placid as they flow through deep green holes. The roar and thunder of the falls are but an echo, and beside the now-mellow Fish Creek the trail ascends to the lovely, open meadows of Tully Hole (9500'). Fish Creek is a pleasant, meandering background to the good campsites at the northwest edge of the meadow. Here the angler should break out his rod for the good-to-excellent fishing for brook, rainbow, and some golden (to 12").

4th Hiking Day: Reverse the steps of the 3rd hiking day, Trip 95, 2.5 miles (4 km).

5th and 6th Hiking Days: Follow the steps of the 3rd and 4th hiking days, Trip 97, 8 miles (12.9 km).

7th and 8th Hiking Days: Follow the steps of the 3rd and 4th hiking days, Trip 96, 11.1 miles (17.9 km).

Mts. Dana and Gibbs, Dana Fork of the Tuolumne River

Trip Cross-reference Table

Trip Number	No. Hiking Days	Season			Pace			Trip Type			
		Early	Mid	Late	Leisurely	Moderate	Strenuous	Round	Shuttle	Loop	Semiloop
1	2		x		x			x			
2	4		x		x			x			
3	6		x		x			x			
4	2		x		x			x			
5	4		x			x		x			
6	5		x			x			x		
7	2		x		x			x			
8	2		x		x				x		
9	3		x		x				x		
10	2		x			x					x
11	2		x	x		x			x		
12	3		x				x		x		
13	4		x		x						x
14	2		x	x	x						x
15	4		x		x				x		
16	6		x	x	x				x		
17	2		x		x			x			
18	2		x		x				x		
19	2	x	x		x			x			
20	4		x	x	x			x			
21	4		x	x	x			x			
22	5		x	x	x						x
23	7		x	x	x					x	
24	7		x	x	x				x		
25	2		x	x	x			x			
26	4		x	x	x			x			
27	2	x	x		x			x			
28	6		x	x	x			x			
29	5		x	x	x				x		
30	5		x	x	x				x		
31	7		x	x	x				x		
32	2		x	x	x			x			

Trip Number	No. Hiking Days	Season			Pace			Trip Type			
		Early	Mid	Late	Leisurely	Moderate	Strenuous	Round	Shuttle	Loop	Semiloop
33	3		x	x	x			x			
34	4		x	x		x					x
35	5		x	x		x					x
36	5	x	x			x			x		
37	2		x	x		x		x			
38	2		x	x		x		x			
39	4		x	x		x		x			
40	3		x	x		x			x		
41	3		x	x		x					x
42	6		x	x			x		x		
43	6		x	x		x		x			
44	8		x	x		x					x
45	2	x	x	x	x			x			
46	4		x	x		x			x		
47	2		x	x	x				x		
48	2	x			x			x			
49	4	x			x			x			
50	2		x	x		x		x			
51	3		x	x		x			x		
52	5		x	x		x			x		
53	2		x	x		x					x
54	2		x	x	x			x			
55	2		x	x	x			x			
56	2		x	x	x			x			
57	4		x	x	x			x			
58	5		x	x	x				x		
59	4		x	x	x				x		
60	5		x	x	x				x		
61	3		x	x	x				x		
62	2		x	x		x		x			
63	2		x	x	x			x			
64	2		x	x	x			x			
65	4		x	x	x						x
66	6		x	x		x					x

Trip Number	No. Hiking Days	Season			Pace			Trip Type			
		Early	Mid	Late	Leisurely	Moderate	Strenuous	Round	Shuttle	Loop	Semiloop
67	7		x	x		x					x
68	5		x	x		x			x		
69	2		x	x	x			x			
70	2		x	x	x			x			
71	3		x	x		x			x		
72	2		x	x		x			x		
73	3		x	x	x					x	
74	3		x	x	x					x	
75	3		x	x	x					x	
76	2		x	x	x			x			
77	3		x	x		x			x		
78	4		x	x	x				x		
79	3		x	x	x						x
80	5		x	x	x				x		
81	4	x			x			x			
82	4	x	x		x			x			
83	5	x	x		x				x		
84	5	x	x		x				x		
85	5	x	x		x						x
86	4	x			x			x			
87	11		x	x		x				x	
88	7		x	x	x				x		
89	2		x		x			x			
90	4		x	x	x			x			
91	2		x	x	x			x			
92	2		x	x	x			x			
93	2		x	x	x			x			
94	2		x	x	x			x			
95	7		x	x	x				x		
96	4			x	x				x		
97	3			x		x			x		
98	2			x		x		x			
99	5			x		x			x		
100	8			x	x				x		

Recommended Reading

Books

American Red Cross, *First Aid Textbook*, New York: Doubleday & Co. 1957.

Bateman, Paul C., and Clyde Wahrhaftig, "Geology of the Sierra Nevada," in *California Division of Mines and Geology bulletin 190*, 1966, pp. 107-72.

Bowen, Ezra, *The High Sierra*, New York: Time-Life Books, 1972.

Brewer, William H. (ed. Francis P. Farquhar), *Up and Down California*, Berkeley: University of California Press, 1966.

Brower, David (ed.), *Gentle Wilderness: The Sierra Nevada*, New York: Sierra Club-Ballantine Books, 1968.

———— , (ed.), *The Sierra Club Wilderness Handbook*, New York: Ballantine Books, 1967.

Evanoff, Vlad, *The Fresh-Water Fisherman's Bible*, Garden City, New York: Doubleday & Co., 1964.

Farquhar, Francis P., *History of the Sierra Nevada*, Berkeley: University of California Press, 1965.

—— — , *Place Names of the High Sierra*. (Out of print)

Gudde, Erwin G., *1000 California Place Names*, Berkeley: University of California Press, 1969.

Hill, Mary, *Geology of the Sierra Nevada*, Berkeley: University of California Press, 1975.

Ingles, Lloyd G., *Mammals of the Pacific States*, Stanford, Calif.: Stanford University Press, 1965.

King, Clarence, *Mountaineering in the Sierra Nevada*, New York: Lippincott, 1963.

Matthes, Francois, *The Incomparable Valley*, Berkeley: University of California Press, 1964.

McDermand, Charles, *Yosemite and Kings Canyon Trout*. (Out of print.)

Muir, John, *My First Summer in the Sierra*, Dunwoody, Ga.: Berg, 1972.

———— , (ed. Frederick Grunsky), *South of Yosemite: Selected Writings of John Muir*, Garden City: Natural History Press, 1968.

Murie, Olaus J., *A Field Guide to Animal Tracks,* Boston: Houghton, 1958.

Niehaus, Theodore, *Sierra Wildflowers,* Berkeley: University of California Press, 1974.

Peattie, Roderick (ed.), *The Sierra Nevada: The Range of Light,* New York: Vanguard Press, 1947. (Out of print.)

Peterson, Roger Tory, *A Field Guide to Western Birds,* Boston: Houghton Mifflin, 1961.

Roper, Steve, *Climber's Guide to the High Sierra.* San Francisco: Sierra Club, 1976.

Roth, Hal, *Pathway in the Sky: The Story of the John Muir Trail,* Berkeley: Howell-North Books, 1965.

Russell, Carl P., *100 Years in Yosemite,* Yosemite Natural History Association, 1968.

Schaffer, Jeffrey P., *Yosemite National Park.* Berkeley: Wilderness Press, 1977.

Storer, Tracy I. and Robert L. Usinger, *Sierra Nevada Natural History,* Berkeley: University of California Press, 1963.

Thomas, Winnie, and Hasse, Bunnelle, *Food for Knapsackers,* San Francisco: Sierra Club, 1971.

Weeden, Norman, *A Sierra Nevada Flora.* Berkeley: Wilderness Press, 1981.

Pamphlets

Hood, Mary and Bill, *Wildflowers of Yosemite,* Yosemite: Flying Spur Press, 1969.

Yosemite Natural History Association,
   Fishes of Yosemite
   Cone-Bearing Trees of Yosemite National Park
   Wildflowers of the Sierra
   Mammals of Yosemite National Park
   Birds of Yosemite

(For out-of-print books, try your library)

Index